The Interwoven Gospels

THE

INTERWOVEN GOSPELS

OR

THE FOUR HISTORIES OF JESUS CHRIST
BLENDED INTO A COMPLETE AND CON-
TINUOUS NARRATIVE IN THE WORDS
OF THE GOSPELS

~~Barry, Tennessee Mission~~

WITH A COMPLETE

INTERLEAVED HARMONY

According to the REVISED VERSION of 1881
with the readings and renderings preferred by the AMERICAN Committee of Revision
incorporated into the text by President Roswell D. Hitchcock, D.D., of the
Union Theological Seminary, New York

COMPILED BY

REV. WILLIAM PITTENGER

AUTHOR OF "ORATORY, SACRED AND SECULAR," "EXTEMPORE SPEECH,"
"THE GREAT LOCOMOTIVE CHASE," ETC.

NEW YORK
JOHN B. ALDEN, PUBLISHER
1890

Copyright, 1889, 1891,

BY

WM. PITTENGER.

PREFACE TO THE NEW EDITION OF "INTERWOVEN GOSPELS AND GOSPEL HARMONY."

THIS new and enlarged edition contains novel features of great value. In addition to the interwoven account which presents in bible words everything in the Four Gospels, all parallel accounts are given on opposite pages, in finer type, so that at a glance their relation is seen. Every clause and word taken from these parallel accounts to make up the interwoven narrative is underlined so that the mode of compilation is made perfectly obvious. In the Transfiguration account, for instance, we have Mark taken as the standard, and all the facts peculiar to Matthew and Luke are woven into it ; then on opposite pages the full accounts by Matthew and Luke are given in fine type, with the words that have been added to Mark exhibited by underlining. The student who uses this work thus gets three important things before him without labor or the possibility of error: the full story combined from all the Gospels; the peculiarities of each Gospel; and the precise points of agreement or divergence between them. Many excellent Gospel Harmonies have been published, and also a few attempts to frame a continuous Gospel narrative; but so far as the present compiler is aware, no attempt has been made to place both the complete consecutive narrative and the Harmony before the eye at once.

PREFACE TO THE ORIGINAL EDITION OF THE "INTERWOVEN GOSPELS."

THE design of this compilation is to take the four biographies of our Lord which are found in the New Testament, and combine them into a single narrative. As an inspired authority, and for the purpose of consultation and study, the common arrangement is no doubt far better than any other. But a mode of presentation which employs only the familiar Gospel words, which can be read in a few hours as a continuous narrative, and yet gives the whole story in a single impression, may be very useful.

Each of the four Gospels is independent, and has certain peculiarities that the others do not possess. It is curious and instructive to notice how some sayings and incidents in the life of Jesus are found in all four of the Gospels, some in three, some in two, and quite a large number in but one. In like manner the same incident will be narrated with greater or less detail in the different places where it occurs. A full conception of this marvelous history cannot be obtained till all the accounts are in some manner fused into one. The diligent student will make this fusion mentally, and perhaps unconsciously; but may not this essential process be greatly hastened by a careful combination printed and placed before the eye? Many persons rest satisfied with thoroughly knowing but one Gospel, while their idea of the others is hazy and imperfect. This is to be regretted. All the accounts are needed to give us the best attainable conception of the earthly life of our Saviour. The reader who omits to give each Gospel its full weight in his conception of the

work of Christ will be the loser. Very often
what is obscure or perplexing in one account
is made clear in another; and thus, when we
know all that the four Evangelists have recorded, and have mentally arranged their accounts in due order, we have the best—or
rather, the least inadequate—view of the
wonderful human life of the Christ.

It is hoped that this volume will interest
and profit two classes of readers, perhaps in
almost equal degree. If put into the hand of
a child as his first introduction to the study
of the New Testament, it will be read as an
ordinary connected history; and when the
Gospels in their common form are afterward
read, the relation of their different parts will
be at once understood, and many otherwise
perplexing questions will never even arise.

But a person who has been diligently reading the Gospels in the New Testament for
years is equally sure to be delighted and instructed when he finds them all combined
into one story, thus putting before his eye
fully and in print what he has long been mentally approximating. There is a fulness in
many particulars, a new light cast on the
story from the order and succession of events,
which is almost invariably a pleasing surprise,
even to the well-informed.

Many attempts have been made to perfect a
combination of the Evangelists in their own
language. The harmonies which give parallel accounts in parallel columns on the same
page are valuable for the study of detached
passages, but are unsuited for consecutive
reading. Some attempts at making a single
narrative have been very ingenious and useful; but none have hitherto been quite satisfactory. Some have attempted too much,
and by the use of cumbrous machinery have
made the result unreadable, thus defeating
their own purpose. The difficulties lie on
every hand, and are much greater than would

appear at first view. If the compiler adds many words of his own to make easy connections, the authority of the Gospel narrative is impaired; on the contrary, many omissions are fatal to completeness; while if every word from the four accounts is brought into the text, the style will be broken and involved, and there will be much wearisome repetition; if no references are given, the reader does not know what portion of the sacred record he is reading, and the sense of authenticity and security is lost; while frequent references, parentheses, and typographical devices disfigure the page and mar the reader's pleasure. These are by no means all the difficulties encountered, but they are sufficient to explain the limited nature of the acceptance that such works have hitherto met.

Whatever may be its fate, the present attempt enjoys several considerable advantages. The issue of the Revised Version of 1881 furnishes valuable aid. It is not only more accurate than the common version, but possesses two qualities which contribute directly toward the success of this undertaking. The renderings are far more *uniform*, and a large number of *spurious readings* have been removed, thus bringing the several Gospels in their English dress more close together, and rendering more easy the work of blending them smoothly. The labor of interweaving is thus reduced fully one half. Another great advantage secured by the Revised Version, is the placing of chapter and verse numbers in the margin, leaving the page to take the usual form of paragraphs. This renders it possible to retain the familiar notation by chapter and verse without change. The readings and renderings preferred by the American Committee of Revisers have been adopted because they carry still further the principle of uniformity in rendering. Fords, Howard & Hulbert have kindly given per-

mission to use their "American Version,"
edited by Roswell D. Hitchcock, President
of Union Theological Seminary, New York.

A very simple device has removed many of
the difficulties that have hitherto proved very
formidable. When parallel accounts occur
they are not woven together on equal terms,
but one of them is selected as the standard—
either that one which is fullest, or which blends
best with what precedes and what follows—
and only the peculiarities of the others are added. The Gospel, chapter, and verses of the
standard account are as fully indicated as if it
stood entirely alone, while the word, clause, or
sentence from another Gospel is introduced
by an inconspicuous character, showing the
book of its origin at a glance. This mode of
completing one account by a few carefully inserted additions has been found, after many
trials, easier and far more satisfactory than to
build up a new text out of the fragments of
two, three, or four accounts. No attempt has
been made to include every word, or every
variation in the mere form of expression.
That would be to sacrifice the substance to
the shadow, and is the rock on which some
learned and laborious compilations have been
wrecked ; but nothing which makes any addition either in fact or in expression has been
knowingly omitted. The reader of this volume will be able to begin with the introduction of St. John and take up event by
event of the Saviour's life in the words of
each Gospel. Where there is one account
only, this is simply inserted ; but where
several occur, the fullest is given, with all the
additions that the others make. In choosing
these additions where they are found in more
than one Gospel, the same principle of choosing the fullest and most important first is
adopted.

The order of time where it could be determined has been followed in all ordinary cases ;

but to preserve the unity of subject, and to avoid cutting the different accounts into minute fragments, the order of subject has sometimes been preferred, with a clearly marked statement of the chronology as well. The compiler does not claim the authority of an original investigator in the field of Gospel harmony, but has carefully studied the works of the great masters in that field, and has made such a selection as seemed best for the purpose in view. The succession of events in the majority of instances has been determined by general consent. Where doubts exist, reasons have been carefully weighed; and where absolute certainty seems not attainable, that arrangement has been preferred which makes the clearest and most intelligible biography, and least disturbs the association of events with which we are familiar in the Gospels themselves. For instance, the Sermon on the Mount has been given as separate from the very similar discourse in Luke, against the views of the majority of harmonists, because this allows the presentation of two noble discourses in unbroken form, keeps for each the position with which Bible readers are already familiar, and permits a more natural arrangement of the early part of our Saviour's ministry. The same considerations apply to the long passage in Luke from the 9th to the 19th chapter, which is by many harmonists broken into fragments and distributed in various places—hardly fair treatment for an evangelist who professes to write " in order." It has seemed much better to follow the leadership of Dr. G. W. Clark in placing these chapters almost in a body—an arrangement probable in itself, and far better for the purpose of biography. A few questions of harmony are treated in notes, and a few specimen modes of reconciling discrepancies— but only a few, for this work is not intended to be a commentary. Agreements are far more numerous than differences, which are only such as to prove the independence of the Gospels; but it is not our purpose to call attention even to the most striking confirmations. If all the marvelous wealth of the four Gospels can be thrown into one smooth and continuous narrative, we will be well content to let the story make its own impression.

The advantages claimed for "The Interwoven Gospels" may perhaps be clearly conceived by imagining the four Evangelists to be reciting orally the wonderful things they had seen and heard. If each in turn told the whole story so far as he recalled it in one uninterrupted effort, we would have some things told but once, some twice, and some four times; the order of events would differ, and there would be many verbal variations. This would be putting their story in the very strongest possible form as evidences in a court of law; though any story less interesting than that of the Gospels would become tedious when told four times over in such a manner. But in this volume one evangelist relates an incident, and the others add the particulars that their memories supply; then another carries the story forward, and is supplemented in like manner; and this is continued until the whole incomparable story, from the Annunciation to the Ascension, is placed before us, without repetitions, and on the authority of the four witnesses. Can there fail to be a gain in ease of reading, and in freshness and unity of impression? No doubt, if we at the same time *lost the original four Gospels*, the evidence upon which rests the history of Christ would be weakened; but we do not lose them, and the convenience with which they may be referred to is one of the merits of the present volume. A reader who uses it will be better able, from comparison with the combined account, to appreciate the characteristics of the several Gospels.

CHARACTERISTICS AND AGREE-
MENTS OF THE GOSPELS.

No one of the four Gospels is in the form of a modern biography. They contain comparatively few notes of time, and do not always observe chronological order. They are professedly incomplete, giving only a partial record of a life which even inspired pens could not fully write. (See John xxi. 25, and the frequent reference to the "many other things that Jesus did.") Naturally they did not always select the same matters for record or the same particulars and phases of the same event. Their complete independence is thus made evident; and in these four vivid, artless, and most truth-like sketches of a marvelous life there is laid a firm basis for faith. The more they are studied the more the conviction grows of the absolute impossibility of the Gospels originating in any other way than through the attempt of honest men to state what came within their own knowledge.

Our space will only permit a bare statement of a few of the characteristics of the several Gospels, without giving the evidence on which the statement is based. Those who are interested can easily continue this line of research with the aid of competent investigators.

Matthew (though a publican) is especially interested in those phases of the life of Jesus which fulfil the Old Testament predictions regarding the Messiah. His is the longest Gospel.

Mark is supposed to write under the dictation of the Apostle Peter, or at least in direct consultation with him. He places less stress on what is said than on what is done; has few long discourses, though many pithy sayings; but in few words *photographs* the surroundings and minute details of the Saviour's "mighty works." The narrative has the hurry and impetuosity of Peter's own character. The word "straightway" is ever recurring. •

Matthew and Mark are mainly occupied with the works of Jesus in Galilee, and their accounts run more nearly parallel than any other two.

Luke, at the outset, claims to set forth events "in order." He is therefore much more full in the introduction to the ministry than the other three, and gives many miracles and parables occurring beyond Jordan which they omit. There is a rounded fulness in his accounts which suits well with his Greek name.

Tradition represents John as writing later than the others, with the especial purpose, indicated in his introduction, of showing the Divinity of Jesus. He alone gives the works done at the several passovers, and thus furnishes the only available means of computing the length of the public ministry of Jesus. It is also natural that the discourses at Jerusalem, the scholastic and priestly capital of the nation, should be more profound and doctrinal than those uttered to Galilean peasants.

A careful study of the relations of the Gospels reveals the wonderful manner in which they supplement each other. Without Matthew we would lack the Sermon on the Mount; without Mark, a hundred striking details which could have come only from an eye-witness; without Luke, the prelude of angels and the parable of the Prodigal Son; without John we would lack the conversations with Nicodemus and the woman of Samaria, and the matchless pathos of the last discourse. All of these, and many more, are presented here in regular order, and with careful consideration, but without the perplexities of minute criticism ; and each narrative is so indicated that the reader will always know, without the trouble of reference, just whose Gospel he is reading and from what source each particular is added.

In preparing this compilation the lovely and mighty figure of JESUS, THE CHRIST of prophecy,—the SON OF MAN, and the SON OF THE LIVING GOD,—has seemed to become more definite, and to draw ever nearer. May this experience extend to all readers !

EXPLANATION OF CHARACTERS
AND DIVISIONS.

1. The letters *, *b*, *c*, and *d* indicate respectively the Gospels of Matthew, Mark, Luke, and John. The words *following* such letters are taken from the corresponding Gospel.

2. At the top of each page and at the beginning of each Section the Gospel and the chapter are given. When a section is not all taken from one Gospel or chapter, the change is indicated in the margin. The verses are also given at the outside margin under the chapters, so that a glance will show the chapter and verse.

3. The marginal readings of the Revised Version are indicated by small figures, and are printed at the bottom of the page. The compiler has left them unchanged except that references to parallel passages or readings are mostly omitted, as the passages referred to are often woven into the text.

4. Words inserted by the compiler to properly connect interwoven passages are enclosed in brackets, thus [and] *,—the star referring to the words " inserted by the compiler" at the bottom of the page. The number of such words is not great.

5. The whole volume is divided into six periods, as follows :

Period   I. The Time oi Preparation.
   "   II. First Year of Public Ministry.
   "   III. Second Year of Public Ministry.
   "   IV. Third Year of Public Ministry.
   "   V. The Passover Week.
   "   VI. After the Resurrection.

To avoid confusion with the ordinary division into chapters and verses which are noted in the margin, chapters are not otherwise employed in this work. Sections (§) take their place. They are 171 in number, are of irregular length, and will be found very convenient for reference. Many indications of localities are given in brackets under the section titles, which if compared with the maps will add greatly to the interest of the narrative.

TABLE FOR FINDING ANY PASSAGE
WHEN CHAPTER AND VERSE
ARE KNOWN.

	Matthew.				
CHAP.	VERSE.	§	CHAP.	VERSE.	§
I.	1–17	3	XVI.	1–12	65
	18–25	8		13–28	67
II.	1–23	11	XVII.	1–13	68
III.	1–12	14		14–23	69
	13–17	15		24–27	70
IV.	1–11	16	XVIII.	1–14	71
	13	56		15–35	72
	13–16	26	XIX.	1–12	109
	12, 17	24		13–15	110
	18–22	27		16–22	111
	23–25	29		23–30	112
V.	1–48	30	XX.	1–16	113
VI.	1–34	30		17–28	114
VII.	1–29	30		29–34	115
VIII.	1–4	31	XXI.	1–11	118
	5–13	43		12–22	123
	14–17	28		23–27	124
	18–27	52		28–32	125
	28–34	53		33–46	126
IX.	1	53	XXII.	1–14	127
	2–8	32		15–22	128
	9–13	33		23–33	129
	14–17	34		34–46	130
	18–26	35	XXIII.	1–36	131
	27–34	36		37–39	132
	35–38	54	XXIV.	1–28	134
X.	1–42	55		29–51	135
XI.	1	55	XXV.	1–13	136
	2–19	45		14–30	137
	20–27	46		31–46	138
	28–30	47	XXVI.	1–6	140
XII.	1–21	39		6–13	139
	22–37	49		14–16	141
	38–50	50		17–20	142
XIII.	1–53	51		21–25	143
	54–58	54		26–30	145
XIV.	1–12	56		31–36	144
	13–21	58		37–46	148
	22–36	59		47–56	149
XV.	1–20	61		57	151
	21–28	62		58	150
	29–31	63		59–68	151
	32–39	64		68–75	150

Matthew.

CHAP.	VERSE.	§	CHAP.	VERSE.	§
XXVII.	1	151	XXVII.	34–44	158
	2	153		45–56	160
	3–10	152		57–66	161
	11–14	153	XXVIII.	1–10	162
	15–26	155		10–15	163
	27–31	156		16–18	169
	32–33	157		19–20	171

Mark.

CHAP.	VERSE.	§	CHAP.	VERSE.	§
I.	1– 8	14	X.	1–12	109
	9–11	15		13–16	110
	12–13	16		17–31	111
	14–15	24		32–45	114
	16–20	27		46–52	115
	21–34	28	XI.	1–11	118
	35–39	29		12–14	122
	40–45	31		15–25	123
II.	1–12	32		26–33	124
	13–17	33	XII.	1–12	126
	18–22	34		13–17	128
	22–28	39		18–27	129
III.	1– 6	39		28–37	130
	7–12	40		38–40	131
	13–19	41		41–44	133
	20–30	49	XIII.	1–23	134
	31–35	50		24–37	135
IV.	1–34	51	XIV.	1–11	139
	35–41	52		12–16	141
V.	1–21	53		17–21	143
	22–43	35		22–25	145
VI.	1– 6	54		26–31	144
	7–13	55		32–42	148
	14–29	56		43–52	149
	30–31	57		53–65	151
	32–44	58		65–72	150
	45–56	59	XV.	1– 5	153
VII.	1–23	61		6–15	155
	24–30	62		16–20	156
	31–37	63		21–23	157
VIII.	1– 9	64		24–32	158
	10–21	65		33–41	160
	22–26	66		41–47	161
	27–38	67	XVI.	1–11	162
IX.	1	67		12–13	164
	2–13	68		14	165
	14–32	69		15–18	170
	33–50	71		19–20	171

Luke.

CHAP.	VERSE.	§	CHAP.	VERSE.	§
I.	1– 4	2	XI.	29–36	82
	5–25	4		37–54	83
	26–38	5	XII.	1–12	84
	39–56	6		13–59	85
	57–80	7		1– 5	87
II.	1– 7	8		6– 9	88
II.	8–20	9	XIII.	10–17	91
	21–40	10		18–21	92
	41–52	13		22–35	93
III.	1–18	14	XIV.	1–24	95
	19–20	22		25–35	96
	21–22	25	XV.	1– 7	97
	23–38	3		8–10	98
IV.	1–13	16		11–32	99
	14–15	24	XVI.	1–13	100
	16–30	26		14–31	101
	31–41	28	XVII.	1–10	102
	42–44	29		11–19	105
V.	1–11	27		20–37	106
	12–16	31	XVIII.	1– 8	107
	17–26	32		9–14	108
	27–32	33		15–17	110
	33–39	34		18–23	111
VI.	1–11	39		24–30	112
	12–16	41		31–34	114
	17–49	42		35–43	115
VII.	1–10	43	XIX.	1–10	116
	11–17	44		11–28	117
	18–35	45		29–40	118
	36–50	48		41–44	119
VIII.	1– 3	48		45–48	123
	4–18	51	XX.	1– 8	124
	19–21	50		9–19	126
	22–25	52		20–26	128
	26–39	53		27–44	129
	40–56	35		45–47	131
IX.	1– 6	55	XXI.	1– 4	133
	7– 9	56		5–26	134
	10–17	58		27–36	135
	18–27	67		37, 38	123
	28–36	68	XXII.	1– 6	139
	37–45	69		7–13	141
	46–50	71		14–20	145
	51–63	73		21–23	143
X.	1–24	77		24–30	142
	25–37	78		31–38	144
	38–42	79		39–46	148
XI.	1–13	80		47–54	149
	14–28	81		54–62	150

Luke.

CHAP.	VERSE.	§	CHAP.	VERSE.	§
XXII.	63-71	151	XXIII.	44-49	160
XXIII.	1- 5	153		50-56	161
	6-12	154	XXIV.	1	161
	13-25	155		2-12	162
	26-31	157		13-35	164
	32-38	158		36-49	165
	39-43	159		50-53	171

John.

CHAP.	VERSE.	§	CHAP.	VERSE.	§
I.	1-18	1		37-50	121
	19-34	17	XIII.	1-20	142
	35-51	18		21-30	143
II.	1-12	19		31-38	144
	13-25	20	XIV.	1-31	146
III.	1-21	21	XV.	1-27	146
	22-36	22	XVI.	1-33	146
IV.	1-42	23	XVII.	1-26	147
	43-45	24	XVIII.	1	148
	46-54	25		2-11	149
V.	1-18	37		12-14	151
	19-47	38		15-18	150
VI.	1-14	58		19-24	151
	15-21	59		25-27	150
	22-71	60		28-38	153
VII.	1	60		39-40	155
	2-10	73	XIX.	1-16	156
	11-53	74		17	157
VIII.	1-11	75		18-27	158
	12-59	76		28-30	160
IX.	1-41	88		31-42	161
X.	1-18	89	XX.	1-18	162
	19-42	90		19-23	163
XI.	1-46	103		24-29	166
XI.	47-57	104		30-31	172
XII.	1-11	139	XXI.	1-14	167
	12-19	118		15-23	168
	20-36	120		24-25	172

GENERAL TABLE OF CONTENTS.

INDEX TO SECTIONS AND GOSPELS.

PERIOD I.—THE TIME OF PREPARATION.

Sec- tion.	Page.	Gospels from which each Section is taken.*	TITLE OF SECTION.
1	1	John.	Preface by John.
2	2	Luke.	Luke's Introduction.
3	3	Matt., Luke.	The Ancestry of Jesus Christ.
4	5	Luke.	The Birth of John Announced.
5	7	"	Birth of Jesus Announced.
6	8	"	Meeting of Mary and Elizabeth
7	9	"	Birth of John.
8	11	Matt., Luke.	Birth of Jesus.
9	12	Luke.	The Shepherds and the Angels.
10	13	"	Jesus Presented in the Temple.
11	15	Matthew.	The Wise Men from the East.
12	16	"	The Journey into Egypt.
13	17	Luke.	Child Jesus in the Temple.
14	18	Luke, Matt., Mark.	Preaching of John Baptist.
15	20	Matt., Mark, Luke.	Baptism of Jesus.
16	21	Matt., Luke, Mark.	The Temptation.

* The leading Gospel is named first.

* The leading Gospel is named first.

* The leading Gospel is named first.

PERIOD V.—THE PASSOVER WEEK.—*Continued.*

* The leading Gospel is named first.

COLORED MAPS.

HOW TO USE "INTERWOVEN GOSPELS."

THE best of all ways is to begin at the beginning and read the whole book consecutively, carefully noting the divisions into periods and sections, and the locations as shown in the text and maps. If time does not permit this, read a period consecutively, with the same attention to details.

Should the student wish to consult any special subject, he may refer to the index at the close of the volume or to the table of contents just preceding this note. If not readily found by subject in these, he may look for the chapter and verse in the table on page xv, and opposite to them he will find the section (*not page*) in which the account is given. If the chapter and verse for which he looked appear in the margin of the text, he will know that his reference was to the standard account; if not, that it was to a parallel account, only the peculiarities of which have been woven into the standard. An instance will make this plain. Wishing to find the account of the feeding of the five thousand, he sees in the index the words "Five thousand fed" opposite section 58, page 88; or he finds the same reference in the table of contents. The latter may be the more convenient if he knows about what period in the Saviour's life the incident occurs. Or if he knows that the account begins at Mark vi. 32, he finds Mark vi. in the first column of page xvi, and opposite 32–34 is 58, the number of the section. Turning to this, he finds, that Mark is the standard, to which additions are made from the other gospels. Had he looked, however, for John, vi. 1–14 he would have found the same reference to section 58; but on turning to that he would possibly be perplexed by finding no mention of John! But he would find several clauses introduced by the small letter "ᵈ;" such as, "ᵈ and this he said to prove, etc.," "ᵈ and when they were all filled, he said unto his disciples, etc." And on the opposite page, also under § 58, he would see, in fine print, the account of John together with that of Matthew and Luke. Underlining would be seen to distinguish the words that have been added to the standard account. Thus the student has all the accounts before his eye at once, with the peculiarities of each clearly indicated.

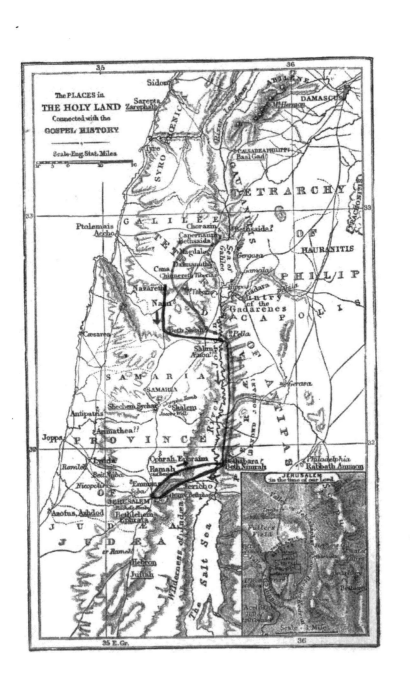

PLATE I.

FROM NAZARETH TO CAPERNAUM. §§ 12–19.

These five maps are arranged to show, by means of colored lines, the journeys of Jesus, and also to call attention to the places and order of time connected with prominent events of his life.

At Capernaum the birth of Jesus was announced. He was born at Bethlehem, carried into Egypt, and afterwards to Nazareth, where the years preceding his public ministry were spent. These first journeys are not indicated by lines.

As shown by the blue line, Jesus journeyed from his home at Nazareth, to the river Jordan, where John was baptizing (§ 15); thence, through the wilderness of Judea (Temptation, § 16), to Jerusalem, and back to Jordan (§§ 17 and 18), where the first disciples were called.

As shown by the red line, Jesus went from Bethabara back to Galilee, where his first miracle was performed, at Cana (§ 19), and then made a brief stay at CAPERNAUM. Thus was completed his first circuit, of which the record is very concise. From this time CAPERNAUM is the starting-point of each circuit, as shown in succeeding plates.

(To face page 1.)

THE INTERWOVEN GOSPELS.

PERIOD I.

The Time of Preparation.

[From the Announcement of the Birth of John the Baptist to the Beginning of Christ's Public Ministry—a period of about thirty-two years.]

§ 1. Preface by John.*

John 1.

1   ᵈ In the beginning was the Word, and the Word was with God, and the Word
2 was God. The same was in the beginning
3 with God. All things were made tl.rough him; and without him ¹ was not anything
4 made that hath been made. In him was life; and the life was the light of men.
5 And the light shineth in the darkness; and the darkness ² apprehended it not.
6 There came a man, sent from God, whose
7 name was John. The same came for witness, that he might bear witness of the light, that all might believe through him.
8 He was not the light, but *came* that he
9 might bear witness of the light. ³ There was the true light, *even the light* which lighteth ⁴ every man, coming into the
10 world. He was in the world, and the world was made through him, and the

KEY.—ᵃ Matthew, ᵇ Mark, ᶜ Luke, ᵈ John.

¹ Or, *was not anything made. That which hath been made was life in him; and the life &c.*
² Or, *overcame.*
³ Or, *The true light, which lighteth every man, was coming.*
⁴ Or, *Every man as he cometh.*

* The introductions to the several Gospels beautifully supplement each other. Luke narrates the events preceding Christ's advent; John declares his divine nature and pre-existence; Matthew (with Luke) gives his ancestral tables; while Mark, in a single sentence, leads at once to the proclamation of the Gospel. The order here adopted differs from most harmonists, who also differ widely among themselves. In these opening sections the clearest arrangement is best.

world knew him not. He came unto ¹his 11
own, and they that were his own received
him not.   But as many as received him, to 12
them gave he the right to become children
of God, *even* to them that believe on his
name : who were ²born, not of ³blood, nor 13
of the will of the flesh, nor of the will of
man, but of God.   And the Word became 14
flesh, and ⁴dwelt among us (and we beheld
his glory, glory as of ⁵the only begotten
from the Father), full of grace and truth.
John beareth witness of him, and crieth, 15
saying, ⁶This was he of whom I said, He
that cometh after me is become before me :
for he was ⁷before me.   For of his fulness 16
we all received, and grace for grace.   For 17
the law was given through Moses ; grace
and truth came through Jesus Christ.   No 18
man hath seen God at any time ; ⁸the only
begotten Son, who is in the bosom of the
Father, he hath declared *him*.

§ 2.   Luke's Introduction.

⁹FORASMUCH as many have taken in 1
hand to draw up a narrative concerning
those matters which have been ¹⁰fulfilled
among us, even as they delivered them 2
unto us, who from the beginning were
eyewitnesses and ministers of the word, it 3
seemed good to me also, having traced the
course of all things accurately from the
first, to write unto thee in order, most excellent Theophilus ; that thou mightest 4
know the certainty concerning the ¹¹things
¹¹wherein thou wast instructed.

KEY.—ª Matthew, ᵇ Mark, ᶜ Luke, ᵈ John.
¹ Gr. *his own things.*   ² Or. *begotten.*
³ Gr. *bloods.*   ⁴ Gr. *tabernacled.*
⁵ Or, *an only begotten from a father.*
⁶ Some ancient authorities read (*this was he that said*).
⁷ Gr. *first in regard of me.*
⁸ Many very ancient authorities read *God only begotten.*
⁹ Or, *fully established.*   ¹⁰ Gr. *words.*
¹¹ Or, *which thou wast taught by word of mouth.*

§ 3. The Ancestry of Jesus Christ.*

Matthew 1.

1   ¹^aTHE book of ²generation of Jesus Christ, the son of, David, the son of Abraham.

2   Abraham begat Isaac; and Isaac begat Jacob; and Jacob begat Judah and his

3 brethren; and Judah begat Perez and Zerah of Tamar; and Perez begat Hezron;

4 and Hezron begat ³Ram; and ³Ram begat Amminadab; and Amminadab begat Nahshon; and Nahshon begat Salmon;

5 and Salmon begat Boaz of Rahab; and Boaz begat Obed of Ruth; and Obed be-

6 gat Jesse; and Jesse begat David the king.

And David begat Solomon of her *that*

7 *had been the wife* of Uriah; and Solomon begat Rehoboam; and Rehoboam begat

8 Abijah; and Abijah begat 'Asa; and 'Asa begat Jehoshaphat; and Jehoshaphat be-

9 gat Joram; and Joram begat Uzziah; and Uzziah begat Jotham; and Jotham begat

10 Ahaz; and Ahaz begat Hezekiah; and Hezekiah begat Manasseh; and Manasseh begat 'Amon; and 'Amon begat Josiah;

11 and Josiah begat Jechoniah and his brethren, at the time of the 'carrying away to Babylon.

12 And after the 'carrying away to Babylon, Jechoniah begat 'Shealtiel; and

13 'Shealtiel begat Zerubbabel; and Zerubbabel begat Abiud; and Abiud begat

14 Eliakim; and Eliakim begat Azor; and Azor begat Sadoc; and Sadoc begat

15 Achim; and Achim begat Eliud; and

KEY.—^a Matthew, ^b Mark, ^c Luke, ^d John.

¹ Or, *The genealogy of Jesus Christ.*
² Or, *birth.*   ³ Gr. *Aram.*   ⁴ Gr. *Asaph.*
⁵ Gr. *Amos.*   ⁶ Or, *removal to Babylon.*
⁷ Gr. *Salathiel.*

* These tables were probably copied from public records which the Jews kept with great care. That of Matthew is generally supposed to present the *legal* descent of Jesus through Joseph; that of Luke, the *actual* descent through Mary.

Matthew 1.

Eliud begat Eleazar ; and Eleazar begat
Matthan ; and Matthan begat Jacob ; and 16
Jacob begat Joseph the husband of Mary, of
whom was born Jesus, who is called Christ.

So all the generations from Abraham 17
unto David are fourteen generations ; and
from David unto the ¹ carrying away to
Babylon fourteen generations ; and from
the ¹ carrying away to Babylon unto the
Christ fourteen generations.   **Luke 3.**

ᶜAnd Jesus himself, when he began *to* 23
teach, was about thirty years of age, being
the son (as was supposed) of Joseph, the
*son** of Heli, the *son* of Matthat, the *son* of 24
Levi, the *son* of Melchi, the *son* of Jannai,
the *son* of Joseph, the *son* of Mattathias, the 25
son of Amos, the *son* of Nahum, the *son* of
Esli, the *son* of Naggai, the *son* of Maath, 26
the *son* of Mattathias, the *son* of Semein,
the *son* of Josech, the *son* of Joda, the *son* of 27
Joanan, the *son* of Rhesa, the *son* of Zerubbabel, the *son* of ² Shealtiel, the *son* of Neri,
the *son* of Melchi, the *son* of Addi, the *son* 28
of Cosam, the *son* of Elmadam, the *son* of
Er, the *son* of Jesus, the *son* of Eliezer, the 29
son of Jorim, the *son* of Matthat, the *son* of
Levi, the *son* of Symeon, the *son* of Judas, 30
the *son* of Joseph, the *son* of Jonam, the *son*
of Eliakim, the *son* of Melæ, the *son* of 31
Menna, the *son* of Mattatha, the *son* of
Nathan, the *son* of David, the *son* of Jesse, 32
the *son* of Obed, the *son* of Boaz, the *son* of
³ Salmon, the *son* of Nahshon, the *son* of 33
Amminadab, ⁴ the *son* of ⁵ Arni, the *son* of

KEY.—ᵃ Matthew, ᵇ Mark, ᶜ Luke, ᵈ John.

¹ Or, *removal to Babylon.*   ² Gr. *Salathiel.*
³ Some ancient authorities write *Sala.*
⁴ Many ancient authorities insert *the* son *of Admin* : and
one writes *Admin* for *Amminadab.*
⁵ Some ancient authorities write *Aram.*

* Commentators usually consider the " son " of Heli as
equivalent to " son-in-law," thus making Heli the father of
Mary.   A few authorities dissent.

Luke 3.

Hezron, the *son* of Perez, the *son* of Judah,
34 the *son* of Jacob, the *son* of Isaac, the *son* of
Abraham, the *son* of Terah, the *son* of
35 Nahor, the *son* of Serug, the *son* of Reu,
the *son* of Peleg, the *son* of Eber, the *son* of
36 Shelah, the *son* of Cainan, the *son* of Arph-
axad, the *son* of Shem, the *son* of Noah, the
37 *son* of Lamech, the *son* of Methuselah, the
son of Enoch, the *son* of Jared, the *son* of
38 Mahalaleel, the *son* of Cainan, the *son* of
Enos, the *son* of Seth, the *son* of Adam, the
son of God.

§ 4. The Birth of John Announced.

[At Jerusalem.]

Luke 1.

5   ᶜTHERE was in the days of Herod, king
of Judæa, a certain priest named Zacharias,
of the course of Abijah: and he had a wife
of the daughters of Aaron, and her name
6   was Elisabeth.   And they were both righteous before God, walking in all the commandments and ordinances of the Lord
7   blameless.   And they had no child, because
that Elisabeth was barren, and they both
were *now* ¹ well stricken in years.
8   Now it came to pass, while he executed
the priest's office before God in the order
9   of his course, according to the custom of
the priest's office, his lot was to enter into
the ²temple of the Lord and burn in-
10 cense.   And the whole multitude of the
people were praying without at the hour
11 of incense.   And there appeared unto
him an angel of the Lord standing on
12 the right side of the altar of incense.   And
Zacharias was troubled when he saw *him*,
13 and fear fell upon him.   But the angel
said unto him, Fear not, Zacharias: because thy supplication is heard, and thy
wife Elisabeth shall bear thee a son, and

KEY.—ᵃ Matthew, ᵇ Mark, ᶜ Luke, ᵈ John.

¹ Gr. *advanced in their days*.   ² Or, *sanctuary*.

thou shalt call his name John.   And thou 14
shalt have joy and gladness; and many
shall rejoice at his birth.   For he shall be 15
great in the sight of the Lord, and he shall
drink no wine nor 'strong drink; and he
shall be filled with the Holy Spirit, even
from his mother's womb.   And many of 16
the children of Israel shall he turn unto the
Lord their God.   And he shall 'go before 17
his face in the spirit and power of Elijah,
to turn the hearts of the fathers to the
children, and the disobedient *to walk* in
the wisdom of the just; to make ready for
the Lord a people prepared *for him*.   And 18
Zacharias said unto the angel, Whereby
shall I know this? for I am an old man,
and my wife 'well stricken in years.   And 19
the angel answering said unto him, I am
Gabriel, that stand in the presence of God;
and I was sent to speak unto thee, and to
bring thee these good tidings.   And be- 20
hold, thou shalt be silent and not able to
speak, until the day that these things shall
come to pass, because thou believedst not
my words, which shall be fulfilled in their
season.   And the people were waiting for 21
Zacharias, and they marvelled 'while he
tarried in the 'temple.   And when he 22
came out, he could not speak unto them:
and they perceived that he had seen a vision in the 'temple: and he continued making signs unto them, and remained dumb.
And it came to pass, when the days of his 23
ministration were fulfilled, he departed
unto his house.

And after these days Elisabeth his wife 24
conceived; and she hid herself five months,
saying, Thus hath the Lord done unto me 25

KEY.— * Matthew, * Mark, * Luke, * John.

[1] Gr. *sikera*.
[2] Some ancient authorities read *come nigh before his face*.
[3] Gr. *advanced in her days*.   [4] Or, *at his tarrying*.
[5] Or, *sanctuary*.

Luke 1.

in the days wherein he looked upon *me*, to take away my reproach among men.

§ 5. The Birth of Jesus Announced.

[At Nazareth.]

Luke 1.

26 ᶜ Now in the sixth month the angel Gabriel was sent from God unto a city of Galilee,
27 named Nazareth, to a virgin betrothed to a man whose name was Joseph, of the house of David; and the virgin's name was
28 Mary.   And he came in unto her, and said, Hail, thou that art ¹highly favoured, the
29 Lord *is* with thee.²   But she was greatly troubled at the saying, and cast in her mind what manner of salutation this might be.
30 And the angel said unto her, Fear not, Mary: for thou hast found ³favour with
31 God.   And behold, thou shalt conceive in thy womb, and bring forth a son, and shalt
32 call his name JESUS.   He shall be great, and shall be called the Son of the Most High: and the Lord God shall give unto
33 him the throne of his father David: and he shall reign over the house of Jacob ⁴for ever; and of his kingdom there shall be
34 no end.   And Mary said unto the angel, How shall this be, seeing I know not a
35 man?   And the angel answered and said unto her, The Holy Spirit shall come upon thee, and the power of the Most High shall overshadow thee: wherefore also ⁶the holy thing which is begotten ⁵shall be called
36 the Son of God.   And behold, Elisabeth thy kinswoman, she also hath conceived a son in her old age: and this is the sixth month with her that ⁷was called barren.

KEY.—ᵃ Matthew, ᵇ Mark, ᶜ Luke, ᵈ John.

¹ Or, *endued with grace.*
² Many ancient authorities add *blessed* art *thou among women.*
³ Or, *grace.*   ⁴ Gr. *unto the ages.*
⁵ Or, *that which is to be born shall be called holy, the Son of God.*   ⁶ Some ancient authorities insert *of thee.*
⁷ Or, *is,*

For no word from God shall be void of 37
power. And Mary said, Behold, the ¹ hand- 38
maid of the Lord; be it unto me according
to thy word. And the angel departed
from her.

§ 6. The Meeting of Mary and Elisabeth.

[In the hill country of Judea.]

⁰ And Mary arose in these days and went 39
into the hill country with haste, into a city
of Judah; and entered into the house of 40
Zacharias and saluted Elisabeth. And it 41
came to pass, when Elisabeth heard the
salutation of Mary, the babe leaped in her
womb; and Elisabeth was filled with the
Holy Spirit; and she lifted up her voice 42
with a loud cry, and said, Blessed *art* thou
among women, and blessed *is* the fruit of
thy womb. And whence is this to me, that 43
the mother of my Lord should come unto
me? For behold, when the voice of thy 44
salutation came into mine ears, the babe
leaped in my womb for joy. And blessed 45
is she that ²believed; for there shall be a
fulfilment of the things which have been
spoken to her from the Lord. And Mary 46
said,

My soul doth magnify the Lord,
And my spirit hath rejoiced in God 47
    my Saviour.
For he hath looked upon the low es- 48
    tate of his ³handmaiden;
For behold, from henceforth all gener-
    ations shall call me blessed.
For he that is mighty hath done to me 49
    great things;
And holy is his name.
And his mercy is unto generations and 50
    generations

KEY.—ᵃ Matthew, ᵇ Mark, ᶜ Luke, ᵈ John.

¹ Gr. *bondmaid.*   ² Or, *believed that there shall be.*
³ Gr. *bondmaiden.*

Luke 1.

On them that fear him.

51   He hath shewed strength with his arm;
He hath scattered the proud [1] in the
imagination of their heart.

52   He hath put down princes from *their*
thrones,
And hath exalted them of low degree.

53   The hungry he hath filled with good
things;
And the rich he hath sent empty away.

54   He hath holpen Israel his servant,
That he might remember mercy

55   (As he spake unto our fathers)
Toward Abraham and his seed for
ever.

56 And Mary abode with her about three
months, and returned unto her house.

§ 7. The Birth of John.

[In the hill country of Judea.]

Luke 1.

57 [c] Now Elisabeth's time was fulfilled that
she should be delivered; and she brought

58 forth a son. And her neighbours and her
kinsfolk heard that the Lord had magni-
fied his mercy towards her; and they re-
59 joiced with her. And it came to pass
on the eighth day, that they came to circumcise the child; and they would have
called him Zacharias, after the name of
60 his father. And his mother answered
and said, Not so; but he shall be called
61 John. And they said unto her, There is
none of thy kindred that is called by this
62 name. And they made signs to his father,
63 what he would have him called. And he
asked for a writing tablet, and wrote, say-
64 ing, His name is John. And they marvelled all. And his mouth was opened
immediately, and his tongue *loosed*, and he
65 spake, blessing God. And fear came on

KEY.—[a] Matthew, [b] Mark, [c] Luke. [d] John.

[1] Or, *by.*

all that dwelt round about them: and all
these sayings were noised abroad throughout all the hill country of Judæa. And 66
all that heard them laid them up in their
heart, saying, What then shall this child
be? For the hand of the Lord was with
him.

And his father Zacharias was filled with 67
the Holy Spirit, and prophesied, saying,

Blessed *be* the Lord, the God of Israel; 68
For he hath visited and wrought re-
demption for his people,
And hath raised up a horn of salvation 69
for us
In the house of his servant David
(As he spake by the mouth of his holy 70
prophets that have been of old),
Salvation from our enemies, and from 71
the hand of all that hate us;
To shew mercy towards our fathers,   72
And to remember his holy covenant;
The oath which he sware unto Abra- 73
ham our father,
To grant unto us that we being deliv- 74
ered out of the hand of our ene-
mies
Should serve him without fear,
In holiness and righteousness before 75
him all our days.
Yea and thou, child, shalt be called the 76
prophet of the Most High:
For thou shalt go before the face of
the Lord to make ready his ways;
To give knowledge of salvation unto 77
his people
In the remission of their sins,
Because of the ¹tender mercy of our 78
God,
²Whereby the dayspring from on high
³shall visit us,

KEY.—ᵃ Matthew, ᵇ Mark, ᶜ Luke, ᵈ John.
¹ Or, *heart of mercy*.   ² Or, *Wherein*.
³ Many ancient authorities read *hath visited us*.

79   To shine upon them that sit in darkness and the shadow of death;
To guide our feet into the way of peace.
80   And the child grew, and waxed strong
in spirit, and was in the deserts till the day
of his shewing unto Israel.

§ 8. The Birth of Jesus.

[At Bethlehem.]

Matthew 1.
18   ^a Now the ¹birth ²of Jesus Christ was on
this wise: When his mother Mary had
been betrothed to Joseph, before they came
together she was found with child of the
19 Holy Spirit. And Joseph* her husband,
being a righteous man, and not willing to
make her a public example, was minded to
20 put her away privily. But when he thought
on these things, behold, an angel of the
Lord appeared unto him in a dream, saying, Joseph, thou son of David, fear not to
take unto thee Mary thy wife: for that
which is ³conceived in her is of the Holy
21 Spirit. And she shall bring forth a son;
and thou shalt call his name JESUS; for it
is he that shall save his people from their
22 sins. Now all this is come to pass, that it
might be fulfilled which was spoken by the
Lord through the prophet, saying,
23   Behold, the virgin shall be with child,
and shall bring forth a son,
And they shall call his name ⁴Imman-
uel;
which is, being interpreted, God with us.
24 And Joseph arose from his sleep, and did
as the angel of the Lord commanded him,
25 and took unto him his wife; and knew her

KEY.—^a Matthew, ^b Mark, ^c Luke, ^d John.

¹ Or, *generation.*
² Some ancient authorities read *of the Christ.*
³ Gr. *begotten.*   ⁴ Gr. *Emmanuel.*

* In Matthew's account Joseph is most prominent; but in
Luke's, Mary occupies the first place.

not till she had brought forth a son : and he
called his name JESUS.　　　　　　　Luke 2.

 ᶜ Now it came to pass in those days, there 1
went out a decree from Cæsar Augustus,
that all ¹ the world should be enrolled.
This was the first enrolment made when 2
Quirinius was governor of Syria.　And all 3
went to enrol themselves, every one to his
own city.　And Joseph also went up from 4
Galilee, out of the city of Nazareth, into
Judæa, to the city of David, which is called
Bethlehem, because he was of the house
and family of David ; to enrol himself with 5
Mary, who was betrothed to him, being
great with child.　And it came to pass, 6
while they were there. the days were fulfilled that she should be delivered.　And 7
she brought forth her firstborn son ; and
she wrapped him in swaddling clothes, and
laid him in a manger, because there was
no room for them in the inn.

§ 9.　The Shepherds and the Angels.

[Near Bethlehem.]

Luke 2.

And there were shepherds in the same 8
country abiding in the field, and keeping
ᵇ watch by night over their flock.　And an 9
angel of the Lord stood by them, and the
glory of the Lord shone round about them :
and they were sore afraid.　And the angel 10
said unto them, Be not afraid ; for behold,
I bring you good tidings of great joy
which shall be to all the people : for there 11
is born to you this day in the city of David
a Saviour, who is ²Christ the Lord.　And 12
this *is* the sign unto you : Ye shall find a
babe wrapped in swaddling clothes, and
lying in a manger.　And suddenly there 13
was with the angel a multitude of the
heavenly host praising God, and saying,

KEY.—ᵃ Matthew, ᵇ Mark, ᶜ Luke, ᵈ John.

¹ Gr. *the inhabited earth.*　　　　² Or, *night-watches,*
² Or, *Anointed Lord.*

Luke 2.

14   Glory to God in the highest,
      And on earth [1]peace among [2]men in
        whom he is well pleased.

15 And it came to pass, when the angels went away from them into heaven, the shepherds said one to another, Let us now go even unto Bethlehem, and see this [4]thing that is come to pass, which the Lord
16 hath made known unto us.   And they came with haste, and found both Mary and Joseph, and the babe lying in the manger.
17 And when they saw it, they made known concerning the saying which was spoken to
18 them about this child.   And all that heard it wondered at the things which were
19 spoken unto them by the shepherds.   But Mary kept all these [3]sayings, pondering
20 them in her heart.   And the shepherds returned, glorifying and praising God for all the things that they had heard and seen, even as it was spoken unto them.

§ 10.   Jesus Presented in the Temple.

[At Jerusalum.]

Luke 2.

21   [c]And when eight days were fulfilled for circumcising him, his name was called JESUS, which was so called by the angel before he was conceived in the womb.
22   And when the days of their purification according to the law of Moses were fulfilled, they brought him up to Jerusalem, to pre-
23 sent him to the Lord (as it is written in the law of the Lord, Every male that openeth the womb shall be called holy to the Lord),
24 and to offer a sacrifice according to that which is said in the law of the Lord, A pair of turtledoves, or two young pigeons.
25 And behold, there was a man in Jerusalem,

KEY.—[a] Matthew, [b] Mark, [c] Luke, [d] John.

[1] Many ancient authorities read *peace, good pleasure among men.*
[2] Gr. *men of good pleasure.*   [3] Or, *saying.*
[4] Or, *things.*

whose name was Simeon; and this man
was righteous and devout, looking for the
consolation of Israel: and the Holy Spirit
was upon him.   And it had been revealed 26
unto him by the Holy Spirit, that he
should not see death, before he had seen
the Lord's Christ.   And he came in the 27
Spirit into the temple: and when the parents brought in the child Jesus, that they
might do concerning him after the custom
of the law, then he received him into his 28
arms, and blessed God, and said,

      Now lettest thou thy [1] servant depart, 29
        O [2] Lord,
      According to thy word, in peace;
      For mine eyes have seen thy salvation, 30
      Which thou hast prepared before the 31
        face of all peoples;
      A light for [3]revelation to the Gentiles, 32
      And the glory of thy people Israel.

And his father and his mother were mar- 33
velling at the things which were spoken
concerning him; and Simeon blessed them, 34
and said unto Mary his mother, Behold,
this *child* is set for the falling and the rising
of many in Israel; and for a sign which is
spoken against; yea and a sword shall 35
pierce through thine own soul; that
thoughts out of many hearts may be revealed.   And there was one Anna, a pro- 36
phetess, the daughter of Phanuel, of the
tribe of Asher (she was 'of a great age,
having lived with a husband seven years
from her virginity, and she had been a 37
widow even unto fourscore and four years),
who departed not from the temple, wor-
shipping with fastings and supplications
night and day.   And coming up at that 38
very hour she gave thanks unto God, and

KEY.—[a] Matthew, [b] Mark, [c] Luke, [d] John. -

[1] Gr. *bondservant*.   [2] Gr. *Master*.
[3] Or, *the unveiling of the Gentiles*.
[4] Gr. *advanced in many days*.

Luke 2.

spake of him to all them that were looking
39 for the redemption of Jerusalem. And
when they had accomplished all things
that were according to the law of the Lord,
they returned into Galilee, to their own
city Nazareth.

40 And the child grew, and waxed strong,
[1] filled with wisdom: and the grace of God
was upon him.

§ 11. The Wise Men from the East.

[Jerusalem and Bethlehem.]

Matthew 2.

1 [a] Now when Jesus was born in Bethlehem of Judæa in the days of Herod the
king, behold, [2] wise men from the east came
2 to Jerusalem, saying, [3] Where is he that is
born King of the Jews? for we saw his star
in the east, and are come to [4] worship him.

3 And when Herod the king heard it, he was
troubled, and all Jerusalem with him.

4 And gathering together all the chief priests
and scribes of the people, he inquired of
them where the Christ should be born.

5 And they said unto him, In Bethlehem of
Judæa: for thus it is written through the
prophet,

6 And thou Bethlehem, land of Judah,
Art in no wise least among the princes
of Judah:
For out of thee shall come forth a gov-
ernor,
Who shall be shepherd of my people
Israel.

7 Then Herod privily called the [2] wise men,
and learned of them carefully [5] what time
8 the star appeared. And he sent them to
Bethlehem, and said, Go and search out

KEY.—[a] Matthew, [b] Mark, [c] Luke, [d] John.

[1] Gr. *becoming full of wisdom.* [2] Gr. *Magi.*
[3] Or, *Where is the King of the Jews that is born?*
[4] The Greek word denotes an act of reverence, whether
paid to man or to God.
[5] Or, *the time of the star that appeared.*

carefully concerning the young child; and
when ye have found *him*, bring me word,
that I also may come and worship him.
And they, having heard the king, went their 9
way; and lo, the star, which they saw in
the east, went before them, till it came and
stood over where the young child was. And 10
when they saw the star, they rejoiced with
exceeding great joy. And they came into 11
the house and saw the young child with
Mary his mother; and they fell down and
worshipped him; and opening their treasures they offered unto him gifts, gold and
frankincense and myrrh. And being 12
warned *of God* in a dream that they should
not return to Herod, they departed into
their own country another way.

§ 12. The Journey into Egypt.

ᵃ Now when they were departed, behold, an 13
angel of the Lord appeareth to Joseph in a
dream, saying, Arise, and take the young
child and his mother, and flee into Egypt,
and be thou there until I tell thee: for Herod will seek the young child to destroy
him. And he arose and took the young 14
child and his mother by night, and departed
into Egypt; and was there until the death 15
of Herod: that it might be fulfilled which
was spoken by the Lord through the prophet, saying, Out of Egypt did I call my son.
Then Herod, when he saw that he was 16
mocked of the ¹ wise men, was exceeding
wroth, and sent forth, and slew all the male
children that were in Bethlehem, and in all
the borders thereof, from two years old and
under, according to the time which he had
carefully learned of the ¹ wise men. Then 17
was fulfilled that which was spoken through
Jeremiah the prophet, saying,

KEY.—ᵃ Matthew, ᵇ Mark. ᶜ Luke, ᵈ John.
¹ Gr. *Magi.*

Matthew 2.

18   A voice was heard in Ramah,
      Weeping and great mourning,
      Rachel weeping for her children;
      And she would not be comforted, be-
        cause they are not.

19 But when Herod was dead, behold, an
angel of the Lord appeareth in a dream to
20 Joseph in Egypt, saying, Arise and take the
young child and his mother, and go into the
land of Israel: for they are dead that
21 sought the young child's life. And he arose
and took the young child and his mother,
22 and came into the land of Israel. But when
he heard that Archelaus was reigning over
Judæa in the room of his father Herod, he
was afraid to go thither; and being warned
of God in a dream, he withdrew into the
23 parts of Galilee, and came and dwelt in a
city called Nazareth: that it might be fulfilled which was spoken through the prophets, that he should be called a Nazarene.

§ 13. The Child Jesus in the Temple.

[At Jerusalem.]

Luke 2.

41   c And his parents went every year to Jeru-
42 salem at the feast of the passover. And
when he was twelve years old, they went up
43 after the custom of the feast; and when they
had fulfilled the days, as they were returning,
the boy Jesus tarried behind in Jerusalem;
44 and his parents knew it not; but supposing
him to be in the company, they went a day's
journey; and they sought for him among
45 their kinsfolk and acquaintance: and when
they found him not, they returned to Jeru-
46 salem, seeking for him. And it came to pass,
after three days they found him in the temple, sitting in the midst of the [1] doctors, both
hearing them, and asking them questions:
47 and all that heard him were amazed at his
48 understanding and his answers. And when

KEY.—a Matthew, b Mark, c Luke, d John.

[1] Or, *teachers.*

they saw him, they were astonished: and
his mother said unto him, [1] Son, why hast
thou thus dealt with us? behold, thy father
and I sought thee sorrowing. And he said 49
unto them, How is it that ye sought me?
knew ye not that I must be [2] in my Father's
house? And they understood not the say- 50
ing which he spake unto them. And he went 51
down with them, and came to Nazareth ;
and he was subject unto them: and his
mother kept all *these* [3] sayings in her heart.

And Jesus advanced in wisdom and [4] stat- 52
ure, and in [5] favour with God and men.

§ 14. Preaching of John the Baptist.

[Near the River Jordan.]

[b] The beginning of the gospel of Jesus 1
Christ the Son of God ; even as it is written 2
in Isaiah the prophet,

Behold, I send my messenger before thy
face,

Who shall prepare thy way.

[c] Now in the fifteenth year of the reign of 1
Tiberius Cæsar, Pontius Pilate being governor of Judæa, and Herod being tetrarch
of Galilee, and his brother Philip tetrarch of
the region of Ituræa and Trachonitis, and
Lysanias tetrarch of Abilene, in the high- 2
priesthood of Annas and Caiaphas, the
word of God came unto John [a] the Baptist,
[c] the son of Zacharias in the wilderness, [a] of
Judæa. [c] And he came into all the region 3
round about Jordan, preaching the baptism
of repentance unto remission of sins; [a] saying, Repent ye, for the kingdom of heaven
is at hand; [c] as it is written in the book of 4
the words of Isaiah the prophet,

The voice of one crying in the wilderness,

KEY.—[a] Matthew, [b] Mark, [c] Luke, [d] John.

[1] Gr. *Child.*

[2] Or, *about my Father's business.* Gr. *in the things of my
Father.*   [3] Or, *things.*   [4] Or, *age.*   [5] Or, *grace.*

§ 14. Preaching of John the Baptist.

Matthew's Account.

Chap. 3.

1 And in those days cometh John the Baptist, preaching
2 in the wilderness of Judæa, saying, Repent ye ; for the
3 kingdom of heaven is at hand. For this is he that was
spoken of by Isaiah the Prophet, saying,
> The voice of one crying in the wilderness,
> Make ye ready the way of the Lord,
> Make his paths straight.

7 But when he saw many of the Pharisees and Sadducees
coming to his baptism, he said unto them, Ye offspring of
vipers, who warned you to flee from the wrath to come?
8 Bring forth therefore fruit worthy of repentance: and
9 think not to say within yourselves, We have Abraham to
our father: for I say unto you, that God is able of these
10 stones to raise up children unto Abraham. And even now
the axe lieth at the root of the trees: every tree therefore
that bringeth not forth good fruit is hewn down, and cast
11 into the fire. I indeed baptize you in water unto repentance: but he that cometh after me is mightier than I,
whose shoes I am not worthy to bear: he shall baptize you
12 in the Holy Spirit and *in* fire: whose fan is in his hand,
and he will thoroughly cleanse his threshing-floor; and he
will gather his wheat into the garner, but the chaff he will
burn up with unquenchable fire.

Mark's Account.

Chap. 1.

1 The beginning of the gospel of Jesus Christ, the Son of
God.

2 Even as it is written in Isaiah the prophet,
> Behold, I send my messenger before thy face,
> Who shall prepare thy way;

3 The voice of one crying in the wilderness,
> Make ye ready the way of the Lord,
> Make his paths straight;

4 John came, who baptized in the wilderness and preached
5 the baptism of repentance unto remission of sins. And
there went out unto him all the country of Judæa, and all
they of Jerusalem; and they were baptized of him in the
6 river Jordan, confessing their sins. And John was clothed
with camel's hair, and *had* a leathern girdle about his loins,
7 and did eat locusts and wild honey. And he preached,
saying, There cometh after me he that is mightier than I,
the latchet of whose shoes I am not worthy to stoop down
8 and unloose. I baptize you in water; but he shall baptize you in the Holy Spirit.

18

Luke 3.

Make ye ready the way of the Lord,
Make his paths straight.

5 Every valley shall be filled,
And every mountain and hill shall be
brought low;
And the crooked shall become straight,
And the rough ways smooth;

6 And all flesh shall see the salvation of

Matthew 3. God.

4 [a] Now John himself had his raiment of
camel's hair, and a leathern girdle about
his loins; and his food was locusts and

5 wild honey. Then went out unto him
Jerusalem, and all Judæa, and all the region

6 round about Jordan; and they were baptized of him in the river Jordan, confessing

Luke 3. their sins.

7 [c] He said therefore to the multitudes [a] of
the Pharisees and Sadducees [c] that went
out to be baptized of him, Ye offspring of
vipers, who warned you to flee from the

8 wrath to come? Bring forth therefore fruits
worthy of [1] repentance, and begin not to say
within yourselves, We have Abraham to
our father: for I say unto you, that God is
able of these stones to raise up children un-

9 to Abraham. And even now is the axe also
laid unto the root of the trees: every tree
therefore that bringeth not forth good fruit

10 is hewn down, and cast into the fire. And
the multitudes asked him, saying, What then

11 must we do? And he answered and said
unto them, He that hath two coats, let him
impart to him that hath none; and he that

12 hath food, let him do likewise. And there
came also [2] publicans to be baptized, and
they said unto him, [3] Master, what must we

13 do? And he said unto them, Extort no
more than that which is appointed you.

KEY.— [a] Matthew, [b] Mark, [c] Luke, [d] John.

[1] Or, *your repentance.*
[2] That is, *collectors or renters of Roman taxes.*
[3] Or, *teacher.*

And [1] soldiers also asked him, saying, And 14
we, what must we do? And he said unto
them, Extort from no man by violence,
neither accuse *any one* wrongfully; and be
content with your wages.

And as the people were in expectation, 15
and all men reasoned in their hearts concerning John, whether haply he were the Christ;
John answered, saying unto them all, I in- 16
deed baptize you with water; but there
cometh he that is mightier than I, the
latchet of whose shoes I am not [2] worthy
[b] to stoop down [c] to unloose: he shall baptize you [3] in the Holy Spirit and *in* fire:
whose fan is in his hand, throughly to 17
cleanse his threshing-floor, and to gather
the wheat into his garner; but the chaff he
will burn up with unquenchable fire.

With many other exhortations therefore 18
preached he [4] good tidings unto the people.

§ 15. Baptism of Jesus.

[The River Jordan.]

[a] Then cometh Jesus [c] when all the people 13
were baptized, [a] from Galilee to the Jordan
unto John, to be baptized of him. But 14
John would have hindered him, saying, I
have need to be baptized of thee, and comest thou to me? But Jesus answering said 15
unto him, Suffer [5] *it* now: for thus it becometh us to fulfil all righteousness. Then he
suffereth him. And Jesus, when he was 16
baptized, went up [o] praying, [a] straightway
from the water: and lo, the heavens were
[b] rent asunder and [a] opened [6] unto him, and
he saw the Spirit of God descending [c] in a
bodily form, [a] as a dove, and coming upon
him; and lo, a voice out of the heavens, say- 17

KEY.—[a] Matthew, [b] Mark, [c] Luke, [d] John.

[1] Gr. *soldiers on service.*   [2] Gr. *sufficient.*
[3] Or, *with.*   [4] Or, *the gospel.*   [5] Or, *me*
[6] Some ancient authorities omit *unto him.*

§ 15. Baptism of Jesus.

Mark's Account.

Chap. 1.

9 And it came to pass in those days, that Jesus came from Nazareth of Galilee, and was baptized of John in the
10 Jordan. And straightway coming up out of the water, he saw the heavens rent asunder, and the Spirit as a dove de-
11 scending upon him: and a voice came out of the heavens, Thou art my beloved Son, in thee I am well pleased.

Luke's Account.

Chap. 3.

21 Now it came to pass, when all the people were baptized, that, Jesus also having been baptized, and praying, the
22 heaven was opened, and the Holy Spirit descended in a bodily form, as a dove, upon him, and a voice came out of heaven, Thou art my beloved Son; in thee I am well pleased.

20

§ 16. The Temptation.

Mark's Account.

Mark 1.

And straightway the Spirit driveth him forth into the 12 wilderness. And he was in the wilderness forty days 13 tempted of Satan; and he was with the wild beasts; and the angels ministered unto him.

Luke's Account.

Luke 4.

And Jesus, full of the Holy Spirit, returned from the 1 Jordan, and was led in the Spirit in the wilderness during forty days, being tempted of the devil. And he did eat 2 nothing in those days: and when they were completed, he hungered. And the devil said unto him, If thou art the 3 Son of God, command this stone that it become bread. And Jesus answered unto him, It is written, Man shall not 4 live by bread alone. And he led him up, and shewed him 5 all the kingdoms of the world in a moment of time. And 6 the devil said unto him, To thee will I give all this authority, and the glory of them: for it hath been delivered unto me; and to whomsoever I will I give it. If thou 7 therefore wilt worship before me, it shall all be thine. And Jesus answered and said unto him, It is written, Thou 8 shalt worship the Lord thy God, and him only shalt thou serve. And he led him to Jerusalem, and set him on the 9 pinnacle of the temple, and said unto him, If thou art the Son of God, cast thyself down from hence: for it is written, 10

He shall give his angels charge concerning thee,
to guard thee:

and, 11

On their hands they shall bear thee up,
Lest haply thou dash thy foot against a stone.

And Jesus answering said unto him, It is said, Thou shalt 12 not try the Lord thy God.

And when the devil had completed every temptation, he 13 departed from him for a season.

21

Matthew 3.

ing, [1] This* is my beloved Son, in whom I am well pleased.

§ 16. The Temptation.

[In the Wilderness of Judea.]

Matthew 4.

1 [c]And Jesus, full of the Holy Spirit, returned from the Jordan and was [a]led up of the Spirit into the wilderness to be tempt-

2 ed of the devil: [b]and he was with the wild beasts. [a]And when he had fasted forty days and forty nights, [c]and did eat nothing in those days, [a]he afterward hungered.

3 And the tempter [c]—the devil—[a]came and said unto him, If thou art the Son of God, command that †these stones become

4 [a]bread. But he answered and said, It is written, Man shall not live by bread alone, but by every word that proceedeth out of

5 the mouth of God. Then the devil taketh him into [c]Jerusalem, [a]the holy city; and he

6 set him on the [a]pinnacle of the temple, and saith unto him, If thou art the Son of God, cast thyself down [c]from hence: [a]for it is written,

> He shall give his angels charge concerning thee [c]to guard thee:
> [a]And on their hands they shall bear thee up,
> Lest haply thou dash thy foot against a stone.

7 Jesus said unto him, Again it is written, Thou shalt not try the Lord thy God.

8 Again, the devil taketh him unto an exceeding high mountain, and sheweth him all the kingdoms of the world, and the glory of

9 them [c]in a moment of time, [a]and he said unto him, All these things will I give thee, if thou wilt fall down and worship me: [c]to

KEY.—[a] Matthew, [b] Mark, [c] Luke, [d] John.

[1] Or, *This is my Son; my beloved in whom I am well pleased.*　　[2] Gr. *loaves.*　　[3] Gr. *wing.*

* In Mark and Luke it is, *Thou art,* etc.

† Luke, *This* stone that *it,* etc.

thee will I give all this authority and the glory of them; for it hath been delivered unto me; and to whomsoever I will, I give it. If thou, therefore, wilt worship before me, it shall all be thine. [a] Then saith Jesus un- 10 to him, Get thee hence, Satan: for it is written, Thou shalt worship the Lord thy God, and him only shalt thou serve. [c] And when the devil had completed every temptation, he departed from him for a season; [a] and behold, angels came and ministered 11 unto him.

KEY.—[a] Matthew, [b] Mark, [c] Luke, [d] John.

PERIOD II.

First Year of Public Ministry.

FROM THE CALLING OF THE FIRST DISCIPLES TO THE SECOND PASSOVER.

[Time—A little more than one year.]

---

§ 17. The Testimony of John.

[Near Jordan.]

John 1.

ᶜAND Jesus himself, when he began to teach, was about thirty years of age.

19 ᵈAnd this is the witness of John, when the Jews sent unto him from Jerusalem priests and Levites to ask him, Who art

20 thou? And he confessed, and denied not; and he confessed, I am not the Christ.

21 And they asked him, What then? Art thou Elijah? And he saith, I am not. Art thou the prophet? And he answered,

22 No. They said therefore unto him, Who art thou? that we may give an answer to them that sent us. What sayest thou of

23 thyself? He said, I am the voice of one crying in the wilderness, Make straight the way of the Lord, as said Isaiah the prophet.

24 ¹And they had been sent from the Phari-

25 sees. And they asked him, and said unto him, Why then baptizest thou, if thou art not the Christ, neither Elijah, neither the

26 prophet? John answered them, saying, I baptize ²in water: in the midst of you

27 standeth one whom ye know not, *even* he

KEY.—ᵃ Matthew, ᵇ Mark, ᶜ Luke, ᵈ John.

¹ Or, *And* certain *had been sent from among the Pharisees.*
² Or, *with*

that cometh after me, the latchet of whose
shoe I am not worthy to unloose.   These 28
things were done in [1]Bethany beyond Jordan, where John was baptizing.

On the morrow he seeth Jesus coming 29
unto him, and saith, Behold, the Lamb of
God, that [2]taketh away the sin of the
world!   This is he of whom I said, After 30
me cometh a man who is become before
me: for he was [3]before me.   And I knew 31
him not; but that he should be made manifest to Israel, for this cause came I baptizing [4]in water.   And John bare witness, 32
saying, I have beheld the Spirit descending as a dove out of heaven; and it abode
upon him.   And I knew him not: but he 33
that sent me to baptize [4]in water, he said
unto me, Upon whomsoever thou shalt see
the Spirit descending, and abiding upon
him, the same is he that baptizeth [4]in the
Holy Spirit.   And I have seen, and have 34
borne witness that this is the Son of God.

§ 18. The First Disciples Called.

[Near Jordan.]

[d]Again on the morrow John was standing, 35
and two of his disciples; and he looked 36
upon Jesus as he walked, and saith, Behold,
the Lamb of God!   And the two disciples 37
heard him speak, and they followed Jesus.
And Jesus turned, and beheld them follow- 38
ing, and saith unto them, What seek ye?
And they said unto him, Rabbi (which is to
say, being interpreted, [5]Master), where abid-
est thou?   He saith unto them, Come, and 39
ye shall see.   They came therefore and saw
where he abode; and they abode with him

KEY.—[a] Matthew, [b] Mark, [c] Luke, [d] John.

[1] Many ancient authorities read *Bethabarah*, some *Betha
rabah*.
[2] Or, *beareth the sin.*   [3] Gr. *first in regard of me.*
[4] Or, *with.*   [5] Or, *Teacher.*

40 that day: it was about the tenth hour. One of the two that heard John *speak*, and followed him, was Andrew, Simon Peter's

41 brother. He findeth first his own brother Simon, and saith unto him, We have found the Messiah (which is, being interpreted, [1]Christ). He brought him unto Jesus.

42 Jesus looked upon him, and said, Thou art Simon the son of [2]John: thou shalt be called Cephas (which is by interpretation, [3]Peter).

43 On the morrow he was minded to go forth into Galilee, and he findeth Philip:

44 and Jesus saith unto him, Follow me. Now Philip was from Bethsaida, of the city of

45 Andrew and Peter. Philip findeth Nathanael, and saith unto him, We have found him, of whom Moses in the law, and the prophets, did write, Jesus of Nazareth, the

46 son of Joseph. And Nathanael said unto him, Can any good thing come out of Nazareth? Philip saith unto him, Come and

47 see. Jesus saw Nathanael coming to him, and saith of him, Behold, an Israelite indeed, in whom is no guile! Nathanael

48 saith unto him, Whence knowest thou me? Jesus answered and said unto him, Before Philip called thee, when thou wast under

49 the fig tree, I saw thee. Nathanael answered him, Rabbi, thou art the Son of

50 God; thou art King of Israel. Jesus answered and said unto him, Because I said unto thee I saw thee underneath the fig tree, believest thou? thou shalt see greater

51 things than these. And he saith unto him, Verily, verily, I say unto you, Ye shall see the heaven opened, and the angels of God ascending and descending upon the Son of man.

KEY.—[a] Matthew, [b] Mark, [c] Luke, [d] John.

[1] That is. *Anointed*.
[2] Gr. *Joanes*: called in Matt. xvi. 17, *Jonah*.
[3] That is, *Rock* or *Stone*.

§ 19. The Marriage at Cana of Galilee.

John 2.

^d And the third day there was a marriage 1 in Cana of Galilee; and the mother of Jesus was there: and Jesus also was bidden, and 2 his disciples, to the marriage.   And when 3 the wine failed, the mother of Jesus saith unto him, They have no wine.   And Jesus 4 saith unto her, Woman, what have I to do with thee? mine hour is not yet come. His mother saith unto the servants, What- 5 soever he saith unto you, do it.   Now 6 there were six waterpots of stone set there after the Jews' manner of purifying, containing two or three firkins apiece. Jesus saith unto them, Fill the waterpots 7 with water.   And they filled them up to the brim.   And he saith unto them, Draw 8 out now, and bear unto the 'ruler of the feast.   And they bare it.   And when 9 the ruler of the feast tasted the water ² now become wine, and knew not whence it was (but the servants who had drawn the water knew), the ruler of the feast calleth the bridegroom, and saith unto 10 him, Every man setteth on first the good wine; and when *men* have drunk freely, *then* that which is worse: thou hast kept the good wine until now.   This begin- 11 ning of his signs did Jesus in Cana of Galilee, and manifested his glory; and his disciples believed on him.

After this he went down to Capernaum, 12 he, and his mother, and *his* brethren, and his disciples: and there they abode not many days.

§ 20. Cleansing the Temple.

[Jerusalem.]

John 2.

^d And the passover of the Jews was at 13 hand, and Jesus went up to Jerusalem.*

KEY.—^a Matthew, ^b Mark, ^c Luke, ^d John.

¹ Or, *steward.*   ² Or, *that it had become.*

* The first passover that Jesus attended as a public

PLATE II.

FROM CAPERNAUM TO JERUSALEM, AND RETURN.

(§§ 20–29.)

As shown by the blue line, Jesus went from Capernaum up to Jerusalem to the first Passover of his ministry (§ 20). Here he met Nicodemus (§ 21); then he went into the country of Judea, near to the place of John's baptizing (§ 22), and there baptized.

As shown by the red line, Jesus returned into Galilee by the way of Jerusalem and Samaria, and near Sychar (§ 23) talked with the women of Samaria; continuing his journey, he healed a nobleman's son at Cana (§ 25); was rejected at Nazareth, his old home (§ 26), and making a circuit through the cities of Galilee, reached Capernaum again, where he wrought many miracles (§§ 27–29). In the vicinity of this city the Sermon on the Mount was preached (§ 30), and a leper cleansed; also the daughter of Jairus was raised from the dead (§ 35), and two blind men restored to sight (§ 36), in Capernaum.

The next journey, which was to the second Passover of the public ministry at Jerusalem, and return to Capernaum, is not delineated on the map, as it is similar to that marked on this plate (§§ 38–40).

(Opposite page 27.)

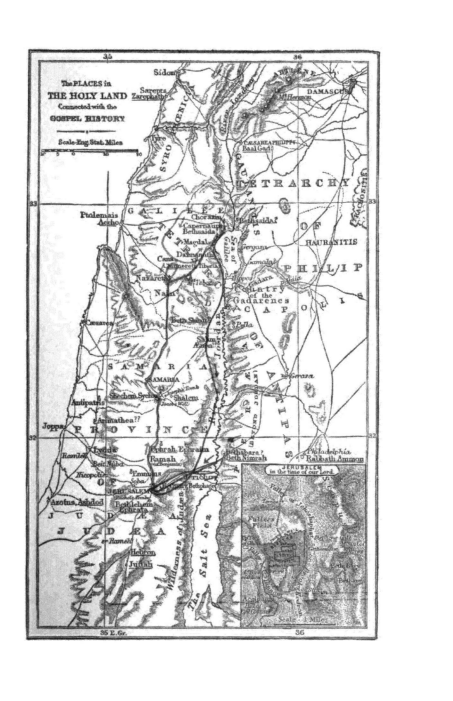

John 2.

14 And he found in the temple those that sold
 oxen and sheep and doves, and the chang-
15 ers of money sitting: and he made a scourge
 of cords, and cast all out of the temple,
 both the sheep and the oxen; and he
 poured out the changers' money, and over-
16 threw their tables; and to them that sold
 the doves he said, Take these things hence;
 make not my Father's house a house of
17 merchandise. His disciples remembered
 that it was written, Zeal for thy house shall
18 eat me up. The Jews therefore answered
 and said unto him, What sign shewest
 thou unto us, seeing that thou doest these
19 things? Jesus answered and said unto
 them, Destroy this ¹ temple, and in three
20 days I will raise it up. The Jews therefore said, Forty and six years was this
 ᵃtemple in building, and wilt thou raise
21 it up in three days? But he spake of the
22 ᵃtemple of his body. When therefore he
 was raised from the dead, his disciples
 remembered that he spake this; and they
 believed the scripture, and the word which
 Jesus had said.
23 Now when he was in Jerusalem at the
 passover, during the feast, many believed
 on his name, beholding his signs which he
24 did. But Jesus did not trust himself unto
25 them, for that he knew all men, and because he needed not that any one should
 bear witness concerning ²man; for he
 himself knew what was in man.

§ 21. Nicodemus.

[Jerusalem.]

John 3.

1 Now there was a man of the Pharisees,
2 named Nicodemus, a ruler of the Jews: the

KEY——ᵃ Matthew, ᵇ Mark, ᵉ Luke, ᵈ John.

¹ Or, *sanctuary.* ² Or, *a man; for . . . the man.*

teacher. It is only by means of the successive passovers
he visited that the duration of his earthly ministry can be
computed. These notes of time are furnished only by
John's Gospel.

same came unto him by night, and said
to him, Rabbi, we know that thou art a
teacher come from God: for no man can
do these signs that thou doest, except God
be with him. Jesus answered and said 3
unto him, Verily, verily, I say unto thee,
Except a man be born ¹anew, he cannot
see the kingdom of God.. Nicodemus 4
saith unto him, How can a man be born
when he is old? can he enter a second time
into his mother's womb, and be born?
Jesus answered, Verily, verily, I say unto 5
thee, Except a man be born of water and
the Spirit, he cannot enter into the kingdom of God.   That which is born of the 6
flesh is flesh; and that which is born of
the Spirit is spirit.   Marvel not that I 7
said unto thee, Ye must be born ¹anew.
²The wind bloweth where it listeth, and 8
thou hearest the voice thereof, but knowest
not whence it cometh, and whither it goeth:
so is every one that is born of the Spirit.
Nicodemus answered and said unto him, 9
How can these things be? Jesus answered 10
and said unto him, Art thou the teacher
of Israel, and understandest not these
things? Verily, verily, I say unto thee, 11
We speak that we do know, and bear witness of that we have seen; and ye receive
not our witness. If I told you earthly 12
things, and ye believe not, how shall ye
believe, if I tell you heavenly things? And 13
no man hath ascended into heaven, but he
that descended out of heaven, *even* the Son
of man, ³who is in heaven.   And as Moses 14
lifted up the serpent in the wilderness, even
so must the Son of man be lifted up: that 15
whosoever ⁴believeth may in him have
eternal life.

KEY.—ᵃ Matthew, ᵇ Mark, ᶜ Luke, ᵈ John.

¹ Or, *from above.*   ² Or, *The Spirit breatheth.*
³ Many ancient authorities omit *who is in heaven.*
⁴ Or, *believeth in him may have*

John 3.

16 For God so loved the world, that he gave his only begotten Son, that whosoever believeth on him should not perish,

17 but have eternal life. For God sent not the Son into the world to judge the world; but that the world should be saved through

18 him. He that believeth on him is not judged: he that believeth not hath been judged already, because he hath not believed on the name of the only begotten

19 Son of God. And this is the judgement, that the light is come into the world, and men loved the darkness rather than the light;

20 for their works were evil. For every one that [1] doeth evil hateth the light, and cometh not to the light, lest his works should

21 be [2] reproved. But he that doeth the truth cometh to the light, that his works may be made manifest, [3] that they have been wrought in God.

§ 22. Jesus and John baptize.

[In the Jordan Valley.]

John 3.

22 [d] After these things came Jesus and his disciples into the land of Judæa; and there

23 he tarried with them, and baptized. And John also was baptizing in Ænon near to Salim, because there [4] was much water there: and they came, and were baptized.

24 For John was not yet cast into prison.

25 There arose therefore a questioning on the part of John's disciples with a Jew about

26 purifying. And they came unto John, and said to him, Rabbi, he that was with thee beyond Jordan, to whom thou hast borne witness, behold, the same baptizeth, and all

27 men come to him. John answered and said, A man can receive nothing, except it

28 have been given him from heaven. Ye

KEY.—[a] Matthew, [b] Mark, [c] Luke, [d] John.

[1] Or, *practiseth.*   [2] Or, *convicted.*
[3] Or, *because.*   [4] Gr. *were many waters.*

yourselves bear me witness, that I said, I am not the Christ, but, that I am sent before him.   He that hath the bride is the bride- 29 groom: but the friend of the bridegroom, who standeth and heareth him, rejoiceth greatly because of the bridegroom's voice: this my joy therefore is made full.   He 30 must increase, but I must decrease.

He that cometh from above is above all: 31 he that is of the earth is of the earth, and of the earth he speaketh: [1] he that cometh from heaven is above all.   What he hath 32 seen and heard, of that he beareth witness; and no man receiveth his witness.   He that 33 hath received his witness hath set his seal to *this*, that God is true.   For he whom 34 God hath sent speaketh the words of God: for he giveth not the Spirit by measure. The Father loveth the Son, and hath given 35 all things into his hand.   He that believeth 36 on the Son hath eternal life; but he that [2] obeyeth not the Son shall not see life, but the wrath of God abideth on him.

§ 23.   The Woman of Samaria.

[d] When therefore the Lord knew how 1 that the Pharisees had heard that Jesus was making and baptizing more disciples than John (although Jesus himself baptized not, 2 but his disciples), he left Judæa, and de- 3 parted again into Galilee.   And he must 4 needs pass through Samaria.   So he com- 5 eth to a city of Samaria, called Sychar, near to the parcel of ground that Jacob gave to his son Joseph: and Jacob's [3] well was there. 6 Jesus therefore, being wearied with his journey, sat [4] thus by the [3] well.   It was

KEY.—[a] Matthew, [b] Mark, [c] Luke, [d] John.

[1] Some ancient authorities read *he that cometh from heaven beareth witness of what he hath seen and heard.*

[2] Or, *believeth not.*

[3] Gr. *spring*: and so in ver. 14; but not in ver. 11, 12.

[4] Or, *as he was.*

John 4.

7 about the sixth hour. There cometh a
woman of Samaria to draw water: Jesus
8 saith unto her, Give me to drink. For his
disciples were gone away into the city to
9 buy food. The Samaritan woman therefore saith unto him, How is it that thou,
being a Jew, asketh drink of me, who am a
Samaritan woman? (¹For Jews have no
10 dealings with Samaritans.) Jesus answered and said unto her, If thou knewest the
gift of God, and who it is that saith to thee,
Give me to drink; thou wouldest have
asked of him, and he would have given thee
11 living water. The woman saith unto him,
'Sir, thou hast nothing to draw with, and
the well is deep: from whence then hast
12 thou that living water? Art thou greater
than our father Jacob, who gave us the
well, and drank thereof himself, and his
13 sons, and his cattle? Jesus answered and
said unto her, Every one that drinketh of
14 this water shall thirst again: but whosoever drinketh of the water that I shall give
him shall never thirst; but the water that
I shall give him shall become in him a well
15 of water springing up unto eternal life. The
woman saith unto him, 'Sir, give me this
water, that I thirst not, neither come all
16 the way hither to draw. Jesus saith unto
her, Go, call thy husband, and come hither.
17 The woman answered and said unto him,
I have no husband. Jesus saith unto her,
18 Thou saidst well, I have no husband: for
thou hast had five husbands; and he whom
thou now hast is not thy husband: this hast
19 thou said truly. The woman saith unto
him, 'Sir, I perceive that thou art a proph-
20 et. Our fathers worshipped in this mountain; and ye say, that in Jerusalem is the

KEY.—ᵃ Matthew, ᵇ Mark, ᶜ Luke, ᵈ John.

¹ Some ancient authorities omit *For Jews have no dealings with Samaritans.*
³ Or. *Lord.*

place where men ought to worship. Jesus 21 saith unto her, Woman, believe me, the hour cometh, when neither in this mountain, nor in Jerusalem, shall ye worship the Father. Ye worship that which ye know 22 not: we worship that which we know: for salvation is from the Jews. But the hour 23 cometh, and now is, when the true worshippers shall worship the Father in spirit and truth: ¹ for such doth the Father seek to be his worshippers. ² God is a Spirit: 24 and they that worship him must worship in spirit and truth. The woman saith unto 25 him, I know that Messiah cometh (who is called Christ): when he is come, he will declare unto us all things. Jesus saith unto 26 her, I that speak unto thee am *he*.

And upon this came his disciples; and 27 they marvelled that he was speaking with a woman; yet no man said, What seekest thou? or, Why speakest thou with her? So 28 the woman left her waterpot, and went away into the city, and saith to the men, Come, see a man, who told me all things 29 that *ever* I did: can this be the Christ? They went out of the city, and were com- 30 ing to him. In the mean while the disci- 31 ples prayed him, saying, Rabbi, eat. But 32 he said unto them, I have meat to eat that ye know not. The disciples therefore said 33 one to another, Hath any man brought him *aught* to eat? Jesus saith unto them, 34 My meat is to do the will of him that sent me, and to accomplish his work. Say not 35 ye, There are yet four months, and *then* cometh the harvest? behold, I say unto you, Lift up your eyes, and look on the fields, that they are ³ white already unto harvest. He that reapeth receiveth wages, and 36

KEY.—ᵃ Matthew, ᵇ Mark, ᶜ Luke, ᵈ John.
¹ Or, *for such the Father also seeketh.*
² Or, *God is spirit.*
³ Or, *white unto harvest. Already he that reapeth &c.*

§ 24. Preaching in Galilee.

Mark's Account.

Chap. 1.

Now after that John was delivered up, Jesus came into 14
Galilee preaching the gospel of God, and saying, The time 15
is fulfilled, and the kingdom of God is at hand: repent ye,
and believe in the gospel.

Luke's Account.

Chap. 4.

And Jesus returned in the power of the Spirit into 14
Galilee: and a fame went out concerning him through all
the region round about. And he taught in their syna- 15
gogues, being glorified of all.

John 4.

gathereth fruit unto life eternal; that he
that soweth and he that reapeth may re-
37 joice together. For herein is the saying
true, One soweth, and another reapeth.
38 I sent you to reap that whereon ye have
not laboured: others have laboured, and
ye are entered into their labour.

39 And from that city many of the Samaritans believed on him because of the word
of the woman, who testified, He told me all
40 things that *ever* I did. So when the Samaritans came unto him, they besought him
to abide with them: and he abode there
41 two days. And many more believed be-
42 cause of his word; and they said to the
woman, Now we believe, not because of
thy speaking: for we have heard for ourselves, and know that this is indeed the
Saviour of the world.

§ 24. Preaching in Galilee.

John 4.

43 ᵈ And after the two days he went forth
44 from thence into Galilee. For Jesus himself testified, that a prophet hath no honour
45 in his own country. So when he came into Galilee, the Galilæans received him,
having seen all the things that he did in
Jerusalem at the feast: for they also went
unto the feast. ᶜAnd a fame went out concerning him through all the region round
about; and he taught in their synagogues
being glorified of all; ᵇ preaching the gospel of God, and saying, The time is fulfilled, and the kingdom of God is at hand;
repent ye, and believe in the gospel.

§ 25. The Nobleman's Son.

[At Cana.]

John 4.

46 ᵈ He came therefore again unto Cana of
Galilee, where he made the water wine.

KEY.—ᵃ Matthew, ᵇ Mark, ᶜ Luke, ᵈ John.

And there was a certain ' nobleman, whose son was sick at Capernaum. When he 47 heard that Jesus was come out of Judæa into Galilee, he went unto him, and besought *him* that he would come down, and heal his son; for he was at the point of death. Jesus therefore said unto him, Ex- 48 cept ye see signs and wonders, ye will in no wise believe. The 'nobleman saith un- 49 to him, ' Sir, come down ere my child die. Jesus saith unto him, Go thy way ; thy son 50 liveth. The man believed the word that Jesus spake unto him, and he went his way. And as he was now going down, his ' ser- 51 vants met him, saying, that his son lived. So he inquired of them the hour when he 52 began to amend. They said therefore unto him, Yesterday at the seventh hour the fever left him. So the father knew that *it* 53 *was* at that hour in which Jesus said unto him, Thy son liveth : and himself believed, and his whole house. This is again the 54 second sign that Jesus did, having come out of Judæa into Galilee.

§ 26. Rejection at Nazareth.

° And he came to Nazareth, where he had 16 been brought up : and he entered, as his custom was, into the synagogue on the sabbath day, and stood up to read. And 17 there was delivered unto him ' the book of the prophet Isaiah. And he opened the ' book, and found the place where it was written,

> The Spirit of the Lord is upon me, 18
> ' Because he anointed me to preach
>   ' good tidings to the poor :
> He hath sent me to proclaim release
>   to the captives,

KEY.—ᵃ Matthew, ᵇ Mark, ᶜ Luke, ᵈ John.

¹ Or, *king's officer.* ² Gr. *Lord.* ³ Or. *bond-servants.*
⁴ Or, *a roll.* ⁵ Or, *roll.* ⁶ Or, *Wherefore.*
⁷ Or, *the gospel.*

Luke 4.

And recovering of sight to the blind,
To set at liberty them that are bruised,

19   To proclaim the acceptable year of
the Lord.

20 And he closed the ¹book, and gave it back
to the attendant, and sat down: and the
eyes of all in the synagogue were fastened

21 on him.   And he began to say unto them,
To-day hath this scripture been fulfilled in

22 your ears.   And all bare him witness, and
wondered at the words of grace which
proceeded out of his mouth: and they said,

23 Is not this Joseph's son?   And he said
unto them, Doubtless ye will say unto me
this parable, Physician, heal thyself : whatsoever we have heard done at Capernaum,

24 do also here in thine own country.   And
he said, Verily I say unto you,   No
prophet is acceptable in his own coun-

25 try.   But of a truth I say unto you,
There were many widows in Israel in the
days of Elijah, when the heaven was shut
up three years and six months, when there

26 came a great famine over all the land ; and
unto none of them was Elijah sent, but
only to ² Zarephath, in the land of Sidon,

27 unto a woman that was a widow.   And
there were many lepers in Israel in the
time of Elisha the prophet ; and none of
them was cleansed, but only Naaman the

28 Syrian.   And they were all filled with
wrath in the synagogue, as they heard

29 these things ; and they rose up, and cast
him forth out of the city, and led him unto
the brow of the hill whereon their city
was built, that they might throw him down

30 headlong.   But he passing through the
midst of them went his way.

13 **Matthew 4.** ª And leaving Nazareth, he came
and dwelt in Capernaum, ᶜ a city of Gali-

KEY.--ª Matthew, ᵇ Mark, ᶜ Luke, ᵈ John.

¹ Or, *roll*.   ² Gr. *Sarepta*.

lee, ^awhich is by the sea, in the borders of 14
Zebulun and Naphtali: that it might be
fulfilled which was spoken through Isaiah
the prophet, saying,

> The land of Zebulun and the land of 15
> Naphtali,
> ¹Toward the sea, beyond Jordan,
> Galilee of the ²Gentiles,
> The people that sat in darkness   16
> Saw a great light,
> And to them that sat in the region
> and shadow of death,
> To them did light spring up.

§ 27.   Catching Fish and Fishermen.

[Near Capernaum.]

^cNow it came to pass, while the multitude 1
pressed upon him and heard the word of
God, that he was standing by the lake of
Gennesaret; and he saw two boats stand- 2
ing by the lake: but the fishermen had
gone out of them, and were washing their
nets. And he entered into one of the boats, 3
which was Simon's, and asked him to put
out a little from the land. And he sat
down and taught the multitudes out of the
boat. And when he had left speaking, he 4
said unto Simon, Put out into the deep,
and let down your nets for a draught. And 5
Simon answered and said, Master, we
toiled all night, and took nothing: but at
thy word I will let down the nets. And 6
when they had this done, they inclosed a
great multitude of fishes; and their nets
were breaking; and they beckoned unto 7
their partners in the other boat, that they
should come and help them. And they
came, and filled both the boats, so that
they began to sink. But Simon Peter, 8

KEY.—^a Matthew, ^b Mark, ^c Luke, ^d John.

¹ Gr. *The way of the sea.*
² Gr. *nations* : and so elsewhere.

§ 27. Catching Fish and Fishermen.

Matthew's Account.

Chap. 4.

18 And walking by the sea of Galilee, he saw two brethren, Simon who is called Peter, and Andrew his brother, cast-

19 ing a net into the sea; for they were fishers. And he saith unto them, Come ye after me, and I will make you

20 fishers of men. And they straightway left the nets, and

21 followed him. And going on from thence he saw other two brethren, James the *son* of Zebedee, and John his brother, in the boat with Zebedee their father, mending

22 their nets; and he called them. And they straightway left the boat and their father, and followed him.

Mark's Account.

Chap. 1.

16 And passing along by the sea of Galilee, he saw Simon and Andrew the brother of Simon, casting a net in the sea.

Luke's Account.

Chap. 5.

9 For he was amazed, and all that were with him, at the

10 draught of the fishes which they had taken; and so were also James and John, sons of Zebedee, who were partners with Simon. And Jesus said unto Simon, Fear not;

11 from henceforth thou shalt catch men. And when they had brought their boats to land, they left all, and followed him.

85

§ 28. Miracles at Capernaum.

Matthew's Account.

Chap. 8.

And when Jesus was come into Peter's house, he saw 14 his wife's mother lying sick of a fever. And he touched 15 her hand, and the fever left her ; and she arose, and min- istered unto him. And when even was come, they brought 16 unto him many possessed with demons : and he cast out the spirits with a word, and healed all that were sick : that 17 it might be fulfilled which was spoken through Isaiah the prophet, saying, Himself took our infirmities, and bare our diseases.

Luke's Account.

Chap. 4.

And he came down to Capernaum, a city of Galilee. 31 And he was teaching them on the sabbath day : and they 32 were astonished at his teaching : for his word was with authority. And in the synagogue there was a man, that 33 had a spirit of an unclean demon ; and he cried out with a loud voice, Ah! what have we to do with thee, thou Jesus 34 of Nazareth? art thou come to destroy us? I know thee who thou art, the Holy One of God. And Jesus rebuked 35 him, saying, Hold thy peace, and come out of him. And when the demon had thrown him down in the midst, he came out of him, having done him no hurt. And amaze- 36 ment came upon all, and they spake together, one with another, saying, What is this word? for with authority and power he commandeth the unclean spirits, and they come out. And there went forth a rumour concerning 37 him into every place of the region round about.

And he rose up from the synagogue, and entered into 38 the house of Simon. And Simon's wife's mother was holden with a great fever ; and they besought him for her. And he stood over her, and rebuked the fever ; and it left 39 her : and immediately she rose up and ministered unto them.

And when the sun was setting, all they that had any 40 sick with divers diseases brought them unto him ; and he laid his hands on every one of them, and healed them. And demons also came out from many, crying out, and 41 saying, Thou art the Son of God. And rebuking them, he suffered them not to speak, because they knew that he was the Christ.

And when it was day, he came out and went into a 42 desert place : and the multitudes sought after him, and came unto him, and would have stayed him, that he should not go from them. But he said unto them, I must preach 43 the good tidings of the kingdom of God to the other cities also : for therefore was I sent.

Luke 5.

when he saw it, fell down at Jesus' knees,
saying, Depart from me ; for I am a sinful
9 man, O Lord. For he was amazed, and
all that were with him, at the draught of
Mark 1. the fishes which they had taken.
17   ᵇ And Jesus said unto them, Come ye
after me, and I will make you to become
18 fishers of men. And straightway they
19 left the nets, and followed him. And going
on a little further, he saw James the *son* of
Zebedee, and John his brother, who also
20 were in the boat mending the nets. And
straightway he called them : and ᶜ when
they had brought their boats to land ᵇ they
left their father Zebedee in the boat with
the hired servants, and went after him.

§ 28. Miracles at Capernaum.

Mark 1.
21   ᵇ And they go into Capernaum ; and
straightway on the sabbath day he entered
22 into the synagogue and taught. And they
were astonished at his teaching : for he
taught them as having authority, and not
as the scribes ; ᶜ for his word was with au-
23 thority. ᵇ And straightway there was in
their synagogue a man with an unclean
spirit *[or] ᶜ demon ; ᵇ and he cried out,
24 ᶜ with a loud voice, ᵇ saying, ᶜ Ah ! ᵇ what
have we to do with thee, thou Jesus of
Nazareth ? art thou come to destroy us ?
I know thee who thou art, the Holy One
25 of God. And Jesus rebuked ¹ him, saying,
Hold thy peace, and come out of him.
26 And the unclean spirit, ᶜ when he had
thrown him down in the midst, ᵇ² tearing
him and crying with a loud voice, came
27 out of him. And they were all amazed, insomuch that they questioned among
themselves, saying, What is this ᶜ word ?

Key.—ᵃ Matthew, ᵇ Mark, ᶜ Luke, ᵈ John.

¹ Or, *it*.   ² Or, *convulsing*.

* A word inserted by the compiler.

[b] a new teaching! with authority [c] and power
[b] he commandeth even the unclean spirits, and they obey him.   And the report of 28 him went out straightway everywhere into all the region of Galilee round about.

And straightway, [1] when they were come 29 out of the synagogue, they came into the house of Simon and Andrew, with James and John.   Now Simon's wife's mother lay 30 sick of a [c] great [b] fever; and straightway they tell him of her : and he came and took her 31 by the hand, [c] and stood over her, and rebuked the fever, [b] and raised her up ; and the fever left her, and she ministered unto them.

And at even, when the sun did set, they 32 brought unto him all that were sick, and them that were [2] possessed with demons. And all the city was gathered together at 33 the door.   And he healed many that were 34 sick with divers diseases, [c] and he laid his hands on every one of them and he healed them, [b] and cast out many demons [a] with a word ; [b] and he suffered not the demons to speak, because they knew him [3] [c] that he was the Christ.

[b] And in the morning, a great while be- 35 fore day, he rose up and went out, and departed into a desert place, and there 36 prayed.   And Simon and they that were with him followed after him ; and they 37 found him, and say unto him, All are seeking thee.   [c] And the multitudes sought after him, and came unto him, and would have stayed him, that he should not go from them.   [b] And he saith unto them, Let 38 us go elsewhere into the next towns, that I may preach [c] the good tidings of the

KEY.—[a] Matthew, [b] Mark, [c] Luke, [d] John.

[1] Some ancient authorities read *when he was come out of the synagogue, he came &c.*
[2] Or, *demoniacs.*
[3] Many ancient authorities add *to be Christ.*

§ 29. The Growing Fame of Jesus.

Mark's Account.

Chap. 1.

And he went into their synagogues throughout all Galilee, 39
preaching and casting out demons.

Luke's Account.

Chap. 4.

And he was preaching in the synagogues of Galilee. 44

89.

Mark 1.

kingdom of God [b]there also ; for to this end came I forth.

§ 29. The Growing Fame of Jesus.

Matthew 4.

23 And [1]Jesus went about in all Galilee, teaching in their synagogues, and preaching the [2]gospel of the kingdom, and healing all manner of disease and all manner of
24 sickness among the people. And the report of him went forth into all Syria : and they brought unto him all that were sick, holden with divers diseases and torments, [3]possessed with demons, and epileptic, and
25 palsied ; and he healed them. And there followed him great multitudes from Galilee and Decapolis and Jerusalem and Judæa and *from* beyond Jordan.

§ 30. The Sermon on the Mount.*

[Probably the " Horns of Hattin," about seven miles from Capernaum.]

Matthew 5.

1 [a]And seeing the multitudes, he went up into the mountain : and when he had sat
2 down, his disciples came unto him : and he opened his mouth and taught them, saying,
3 Blessed are the poor in spirit: for theirs is the kingdom of heaven.
4 [a]Blessed are they that mourn : for they shall be comforted.

KEY.—[a] Matthew, [b] Mark, [c] Luke, [d] John.

[1] Some ancient authorities read *he.*
[2] Or, *good tidings :* and so elsewhere.
[3] Or, *demoniacs.*
[4] Some ancient authorities transpose ver. 4 and 5.

* Most harmonists treat the Sermon on the Mount as identical with the discourse of Luke 6. Several of weight, however, as Greswell, Doddridge, Clark, Alexander, and others, regard them as utterances separated by a considerable interval. We prefer this arrangement not only because of the strong arguments by which it is supported, but also because it leaves unchanged the familiar beauty of this marvellous passage. " The Sermon on the Plain" (§ 42) is a noble but much briefer discourse.

Blessed are the meek: for they shall in- 5
herit the earth.

Blessed are they that hunger and thirst 6
after righteousness: for they shall be
filled.

Blessed are the merciful: for they shall 7
obtain mercy.

Blessed are the pure in heart: for they 8
shall see God.

Blessed are the peacemakers: for they 9
shall be called sons of God.

Blessed are they that have been perse- 10
cuted for righteousness' sake: for theirs is
the kingdom of heaven. Blessed are ye 11
when *men* shall reproach you, and persecute you, and say all manner of evil
against you falsely, for my sake. Rejoice, 12
and be exceeding glad: for great is your
reward in heaven: for so persecuted they
the prophets that were before you.

Ye are the salt of the earth: but if the 13
salt have lost its savour, wherewith shall
it be salted? it is thenceforth good for
nothing, but to be cast out and trodden
under foot of men. Ye are the light of 14
the world. A city set on a hill cannot be
hid. Neither do *men* light a lamp, and 15
put it under the bushel, but on the stand;
and it shineth unto all that are in the
house. Even so let your light shine 16
before men, that they may see your good
works, and glorify your Father who is in
heaven.

Think not that I came to destroy the 17
law or the prophets: I came not to destroy, but to fulfil. For verily I say unto 18
you, Till heaven and earth pass away, one
jot or one tittle shall in no wise pass away
from the law, till all things be accom- 19
plished. Whosoever therefore shall break
one of these least commandments, and shall
teach men so, shall be called least in the

KEY.—* Matthew, *b* Mark, *c* Luke, *d* John.

Matthew 5.

kingdom of heaven: but whosoever shall
do and teach them, he shall be called great
20 in the kingdom of heaven.   For I say unto
you, that except your righteousness shall
exceed *the righteousness* of the scribes and
Pharisees, ye shall in no wise enter into
the kingdom of heaven.

21   Ye have heard that it was said to them
of old time, Thou shalt not kill; and whosoever shall kill shall be in danger of the
22 judgment: but I say unto you, that every
one who is angry with his brother[1] shall
be in danger of the judgement; and whosoever shall say to his brother, [2] Raca, shall
be in danger of the council; and whosoever shall say, [3] Thou fool, shall be in dan-
23 ger [4] of the [5] hell of fire.   If therefore thou
art offering thy gift at the altar, and there
rememberest that thy brother hath aught
24 against thee, leave there thy gift before
the altar, and go thy way, first be reconciled to thy brother, and then come and
25 offer thy gift.   Agree with thine adversary quickly, while thou art with him in
the way; lest haply the adversary deliver
thee to the judge, and the judge [6] deliver
thee to the officer, and thou be cast into
26 prison.   Verily I say unto thee, Thou shalt
by no means come out thence, till thou
have paid the last farthing.

27   Ye have heard that it was said, Thou
28 shalt not commit adultery: but I say unto
you, that every one that looketh on a
woman to lust after her hath committed
29 adultery with her already in his heart.   And
if thy right eye causeth thee to stumble,
pluck it out, and cast it from thee: for it

KEY.—[a] Matthew, [b] Mark, [c] Luke, [d] John.

[1] Many ancient authorities insert *without cause*.
[2] An expression of contempt.
[3] Or, *Moreh*, a Hebrew expression of condemnation.
[4] Gr. *unto* or *into*.
[5] Gr. *Gehenna of fire*.
[6] Some ancient authorities omit *deliver thee*.

is profitable for thee that one of thy members should perish, and not thy whole
body be cast into ¹hell.   And if thy right 30
hand causeth thee to stumble, cut it off,
and cast it from thee: for it is profitable
for thee that one of thy members should
perish, and not thy whole body go into
hell.   It was said also, Whosoever shall 31
put away his wife, let him give her a writing of divorcement: but I say unto you, 32
that every one that putteth away his wife,
saving for the cause of fornication, maketh
her an adulteress: and whosoever shall
marry her when she is put away committeth adultery.

Again, ye have heard that it was said to 33
them of old time, Thou shalt not forswear
thyself, but shalt perform unto the Lord
thine oaths: but I say unto you, Swear not 34
at all; neither by the heaven, for it is the
throne of God; nor by the earth, for it is 35
the footstool of his feet; nor ²by Jerusalem, for it is the city of the great King.
Neither shalt thou swear by thy head, for 36
thou canst not make one hair white or
black.   ³But let your speech be, Yea, yea; 37
Nay, nay: and whatsoever is more than
these is of ⁴the evil *one*.

Ye have heard that it was said, An eye 38
for an eye, and a tooth for a tooth: but I 39
say unto you, Resist not ⁴him that is evil:
but whosoever smiteth thee on thy right
cheek, turn to him the other also.   And if 40
any man would go to law with thee, and
take away thy coat, let him have thy cloke
also.   And whosoever shall ⁵compel thee 41
to go one mile, go with him twain.   Give 42
to him that asketh thee, and from him that
would borrow of thee turn not thou away.

KEY.—ᵃ Matthew, ᵇ Mark, ᶜ Luke, ᵈ John.

¹ Gr. *Gehenna*.   ² Or, *toward*
³ Some ancient authorities read *But your speech shall be*.
⁴ Or, *evil*.   ⁵ Gr. *impress*.

Matthew 5.

43 Ye have heard that it was said, Thou
shalt love thy neighbour, and hate thine

44 enemy: but I say unto you. Love your
enemies, and pray for them that persecute

45 you; that ye may be sons of your Father
who is in heaven: for he maketh his sun
to rise on the evil and the good, and send-

46 eth rain on the just and the unjust. For if
ye love them that love you, what reward
have ye? do not even the [1] publicans the

47 same? And if ye salute your brethren
only, what do ye more *than others?* do not

48 even the Gentiles the same? Ye therefore
shall be perfect, as your heavenly Father

Matthew 6. is perfect.

1 Take heed that ye do not your righteousness before men, to be seen of them:
else ye have no reward with your Father
who is in heaven.

2 When therefore thou doest alms, sound
not a trumpet before thee, as the hypocrites do in the synagogues and in the
streets, that they may have glory of men.
Verily I say unto you, They have received

3 their reward. But when thou doest alms,
let not thy left hand know what thy right

4 hand doeth: that thine alms may be in
secret: and thy Father who seeth in secret
shall recompense thee.

5 And when ye pray, ye shall not be as
the hypocrites: for they love to stand and
pray in the synagogues and in the corners
of the streets, that they may be seen of
men. Verily I say unto you, They have

6 received their reward. But thou, when
thou prayest, enter into thine inner chamber, and having shut thy door, pray to thy
Father who is in secret, and thy Father
who seeth in secret shall recompense thee.

7 And in praying use not vain repetitions, as

KEY.—[a] Matthew, [b] Mark, [c] Luke, [d] John.

[1] That is, *collectors or renters of Roman taxes*: and so elsewhere.

the Gentiles do: for they think that they
shall be heard for their much speaking.
Be not therefore like unto them: for 8
[1] your Father knoweth what things ye
have need of, before ye ask him. After 9
this manner therefore pray ye: Our
Father who art in heaven, Hallowed be
thy name. Thy kingdom come. **Thy** 10
will be done, as in heaven, so on **earth.**
Give us this day [2] our daily bread. **And** 11
forgive us our debts, as we also have for- 12
given our debtors. And bring us not into 13
temptation, but deliver us from [3] the evil
one. For if ye forgive men their tres- 14
passes, your heavenly Father will also
forgive you. But if ye forgive not men 15
their trespasses, neither will your Father
forgive your trespasses.

Moreover when ye fast, be not, as the 16
hypocrites, of a sad countenance: for they
disfigure their faces, that they may be seen
of men to fast. Verily I say unto you,
They have received their reward. But 17
thou, when thou fastest, anoint thy head,
and wash thy face; that thou be not seen 18
of men to fast, but of thy Father who is in
secret: and thy Father, who seeth in
secret, shall recompense thee.

Lay not up for yourselves treasures upon 19
the earth, where moth and rust doth consume, and where thieves [5] break through
and steal: but lay up for yourselves 20
treasures in heaven, where neither moth · '
nor rust doth consume, and where thieves
do not [5] break through nor steal: for where 21
thy treasure is, there will thy heart be also.

KEY.—[a] Matthew, [b] Mark, [c] Luke, [d] John.

[1] Some ancient authorities read *God your Father*.
[2] Gr. *our bread for the coming day*, or, *our needful bread*.
[3] Or, *evil*
[4] Many authorities, some ancient, but with variations,
add *For thine is the kingdom, and the power, and the glory,
for ever. Amen.*
[5] Gr. *dig through*.

Matthew 6.

22 The lamp of the body is the eye: if therefore thine eye be single, thy whole body
23 shall be full of light. But if thine eye be evil, thy whole body shall be full of darkness. If therefore the light that is in thee be darkness, how great is the darkness!
24 No man can serve two masters: for either he will hate the one, and love the other; or else he will hold to one, and despise the other. Ye cannot serve God and mam-
25 mon. Therefore I say unto you, Be not anxious for your life, what ye shall eat, or what ye shall drink; nor yet for your body, what ye shall put on. Is not the life more than the food, and the body than the
26 raiment? Behold the birds of the heaven, that they sow not, neither do they reap, nor gather into barns; and your heavenly Father feedeth them. Are not ye of
27 much more value than they? And which of you by being anxious can add one cubit
28 unto ¹ the measure of his life? And why are ye anxious concerning raiment? Consider the lilies of the field, how they grow;
29 they toil not, neither do they spin: yet I say unto you, that even Solomon in all his glory was not arrayed like one of these.
30 But if God doth so clothe the grass of the field, which to-day is, and to-morrow is cast into the oven, *shall he* not much more
31 *clothe* you, O ye of little faith? Be not therefore anxious, saying, What shall we eat? or, What shall we drink? or, Where-
32 withal shall we be clothed? For after all these things do the Gentiles seek; for your heavenly Father knoweth that ye
33 have need of all these things. But seek ye first his kingdom, and his righteousness; and all these things shall be added unto
34 you. Be not therefore anxious for the

KEY.—ᵃ Matthew, ᵇ Mark, ᶜ Luke, ᵈ John.

¹ Or, *his stature.*

Matthew 6.

morrow : for the morrow will be anxious
for itself. Sufficient unto the day is the
evil thereof. **Matthew 7.**

Judge not, that ye be not judged. For 1
with what judgement ye judge, ye shall be
judged : and with what measure ye mete, 2
it shall be measured unto you. And why 3
beholdest thou the mote that is in thy
brother's eye, but considerest not the beam
that is in thine own eye? Or how wilt 4
thou say to thy brother, Let me cast out
the mote out of ·thine eye; and lo, the
beam is in thine own eye? Thou hypo- 5
crite, cast out first the beam out of thine
own eye; and then shalt thou see clearly
to cast out the mote out of thy brother's
eye.

Give not that which is holy unto the 6
dogs, neither cast your pearls before the
swine, lest haply they trample them under,
their feet, and turn and rend you.

Ask, and it shall be given you; seek, 7
and ye shall find; knock, and it shall be
opened unto you : for every one that asketh 8
receiveth; and he that seeketh findeth;
and to him that knocketh it shall be opened.
Or what man is there of you, who, if his 9
son shall ask him for a loaf, will give him
a stone; or if he shall ask for a fish, will 10
give him a serpent? If ye then, being 11
evil, know how to give good gifts unto
your children, how much more shall your
Father who is in heaven give good things
to them that ask him? All things there- 12
fore whatsoever ye would that men should
do unto you, even so do ye also unto them :
for this is the law and the prophets.

Enter ye in by the narrow gate: for 13
wide ¹is the gate, and broad is the way,
that leadeth to destruction, and many are

KEY.—ᵃ Matthew, ᵇ Mark, ᶜ Luke, ᵈ John.

¹ Some ancient authorities omit *is the gate.*

14 they that enter in thereby. ¹ For narrow
is the gate, and straitened the way, that
leadeth unto life, and few are they that
find it.

15 Beware of false prophets, that come to
you in sheep's clothing, but inwardly are
16 ravening wolves. By their fruits ye shall
know them. Do *men* gather grapes of
17 thorns, or figs of thistles? Even so every
good tree bringeth forth good fruit; but
the corrupt tree bringeth forth evil fruit.
18 A good tree cannot bring forth evil fruit,
neither can a corrupt tree bring forth good
19 fruit. Every tree that bringeth not forth
good fruit is hewn down, and cast into the
20 fire. Therefore by their fruits ye shall
21 know them. Not every one that saith
unto me, Lord, Lord, shall enter into the
kingdom of heaven; but he that doeth the
22 will of my Father who is in heaven. Many
will say to me in that day, Lord, Lord, did
we not prophesy by thy name, and by thy
name cast out demons, and by thy name do
23 many² mighty works? And then will I pro-
fess unto them, I never knew you: depart
24 from me, ye that work iniquity. Every
one therefore who heareth these words of
mine, and doeth them, shall be likened
unto a wise man, who built his house upon
25 the rock: and the rain descended, and the
floods came, and the winds blew, and beat
upon that house; and it fell not: for it was
26 founded upon the rock. And every one
that heareth these words of mine, and
doeth them not, shall be likened unto a
foolish man, who built his house upon the
27 sand: and the rain descended, and the
floods came, and the winds blew, and
smote upon that house; and it fell: and
great was the fall thereof.

KEY.—ᵃ Matthew, ᵇ Mark, ᶜ Luke, ᵈ John.

¹ Many ancient authorities read *How narrow is the gate,*
&c.   ² Gr. *powers.*

Matthew 6.

˙ And it came to pass, when Jesus ended 28 these words, the multitudes were aston- ished at his teaching : for he taught them 29 as *one* having authority, and not as their scribes.

Matthew 8.

And when he was come down from the 1 mountain, great multitudes followed him.

§ 31.   A Leper Cleansed.

[An unnamed city of Galilee.]

Mark 1.

ᵇAnd ᶜwhile he was in one of the cities 40 ᵇthere cometh to him a leper, ᶜfull of lep- rosy, ᵇbeseeching him, ¹and kneeling down* to him, and saying unto him, If thou wilt, thou canst make me clean. And being moved with compassion, he 41 stretched forth his hand, and touched him, and saith unto him, I will; be thou made clean.   And straightway the leprosy de- 42 parted from him, and he was made clean. And he ²strictly charged him, and straight- 43 way sent him out, and saith unto him, See 44 thou say nothing to any man : but go, shew thyself to the priest, and offer for thy cleansing the things which Moses com- manded, for a testimony unto them.   But 45 he went out, and began to publish it much, and ᶜso much the more went abroad the re- port concerning the matter ; and great mul- titudes came together to hear him and to be healed of their infirmities ; ᵇinsomuch that ³Jesus could no more openly enter into ⁴a

KEY.—ᵃ Matthew, ᵇ Mark, ᶜ Luke, ᵈ John.

¹ Some ancient authorities omit *and kneeling down to him.*
² Or, *sternly*   ⁴ Or, *the city.*
³ Gr. *he.*

* Matthew says, "worshipped him," and Luke, "he fell on his face."   These are fair specimens of minute verbal differences frequently found in parallel accounts.   It was not impossible for the man to prostrate himself, and then rise on his knees to prefer his petition, while both are pos- tures of worship.

§ 31. A Leper Cleansed.

Matthew's Account.

Chap. 8.

1 And when he was come down from the mountain, great
2 multitudes followed him. And behold, there came to him
, a leper and worshipped him, saying, Lord, if thou wilt,
3 thou canst make me clean. And he stretched forth his
hand, and touched him, saying, I will ; be thou made
4 clean. And straightway his leprosy was cleansed. And
Jesus saith unto him, See thou tell no man ; but go, shew
thyself to the priest, and offer the gift that Moses commanded, for a testimony unto them.

Luke's Account.

Chap. 5.

12 And it came to pass, while he was in one of the cities,
behold, a man full of leprosy: and when he saw Jesus, he
fell on his face, and besought him, saying, Lord, if thou
13 wilt, thou canst make me clean. And he stretched forth
his hand, and touched him, saying, I will ; be thou made
clean. And straightway the leprosy departed from him.
14 And he charged him to tell no man: but go thy way, and
shew thyself to the priest, and offer for thy cleansing, according as Moses commanded, for a testimony unto them.
15 But so much the more went abroad the report concerning
him: and great multitudes came together to hear, and to
16 be healed of their infirmities. But he withdrew himself
in the deserts, and prayed.

§ 32. A Palsied Man Healed.

Matthew's Account.

And behold, they brought to him a man sick of the 2 palsy, lying on a bed: and Jesus seeing their faith said unto the sick of the palsy, Son, be of good cheer; thy sins are forgiven. And behold, certain of the scribes said with- 3 in themselves, This man blasphemeth. And Jesus know- 4 ing their thoughts said, Wherefore think ye evil in your hearts? For whether is easier, to say, Thy sins are for- 5 given; or to say, Arise, and walk? But that ye may know 6 that the Son of man hath authority on earth to forgive sins (then saith he to the sick of the palsy), Arise, and take up thy bed, and go unto thy house. And he arose, and de- 7 parted to his house. But when the multitudes saw it, they 8 were afraid, and glorified God, who had given such author- ity unto men.

Luke's Account.

And it came to pass on one of those days, that he was 17 teaching; and there were Pharisees and doctors of the law sitting by, who were come out of every village of Galilee and Judæa and Jerusalem: and the power of the Lord was with him to heal. And behold, men bring on a bed a man 18 that was palsied: and they sought to bring him in, and to lay him before him. And not finding by what _way_ they 19 might bring him in because of the multitude, they went up to the housetop, and let him down through the tiles with his couch into the midst before Jesus. And seeing their 20 faith, he said, Man, thy sins are forgiven thee. And the 21 scribes and the Pharisees began to reason, saying, Who is this that speaketh blasphemies? Who can forgive sins, but God alone? But Jesus perceiving their reasonings, 22 answered and said unto them, What reason ye in your hearts? Whether is easier, to say, Thy sins are forgiven 23 thee; or to say, Arise and walk? But that ye may know 24 that the Son of man hath authority on earth to forgive sins (he said unto him that was palsied), I say unto thee, Arise, and take up thy couch, and go unto thy house. And immediately he rose up before them, and took up 25 that whereon he lay, and departed to his house, glorifying God. And amazement took hold on all, and they glori- 26 fied God; and they were filled with fear, saying, We have seen strange things to-day.

Mark 1.

city, but was without in desert places: and they came to him from every quarter. ᶜBut he withdrew himself in the deserts, and prayed.

§ 32. A Palsied Man Healed.

[Capernaum.]

Mark 2.

1   ᵇAnd when he entered again into Capernaum after some days, it was noised that

2 he was ¹in the house. And many were gathered together, so that there was no longer room *for them*, no, not even about the door: and he spake the word unto them. ᶜAnd there were Pharisees and doctors of the law sitting by, who were come out of every village of Galilee, and Judea, and Jerusalem; and the power of

3 the Lord was with him to heal. ᵇAnd they come, bringing unto him a man sick of

4 the palsy, borne of four. And when they could not ˢcome nigh unto him for the crowd, they ᶜwent up to the housetop and ᵇuncovered the roof where he was: and when they had broken it up, they let down ᶜthrough the tiles ᵇthe ˢbed whereon the

5 sick of the palsy lay. And Jesus seeing their faith saith unto the sick of the palsy,

6 ˢSon, thy sins are forgiven ᶜthee. ᵇBut there were certain of the scribes ᶜand Pharisees ᵇsitting there, and reasoning in their hearts,

7 Why doth this man thus speak? he blasphemeth: who can forgive sins but one,

8 *even* God? And straightway Jesus, perceiving in his spirit that they so reasoned within themselves, saith unto them, Why reason ye these things in your hearts?

9 Whether is easier, to say to the sick of the palsy, Thy sins are forgiven: or to say,

KEY. —ˢ Matthew, ᵇ Mark, ᶜLuke, ᵈ John.

¹ Or, *at home*
² Many ancient authorities read *bring him unto him*
³ Or, *pallet*   ⁴ Gr. *Child.*

Mark 2.

Arise, and take up thy ¹bed, and walk?
But that ye may know that the Son of man 10
hath authority on earth to forgive sins (he
saith to the sick of the palsy), I say unto 1.1
thee, Arise, take up thy ¹bed, and go unto
thy house. And ᶜimmediately ᵇhe arose, 12
and straightway took up the ¹bed, and
went forth before them all; insomuch that
they were all amazed, and glorified God,
ᵃwho had given such authority unto men,
ᵇsaying, We never saw it on this fashion;
ᶜand they were filled with fear, saying, We
have seen strange things to day.

§ 33. Call of Levi.

[Capernaum.]

Mark 2.

ᵇAnd ᵃas Jesus passed by from thence 13
ᵇhe went forth again by the sea side; and
all the multitude resorted unto him, and
he taught them. And as he passed by, he 14
saw Levi* the *son* of Alphæus sitting at
the place of toll, and he saith unto him,
Follow me. And he arose, ᶜforsook all,
ᵇand followed him. ᶜAnd Levi made him 15
a great feast in his house: and there was a
great multitude of publicans and of others
that were sitting at meat with them, ᵇfor
there were many, and they followed him
And the scribes ²of the Pharisees, when 16
they saw that he was eating with the sinners and publicans, said unto his disciples,
³He eateth ⁴and drinketh with publicans
and sinners. And when Jesus heard it, he 17
saith unto them, They that are ⁵whole have

KEY.—ᵃ Matthew, ᵇ Mark, ᶜ Luke, ᵈ John

¹ Or, *pallet.*
² Some ancient authorities read *and the Pharisees*
³ Or, How is it *that he eateth . . . sinners?*
⁴ Some ancient authorities omit *and drinketh*
⁵ Gr *strong*

* In Matthew this name is given as *Matthew* Two **names**
for one person were not uncommon.

§ 33. Call of Levi.

Matthew's Account.

Chap. 9.

9   And as Jesus passed by from thence, he saw a man, called Matthew, sitting at the place of toll : and he saith unto him, Follow me.   And he arose, and followed him.

10   And it came to pass, as he sat at meat in the house, behold, many publicans and sinners came and sat down with

11   Jesus and his disciples.   And when the Pharisees saw it, they said unto his disciples, Why eateth your Master with

12   the publicans and sinners ?   But when he heard it, he said, They that are whole have no need of a physician, but they

13   that are sick.   But go ye and learn what *this* meaneth, I desire mercy, and not sacrifice : for I came not to call the righteous, but sinners.

Mark's Account.

Chap. 2.

15   And he arose and followed him.   And it came to pass, that he was sitting at meat in his house, and many publicans and sinners sat down with Jesus and his disciples : for there were many, and they followed him.

Luke's Account.

Chap. 5.

27   And after these things he went forth, and beheld a publican, named Levi, sitting at the place of toll, and said unto

28   him, Follow me.   And he forsook all, and rose up and

29   followed him.   And Levi made him a great feast in his house : and there was a great multitude of publicans and

30   of others that were sitting at meat with them.   And the Pharisees and their scribes murmured against his disciples, saying, Why do ye eat and drink with the publicans and

31   sinners ?   And Jesus answering said unto them, They that are whole have no need of a physician ; but they that are

32   sick.   I am not come to call the righteous but sinners to repentance.

§ 34. Dispute about Fasting.

Matthew's Account.

Chap. 9.

Then come to him the disciples of John, saying, Why 14 do we and the Pharisees fast oft, but thy disciples fast not? And Jesus said unto them, Can the sons of the bride- 15 chamber mourn, as long as the bridegroom is with them? but the days will come, when the bridegroom shall be taken away from them, and then will they fast. And no man 16 putteth a piece of undressed cloth upon an old garment; for that which should fill it up taketh from the garment, and a worse rent is made. Neither do *men* put new wine 17 into old wine-skins : else the skins burst, and the wine is spilled, and the skins perish : but they put new wine into fresh wine-skins, and both are preserved.

Luke's Account.

Chap. 5.

And they said unto him, The disciples of John fast 33 often, and make supplications ; likewise also the *disciples* of the Pharisees ; but thine eat and drink. And Jesus 34 said unto them, Can ye make the sons of the bride-chamber fast, while the bridgroom is with them? But 35 the days will come ; and when the bridegroom shall be taken away from them, then will they fast in those days. And he spake also a parable unto them; No man rend- 36 eth a piece from a new garment and putteth it upon an old garment ; else he will rend the new, and also the piece from the new will not agree with the old. And no 37 man putteth new wine into old wine-skins ; else the new wine will burst the skins, and itself will be spilled, and the skins will perish. But new wine must be put into fresh 38 wine-skins. And no man having drunk old *wine* desir- 39 eth new : for he saith, The old is good.

51

Mark 2.

no need of a physician, but they that are
sick : ª But go ye and learn what this meaneth, I desire mercy, and not sacrifice ; ᵇ I
came not to call the righteous, but sinners
ᶜ to repentance.

§ 34. Dispute about Fasting.

[Capernaum.]

Mark 2.

18   ᵇAnd John's disciples and the Pharisees
were fasting : and they come and say unto
him, Why do John's disciples and the disciples of the Pharisees fast ᶜ often and make
19 supplications, ᵇ but thy disciples fast not?
And Jesus said unto them, Can the sons
of the bride-chamber fast, *[and] ª mourn
ᵇ while the bridegroom is with them? as
long as they have the bridegroom with
20 them, they cannot fast. But the days
will come, when the bridegroom shall be
taken away from them, and then will they
21 fast in that day. No man seweth a piece
of undressed cloth on an old garment : else
that which should fill it up taketh from it,
the new from the old, and a worse rent is
made : ᶜ also the piece from the new will
22 not agree with the old. ᵇ And no man putteth new wine into old ¹ wine-skins : else
the wine will burst the skins, and the wine
perisheth, and the skins : but *they put* new
wine into fresh wine-skins. ᶜAnd no man
having drunk old wine desireth new ;
for he saith, the old is good.

§ 35. Jairus.

[Capernaum.]

Mark 5.

22   ᵇ And there cometh one of the rulers of
the synagogue, Jairus by name ; and see-
23 ing him, he falleth at his feet, and be-

Key.—ª Matthew, ᵇ Mark, ᶜ Luke, ᵈ John.

¹ That is *skins used as bottles.*

* A word inserted by the compile

seecheth him much, [c]to come into his house ; for he had an only daughter about twelve years of age, and she lay a dying ; [b] saying, My little daughter is at the point of death : *I pray thee,* that thou come and lay thy hands on her, that she may be [1] made whole, and live. And he [a]arose, and 24 [b] went with him, [a] and so did his disciples ; [b] and a great multitude followed him, and they thronged him.

And a woman, who had an issue of blood 25 twelve years, and had suffered many 26 things of many physicians, and had spent all that she had, and was nothing bettered, but rather grew worse, having heard the 27 things concerning Jesus, came in the crowd behind, and touched [c]the border of [b] his garment. For she said, [a] with in her- 28 self, [b] If I touch but his garments, I shall be [1] made whole. And straightway the foun- 29 tain of her blood was dried up ; and she felt in her body that she was healed of her [2] plague. And straightway Jesus, perceiv- 30 ing in himself that the power *proceeding* from him had gone forth, turned him about in the crowd, and said, Who touched my garments ? [c]And when all denied, Peter said, and they that were with him, [b] Thou seest the multitude thronging thee, 31 and sayest thou, Who touched me ? [c] But Jesus said, Some one did touch me : for I perceived that power had gone forth from me. [b] And he looked round about to 32 see her that had done this thing. But the woman [c]saw she was not hid ; [b]fearing and trembling, knowing what had been done 33 to her, *[she] came and fell down before him, and [c]declared in the presence of all the people for what cause she touched him

KEY.—[a] Matthew, [b] Mark, [c] Luke, [d] John.

[1] Or, *saved.*   [2]Gr. *scourge.*
* A word inserted by the compiler.

§ 35. Jairus.

Matthew's Account.

Chap. 9.

18 While he spake these things unto them, behold, there came a ruler, and worshipped him, saying, My daughter is even now dead : but come and lay thy hand upon her,
19 and she shall live. And Jesus arose, and followed him,
20 and *so did* his disciples. And behold, a woman, who had an issue of blood twelve years, came behind him, and
21 touched the border of his garment : for she said within herself, If I do but touch his garment, I shall be made whole.

22 But Jesus turning and seeing her said, Daughter, be of good cheer; thy faith hath made thee whole. And the woman was made whole from that hour.

Luke's Account.

Chap. 8.

40 And as Jesus returned, the multitude welcomed him ;
41 for they were all waiting for him. And behold, there came a man named Jairus, and he was a ruler of the synagogue : and he fell down at Jesus' feet, and besought him
42 to come into his house ; for he had an only daughter, about twelve years of age, and she lay a dying. But as he went the multitudes thronged him.
43 And a woman having an issue of blood twelve years, who had spent all her living upon physicians, and could not be
44 healed of any, came behind him, and touched the border of his garment : and immediately the issue of her blood
45 stanched. And Jesus said, Who is it that touched me ? And when all denied, Peter said, and they that were with him, Master, the multitudes press thee and crush *thee.*
46 But Jesus said, Some one did touch me : for I perceived
47 that power had gone forth from me. And when the woman saw that she was not hid, she came trembling, and falling down before him declared in the presence of all the people for what cause she touched him, and how she
48 was healed immediately. And he said unto her, Daughter, thy faith hath made thee whole; go in peace.

§ 35. Jairus.—(*Continued.*)

Matthew's Account.

Chap. 9.

And when Jesus came into the ruler's house, and saw the 23
flute-players, and the crowd making a tumult, he said, 24
<u>Give place</u>: for the damsel is not dead, but sleepeth.
And they laughed him to scorn. But when the crowd 25
was put forth, he entered in, and took her by the hand;
and the damsel arose. <u>And the fame hereof went forth</u> 26
<u>into all that land.</u>

Luke's Account.

Chap. 8.

While he yet spake, there cometh one from the ruler of 49
the synagogue's *house*, saying, Thy daughter is dead; trouble not the Master. But Jesus hearing it, answered him, 50
Fear not: only believe, <u>and she shall be made whole.</u> And 51
when he came to the house, he suffered not any man to
enter in with him, save Peter, and John, and James, and
the father of the maiden and her mother. And all were 52
weeping, and bewailing her: but he said, Weep not; for
she is not dead, but sleepeth. And they laughed him to 53
scorn, <u>knowing that she was dead.</u> But he, taking her by 54
the hand, called, saying, Maiden, arise. <u>And her spirit</u> 55
<u>returned,</u> and she rose up immediately: and he commanded
that *something* be given her to eat. And her parents were 56
amazed: but he charged them to tell no man what had been
done.

53

and how she was healed immediately.

34 [b] And he said unto her, Daughter, [a] be of good cheer; [b] thy faith hath [1] made thee whole; go in peace, and be whole of thy [2] plague. [a] And the woman was made whole from that hour.

35 [b] While he yet spake, they come from the ruler of the synagogue's *house*, saying, Thy daughter is dead : why troublest thou

36 the [3] Master any further? But Jesus, [4] not heeding the word spoken, saith unto the ruler of the synagogue, Fear not, only be-

37 lieve, [c] and she shall be made whole. [b] And he suffered no man to follow with him, save Peter, and James, and John the

38 brother of James. And they come to the house of the ruler of the synagogue; and he beholdeth a tumult, [a] flute-players, [b] and

39 *many* weeping and wailing greatly. And when he was entered in, he saith unto them, Why make ye a tumult, and weep? [a] give place; [b] the child is not dead, but

40 sleepeth. And they laughed him to scorn, [c] knowing that she was dead. [b] But he, having put them all forth, taketh the father of the child and her mother and them that were with him, and goeth in

41 where the child was. And taking the child by the hand, he saith unto her, Talitha cumi; which is, being interpreted, Damsel, I say unto thee, Arise. [c] And her spirit

42 returned. [b] And straightway the damsel rose up, and walked; for she was twelve years old. And they were amazed

43 straightway with a great amazement. And he charged them much that no man should know this : and he commanded that *something* should be given her to eat. [a] And the fame hereof went forth into all that land.

KEY.—[a] Matthew, [b] Mark, [c] Luke, [d] John.

[1] Or, *saved thee.*   [2] Or, *scourge.*
[3] Or, *Teacher.*   [4] Or, *overhearing.*

§ 36. Two Blind Men.

[Capernaum.]

Matthew 9.

[a] And as Jesus passed by from thence, two 27 blind men followed him, crying out, and saying, Have mercy on us, thou son of David. And when he was come into the 28 house, the blind men came to him: and Jesus saith unto them, Believe ye that I am able to do this? They say unto him, Yea, Lord. Then touched he their eyes, 29 saying, According to your faith be it done unto you. And their eyes were opened. 30 And Jesus [1] strictly charged them, saying, See that no man know it. But they went 31 forth, and spread abroad his fame in all that land.

And as they went forth, behold, there 32 was brought to him a dumb man possessed with a demon. And when the demon was 33 cast out, the dumb man spake: and the multitudes marvelled, saying, It was never so seen in Israel. But the Pharisees said, 34 [2] By the prince of the demons casteth he out demons.

KEY.—[a] Matthew, [b] Mark, [c] Luke, [d] John.

[1] Or, *sternly.*   [2] Or, *In.*   •

PERIOD III.

Second Year of Public Ministry.

[From Second to Third Passover—one year.]

---

§ 37. Pool of Bethesda.

[At Jerusalem.]

John 5.

1 ^dAfter these things there was ¹ a feast of
the Jews; and Jesus went up to Jerusalem.

2 Now there is in Jerusalem by the sheep
gate a pool, which is called in Hebrew

3 ² Bethesda, having five porches. In these
lay a multitude of them that were sick,

5 blind, halt, withered ². And a certain man
was there, who had been thirty and eight

6 years in his infirmity. When Jesus saw
him lying, and knew that he had been now
a long time *in that case*, he saith unto him,

7 Wouldst thou be made whole? The sick
man answered him, 'Sir, I have no man,
when the water is troubled, to put me into
the pool: but while I am coming, another

8 steppeth down before me. Jesus saith
unto him, Arise, take up thy ' bed, and

9 walk. And straightway the man was
made whole, and took up his ' bed and
walked.

KEY.—^a Matthew, ^b Mark, ^c Luke, ^d John.

¹ Many ancient authorities read *the feast.*

² Some ancient authorities read *Bethsaida*, others, *Beth-zatha.*

³ Many ancient authorities insert, wholly or in part, *waiting for the moving of the water: ⁴ for an angel of the Lord went down at certain seasons into the pool, and troubled the water: whosoever then first after the troubling of the water stepped in was made whole, with whatsoever disease he was holden.*

⁴ Or, *Lord.*　　　　　⁵ Or, *pallet.*

Now it was the sabbath on that day. So 10
the Jews said unto him that was cured, It
is the sabbath, and it is not lawful for thee
to take up thy ¹bed. But he answered 11
them, He that made me whole, the same
said unto me, Take up thy ¹bed, and walk.
They asked him, Who is the man that said 12
unto thee, Take up *thy* ¹*bed*, and walk?
But he that was healed knew not who it 13
was: for Jesus had conveyed himself away,
a multitude being in the place. After- 14
ward Jesus findeth him in the temple, and
said unto him, Behold, thou art made
whole: sin no more, lest a worse thing be-
fall thee. The man went away, and told 15
the Jews that it was Jesus who had made
him whole. And for this cause did the 16
Jews persecute Jesus, because he did these
things on the sabbath. But Jesus answered 17
them, My father worketh even until now,
and I work. For this cause therefore the 18
Jews sought the more to kill him, because
he not only brake the sabbath, but also
called God his own Father, making himself equal with God.

§. 38. Discourse about the Father.

[At Jerusalem.]

ᵈ Jesus therefore answered and said unto 19
them,

Verily, verily, I say unto you, The Son
can do nothing of himself, but what he
seeth the Father doing: for what things
soever he doeth, these the Son also doeth
in like manner. For the Father loveth the 20
Son, and sheweth him all things that himself doeth: and greater works than these
will he shew him, that ye may marvel.
For as the Father raiseth the dead and 21
quickeneth them, even so the Son also

KEY.—ᵃ Matthew, ᵇ Mark, ᶜ Luke, ᵈ John.

¹ Or, *pallet.*

22 quickeneth whom he will. For neither doth the Father judge any man, but he hath given all judgement unto the Son; that all may honour the Son, even as they

23 honour the Father. He that honoureth not the Son honoureth not the Father that

24 sent him. Verily, verily, I say unto you, He that heareth my word, and believeth him that sent me, hath eternal life, and cometh not into judgement, but hath

25 passed out of death into life. Verily, verily, I say unto you, The hour cometh, and now is, when the dead shall hear the voice of the Son of God; and they that

26 hear shall live. For as the Father hath life in himself, even so gave he to the Son

27 also to have life in himself: and he gave him authority to execute judgement, be-

28 cause he is a son of man. Marvel not at this: for the hour cometh, in which all that

29 are in the tombs shall hear his voice, and shall come forth; they that have done good, unto the resurrection of life; and they that have ¹ done evil, unto the resurrection of judgement.

30   I can of myself do nothing: as I hear, I judge: and my judgment is righteous; because I seek not mine own will, but the

31 will of him that sent me. If I bear witness

32 of myself, my witness is not true. It is another that beareth witness of me; and I know that the witness which he witnesseth

33 of me is true. Ye have sent unto John, and he hath borne witness unto the truth.

34 But the witness which I receive is not from man: howbeit I say these things, that

35 ye may be saved. He was the lamp that burneth and shineth: and ye were willing

36 to rejoice for a season in his light. But the witness which I have is greater than

KEY.—ᵃ Matthew, ᵇ Mark, ᶜ Luke, ᵈ John.

¹ Or, *practised*.

that of John: for the works which the Father hath given me to accomplish, the very works that I do, bear witness of me, that the Father hath sent me. And the 37 Father that sent me, he hath borne witness of me. Ye have neither heard his voice at any time, nor seen his form. And ye have 38 not his word abiding in you: for whom he sent, him ye believe not. ' Ye search the 39 scriptures, because ye think that in them ye have eternal life; and these are they which bear witness of me; and ye will not 40 come to me, that ye may have life. I re- 41 ceive not glory from men. But I know 42 you, that ye have not the love of God in yourselves. I am come in my Father's 43 name, and ye receive me not: if another shall come in his own name, him ye will receive. How can ye believe, who receive 44 glory one of another, and the glory that *cometh* from *the only God ye seek not? 45 Think not that I will accuse you to the Father: there is one that accuseth you, *even* Moses, on whom ye have set your hope. For if ye believed Moses, ye would 46 believe me; for he wrote of me. But if ye 47 believe not his writings, how shall ye believe my words?

§ 39. Dispute about the Sabbath.

[Journeying toward Galilee.]

ªAt that season Jesus went on the sabbath 1 day through the cornfields; and his disciples were an hungred, and began ᵇas they went, ªto pluck ears of corn, and to eat, ᶜrubbing them in their hands. ªBut the 2 Pharisees, when they saw it, said unto him, Behold, thy disciples do that which it is not lawful to do upon the sabbath. But he 3

KEY.—ª Matthew, ᵇ Mark, ᶜ Luke, ᵈ John.

² Or, *Search the scriptures.*
³ Some ancient authorities read *the only* one.

§ 39. Dispute about the Sabbath.

Matthew's Account.

Chap. 12.
8 For the Son of man is lord of the sabbath.

Mark's Account.

Chap. 2.
23 And it came to pass, that he was going on the sabbath
day through the cornfields; and his disciples began, as they
24 went, to pluck the ears of corn. And the Pharisees said
unto him, Behold, why do they on the sabbath day that
25 which is not lawful? And he said unto them, Did ye
never read what David did, when he had need, and was an
26 hungred, he, and they that were with him? How he entered into the house of God when Abiathar was high priest,
and did eat the shew-bread, which it is not lawful to eat
save for the priests, and gave also to them that were with
27 him? And he said unto them, The sabbath was made for
28 man, and not man for the sabbath: so that the Son of
man is lord even of the sabbath.

Luke's Account.

Chap. 6.
1 Now it came to pass on a sabbath, that he was going
through the cornfields; and his disciples plucked the ears
2 of corn, and did eat, rubbing them in their hands. But certain of the Pharisees said, Why do ye that which it is not
lawful to do on the sabbath day?
3 And Jesus answering them said, Have ye not read even
this, what David did, when he was an hungred, he, and
4 they that were with him; how he entered into the house of
God, and did take and eat the shewbread, and gave also to
them that were with him; which it is not lawful to eat save
5 for the priests alone? And he said unto them, The Son of
man is lord of the sabbath.

[*Continued on duplicate page 59.*]

§ 39. Dispute about the Sabbath.—(*Continued.*)

Mark's Account.

Chap. 3.

And he entered again into the synagogue; and there was a man there who had his hand withered. And they watched him, whether he would heal him on the sabbath day; that they might accuse him. And he saith unto the 3 man that had his hand withered, Stand forth. And he 4 saith unto them, Is it lawful on the sabbath day to do good, or to do harm? to save a life, or to kill? But they held their peace. And when he had looked round about on 5 them with anger, being grieved at the hardening of their heart, he saith unto the man, Stretch forth thy hand. And he stretched it forth: and his hand was restored. And the 6 Pharisees went out, and straightway with the Herodians took counsel against him, how they might destroy him.

Luke's Account.

Chap. 6

And it came to pass on another sabbath, that he entered 6 into the synagogue and taught: and there was a man there, and his right hand was withered. And the scribes and the 7 Pharisees watched him, whether he would heal on the sabbath; that they might find how to accuse him. But he 8 knew their thoughts: and he said to the man that had his hand withered, Rise up, and stand forth in the midst. And he arose and stood forth. And Jesus said unto them, I ask 9 you, Is it lawful on the sabbath to do good, or to do harm? to save a life, or to destroy it? And he looked round about 10 on them all, and said unto him, Stretch forth thy hand. And he did *so*: and his hand was restored. But they were 11 filled with madness; and communed one with another what they might do to Jesus.

59

said unto them, Have ye not read what
David did, when he [b] had need and [a] was an
hungred, and they that were with him;
4 how he entered into the house of God,
[b] when Abiathar was high priest, [a] and [1] did
eat the shewbread, which it was not lawful
for him to eat, neither for them that were
5 with him, but only for the priests? Or
have ye not read in the law, how that on
the sabbath day the priests in the temple
6 profane the sabbath, and are guiltless? But
I say unto you, that [2] one greater than the
7 temple is here. But if ye had known what
this meaneth, I desire mercy, and not sacrifice, ye would not have condemned the
guiltless. [b] And he said unto them, The
sabbath was made for man, and not man for
the sabbath: so that the Son of man is lord
even of the sabbath.
9   [a] And he departed thence, and went into
their **synagogue** [c] on another sabbath and
taught: and there was a man there and his
right hand was withered.   And the scribes
and the Pharisees [a] asked him, saying, Is it
lawful to heal on the sabbath day? that they
11 might accuse him. And he said unto them,
What man shall there be of you, that shall
have one sheep, and if this fall into a pit on
the sabbath day, will he not lay hold on it,
12 and lift it out? How much then is a man
of more value than a sheep! Wherefore it
is lawful to do good on the sabbath day.
[b] But they held their peace. And when he
had looked round about on them with anger, being grieved at the hardening of their
heart, he saith unto the man, [c] Rise up and
stand forth in the midst; and he arose and
13 stood forth. [a] Then saith he to the man,
Stretch forth thy hand. And he stretched

KEY.—[a] Matthew, [b] Mark, [c] Luke, [d] John.

[1] Some ancient authorities read *they did eat.*
[2] Gr. *a greater thing.*

it forth; and it was restored whole, as the
other.   But the Pharisees went out, and 14
took counsel ᵇ with the Herodians ᵃ against
him, how they might destroy him.   And 15
Jesus perceiving *it* withdrew from thence:
and many followed him; and he healed
them all, and charged them that they 16
should not make him known: that it might 17
be fulfilled which was spoken through
Isaiah the prophet, saying,

> Behold, my servant whom I have 18
>   chosen;
> My beloved in whom my soul is well
>   pleased:
> I will put my Spirit upon him,
> And he shall declare judgement to the
>   Gentiles.
> He shall not strive, nor cry aloud;   19
> Neither shall any one hear his voice in
>   the streets.
> A bruised reed shall he not break,   20
> And smoking flax shall he not quench,
> Till he send forth judgement unto vic-
>   tory.
> And in his name shall the Gentiles 21
>   hope.

§ 40.   Gathering at the Sea.

[The sea of Galilee.]

ᵇAnd Jesus with his disciples withdrew 7
to the sea: and a great multitude from
Galilee followed: and from Judæa, and 8
from Jerusalem, and from Idumæa, and beyond Jordan, and about Tyre and Sidon, a
great multitude, hearing ᶦwhat great
things he did, came unto him.   And he 9
spake to his disciples, that a little boat
should wait on him because of the crowd,
lest they should throng him: for he had 10

KEY.—ᵃ Matthew, ᵇ Mark, ᶜ Luke, ᵈ John.

¹ Or, *all the things that he did.*

PLATE III.

§§ 52–59.

At or near Capernaum, Jesus chooses his disciples and
delivers the Sermon on the Plain, with many other discourses,
and performs several miracles (§§ 40–52).

As shown by the blue line Jesus crosses the Sea of Galilee,
stilling the tempest on the way, and sends demons into the
swine on the eastern coast (§§ 52 and 53). He then revisits
Nazareth (§ 54), and afterwards sends forth his disciples (§ 55).

As shown by the red line, Jesus comes to Bethsaida and
feeds 5000 (§ 58), walks on the sea (§ 59), and discourses on
the bread of life, at Capernaum.

(Opposite page 61.)

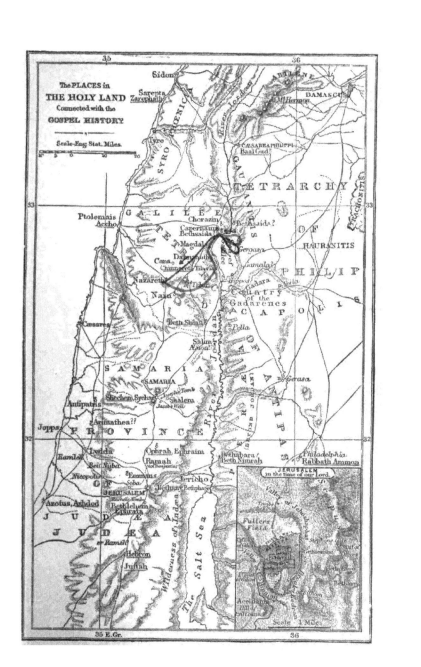

The PLACES in
THE HOLY LAND
Connected with the
GOSPEL HISTORY

Scale-Eng Stat. Miles.

§ 41. The Disciples Chosen.

Mark's Account.

Chap. 3.

And he goeth up into the mountain, and calleth unto him 13
whom he himself would: and they went unto him. And 14
he appointed twelve, that they might be with him, and that
he might send them forth to preach, and to have authority
to cast out demons.

Luke's Account.

Chap. 6.

And it came to pass in these days, that he went out into 12
the mountain to pray; and he continued all night in prayer
to God. And when it was day, he called his disciples: and 13
he chose from them twelve, whom also he named apostles;
Simon, whom he also named Peter, and Andrew his brother, 14
and James and John, and Philip and Bartholomew, and 15
Matthew and Thomas, and James *the son* of Alphæus, and
Simon who was called the Zealot, and Judas *the son* of 16
James, and Judas Iscariot, who became a traitor;

61

Mark 3.

healed many; insomuch that as many as
had ¹ plagues ² pressed upon him that they
11 might touch him.   And the unclean spirits,
whensoever they beheld him, fell down before him, and cried, saying, Thou art the
12 Son of God.   And he charged them much
that they should not make him known.

§ 41. The Disciples Chosen.

[Near Capernaum.]

Mark 3.

13   ᵇAnd he goeth up into the mountain, ᶜto
pray: and he continued all night in prayer
unto God.   And when it was day, he called
his disciples, and he chose from them
twelve whom he named apostles, ᵇthat
they might be with him, and that he might
15 send them forth to preach, and to have
16 authority to cast out demons: and Simon
17 he surnamed Peter; and James the *son* of
Zebedee, and John the brother of James;
and them he surnamed Boanerges, which
18 is, Sons of thunder: and Andrew, and
Philip, and Bartholomew, and Matthew,
and Thomas, and James the *son* of Alphæus,
and Thaddæus, and Simon the ³Cananæan,
19 and Judas Iscariot, who also betrayed him;
17 **Luke 6.** ᶜand he came down with them, and
stood on a level place, and a great multitude
of his disciples, and a great number of the
people from all Judæa and Jerusalem, and
the sea coast of Tyre and Sidon, who çame
to hear him, and to be healed of their dis-
18 eases; and they that were troubled with
19 unclean spirits were healed.   And all the
multitude sought to touch him; for power
came forth from him, and healed *them*
all.

KEY.—ᵃ Matthew, ᵇ Mark, ᶜ Luke, ᵈ John.

¹ Gr. *scourges*.   ² Gr. *fell*.   ³ Or, *Zealot*.

§ 42. Sermon on the Plain.*

[Near Capernaum.]

Luke 6.

^cAnd he lifted up his eyes on his disci- 20
ples, and said, Blessed *are* ye poor : for
yours is the kingdom of God. Blessed *are* 21
ye that hunger now : for ye shall be filled.
Blessed *are* ye that weep now : for ye shall
laugh.   Blessed are ye, when man shall 22
hate you, and when they shall separate
you *from their company*, and reproach you,
and cast out your name as evil, for the Son
of man's sake. Rejoice in that day, and 23
leap *for joy* : for behold, your reward is
great in heaven : for in the same manner
did their fathers unto the prophets. But 24
woe unto you that are rich ! for ye have received your consolation. Woe unto you, 25
ye that are full now ! for ye shall hunger.
Woe *unto you*, ye that laugh now ! for ye
shall mourn and weep. Woe *unto you*, 26
when all men shall speak well of you ! for
in the same manner did their fathers to the
false prophets.

But I say unto you who hear, Love 27
your enemies, do good to them that hate
you, bless them that curse you, pray for 28
them that despitefully use you. To him 29
that smiteth thee on the *one* cheek offer also
the other ; and from him that taketh away
thy cloke withhold not thy coat also. Give 30
to every one that asketh thee ; and of him
that taketh away thy goods ask them not
again. And as ye would that men should 31
do to you, do ye also to them likewise.
And if ye love them that love you, what 32

KEY.—^a Matthew, ^b Mark, ^c Luke, ^d John.

* This discourse, though so much shorter, is very similar
in general character to the Sermon on the Mount. But it
was spoken in a level place (v. 17); the beatitudes are in the
second person, and are followed by corresponding woes;
and Matthew puts the list of the twelve disciples and their
commission apparently long after the Sermon on the Mount.
The arrangement here given seems more easy and natural.

Luke 6.

thank have ye? for even sinners love those
33 that love them.   And if ye do good to
them that do good to you, what thank
have ye? for even sinners do the same.
34 And if ye lend to them of whom ye hope
to receive, what thank have ye? even sinners lend to sinners, to receive again as
35 much.   But love your enemies, and do
them good, and lend, 'never despairing;
and your reward shall be great, and ye
shall be sons of the Most High: for he is
36 kind toward the unthankful and evil.   Be
ye merciful, even as your father is merci-
37 ful.   And judge not, and ye shall not be
judged: and condemn not, and ye shall
not be condemned: release, and ye shall
38 be released: give, and it shall be given
unto you: good measure, pressed down,
shaken together, running over, shall they
give into your bosom.   For with what
measure ye mete it shall be measured to
you again.
39   And he spake also a parable unto them,
Can the blind guide the blind? shall they
40 not both fall into a pit?   The disciple is
not above his ²master: but every one when
he is perfected shall be as his ²master.
41 And why beholdest thou the mote that is
in thy brother's eye, but considerest not
42 the beam that is in thine own eye?   Or
how canst thou say to thy brother,
Brother, let me cast out the mote that is
in thine eye, when thou thyself beholdest
not the beam that is in thine own eye?
Thou hypocrite, cast out first the beam out
of thine own eye, and then shalt thou see
clearly to cast out the mote that is in thy
43 brother's eye.   For there is no good tree
that bringeth forth corrupt fruit; nor
again a corrupt tree that bringeth forth

KEY.—ᵃ Matthew, ᵇ Mark, ᶜ Luke, ᵈ John.

¹ Some ancient authorities read *despairing of no man.*
² Or, *teacher.*

Luke 6.

good fruit.   For each tree is known by its 44
own fruit.   For of thorns men do not
gather figs, nor of a bramble bush gather
they grapes.   The good man out of the 45
good treasure of his heart bringeth forth
that which is good; and the evil *man* out
of the evil *treasure* bringeth forth that
which is evil: for out of the abundance of
the heart his mouth speaketh.

And why call ye me, Lord, Lord, and 46
do not the things which I say?   Every 47
one that cometh unto me, and heareth my
words, and doeth them, I will shew you
to whom he is like: he is like a man build- 48
ing a house, who digged and went deep,
and laid a foundation upon the rock: and
when a flood arose, the stream brake
against that house, and could not shake
it: ¹ because it had been well builded.
But he that heareth, and doeth not, is like 49
a man that built a house upon the earth
without a foundation; against which the
stream brake, and straightway it fell in;
and the ruin of that house was great.

§ 43.   The Centurion's Servant.*

[Capernaum.]

Luke 7.

ᶜAfter he had ended all his sayings in the 1
ears of the people, he entered into Capernaum.

And a certain centurion's ²servant, who 2
was ³dear unto him, was sick ᵃ of the palsy,
grievously tormented, ᶜand at the point of
death.   And when he heard concerning 3
Jesus, he sent unto him elders of the Jews,

KEY.—ᵃ Matthew, ᵇ Mark, ᶜ Luke, ᵈ John.

¹ Many ancient authorities read *for it had been founded
upon the rock.*
² Gr. *bondservant.*
³ Or, *precious to him.* Or, *honourable with him.*

*In Matthew, the Centurion is represented as himself
coming to Jesus.   This may be explained on the legal
principle that what a man does or says by his agents he
does or says himself.

§ 43. The Centurion's Servant.

Matthew's Account.

Chap. 8.

5 And when he was entered into Capernaum, there came
6 unto him a centurion, beseeching him, and saying, Lord,
my servant lieth in the house sick of the palsy, grievously
7 tormented.   And he saith unto him, I will come and heal
8 him.   And the centurion answered and said, Lord, I am not
worthy that thou shouldest come under my roof : but only
9 say the word, and my servant shall be healed.   For I also
am a man under authority, having under myself soldiers :
and I say to this one, Go, and he goeth ; and to another,
Come, and he cometh ; and to my servant, Do this, and he
10 doeth it.   And when Jesus heard it, he marvelled, and
said to them that followed, Verily I say unto you, I have
not found so great faith, no, not in Israel.

Luke's Account.

Chap. 7.

10 And they that were sent, returning to the house, found
the servant whole.

64

asking him that he would come and save
4 his [1] servant.   And they, when they came
to Jesus, besought him earnestly, saying,
He is worthy that thou shouldest do this
5 for him: for he loveth our nation, and
6 himself built us our synagogue.   And
Jesus went with them.   And when he was
now not far from the house, the centurion
sent friends to him, saying unto him, Lord,
trouble not thyself: for I am not [2] worthy
that thou shouldest come under my roof:
7 wherefore neither thought I myself worthy
to come unto thee: but [3] say the word, and
8 my [4] servant shall be healed.   For I also
am a man set under authority, having
under myself soldiers: and I say to this
one, Go, and he goeth; and to another,
Come, and he cometh; and to my [1] ser-
9 vant, Do this, and he doeth it.   And when
Jesus heard these things, he marvelled at
him, and turned and said unto the multitude that followed him, I say unto you, I
have not found so great faith, no, not in
11 **Matthew 8.**   Israel.   [a]And I say unto you,
that many shall come from the east and the
west, and shall [5] sit down with Abraham,
and Isaac, and Jacob, in the kingdom of
12 heaven: but the sons of the kingdom shall
be cast forth into the outer darkness: there
shall be the weeping and gnashing of teeth.
13 And Jesus said unto the centurion, Go
thy way; as thou hast believed, *so* be it
done unto thee.   And the [1] servant was
healed in that hour.

§ 44.   The Widow's Son.

[Near Nain.]

Luke 7.

11   [c]And it came to pass [6] soon afterwards,
that he went to a city called Nain; and his

KEY.—[a] Matthew, [b] Mark, [c] Luke, [d] John.

[1] Gr. *bondservant.*   [2] Gr. *sufficient.*
[3] Gr. *say with a word.*   [4] Or, *boy.*   [5] Gr. *recline.*
[6] Many ancient authorities read *on the next day.*

Luke 7.

disciples went with him, and a great multitude.   Now when he drew near to the 12
gate of the city, behold, there was carried
out one that was dead, the only son of his
mother, and she was a widow : and much
people of the city was with her.   And 13
when the Lord saw her, he had compassion on her, and said unto her, Weep not.
And he came nigh and touched the bier : 14
and the bearers stood still.   And he said,
Young man, I say unto thee, Arise.   And 15
he that was dead sat up, and began to
speak.   And he gave him to his mother.
And fear took hold on all : and they glori- 16
fied God, saying, A great prophet is arisen
among us : and, God hath visited his
people.   And this report went forth con- 17
cerning him in the whole of Judæa, and
all the region round about.

§ 45. John's Questioning.

Luke 7.

cAnd the disciples of John told him a in 18
the prison c of all these things.   And John 19
calling unto him [1] two of his disciples sent
them to the Lord, saying, Art thou he
that cometh, or look we for another?   And 20
when the men were come unto him, they
said, John the Baptist hath sent us unto
thee, saying, Art thou he that cometh, or
look we for another?   In that hour he 21
cured many of diseases and [2]plagues and
evil spirits ; and on many that were blind
he bestowed sight.   And he answered and 22
said unto them, Go your way, and tell
John what things ye have seen and heard ;
the blind receive their sight, the lame
walk, the lepers are cleansed, and the deaf
hear, the dead are raised up, the poor have
[3]good tidings preached to them.   And 23

KEY.—a Matthew, b Mark, c Luke, d John

[1] Gr. certain two.   [2] Gr. scourges.
[3] Or, the gospel.

§ 45. John's Questioning.

Matthew's Account.

Chap. 11.

2   Now when John heard <u>in the prison</u> the works of the
3 Christ, he sent by his disciples, and said unto him, Art
4 thou he that cometh, or look we for another? And Jesus
  answered and said unto them, Go your way and tell John
5 the things which ye do hear and see : the blind receive
  their sight, and the lame walk, the lepers are cleansed, and
  the deaf hear, and the dead are raised up, and the poor have
6 good tidings preached to them. And blessed is he, who-
7 soever shall find none occasion of stumbling in me. And
  as these went their way, Jesus began to say unto the multitudes concerning John, What went ye out into the wilder-
8 ness to behold? a reed shaken with the wind? But what
  went ye out for to see? a man clothed in soft *raiment*?
  Behold, they that wear soft *raiment* are in kings' houses.
9 But wherefore went ye out? to see a prophet? Yea, I say
10 unto you, and much more than a prophet. This is he, of
  whom it is written,
     Behold, I send my messenger before thy face,
     Who shall prepare thy way before thee.
11 Verily I say unto you, Among them that are born of women
  there hath not <u>arisen</u> a greater than John the Baptist : yet
  he that is but <u>little</u> in the kingdom of heaven is greater
  than he.
16   But whereunto shall I liken this generation? It is like
  unto children sitting in the marketplaces, that call unto
17 their fellows, and say, We piped unto you, and ye did not
18 dance ; we wailed, and ye did not mourn. For John came
  neither eating nor drinking, and they say, He hath a
19 demon. The Son of man came eating and drinking, and
  they say, Behold, a gluttonous man, and a winebibber, a
  friend of publicans and sinners ! And wisdom is justified
  <u>by her works.</u>

Luke 7.

blessed is he, whosoever shall find none occasion of stumbling in me.

24 And when the messengers of John were departed, he began to say unto the multitudes concerning John, What went ye out into the wilderness to behold? a reed

25 shaken with the wind? But what went ye out to see? a man clothed in soft raiment? Behold, they that are gorgeously apparelled, and live delicately, are in kings'

26 courts. But what went ye out to see? a prophet? Yea, I say unto you, and much

27 more than a prophet. This is he of whom it is written,

> Behold, I send my messenger before thy face,
> Who shall prepare thy way before thee.

28 ᵃVerily, ᶜI say unto you, Among them that are born of women there is none ᵃarisen ᶜgreater than John : yet he that is ¹ but little in the kingdom of God is greater than he.

12 **Matthew 11.** ᵃAnd from the days of John the Baptist until now the kingdom of heaven suffereth violence, and men of violence take

13 it by force. For all the prophets and

14 the law prophesied until John. And if

15 ye are willing to receive ²*it*, this is Elijah, who is to come. He that hath

Luke 7. ears ³to hear, let him hear.

29 ᶜAnd all the people when they heard, and the publicans, justified God, ⁴being

30 baptized with the baptism of John. But the Pharisees and the lawyers rejected for themselves the counsel of God, ⁵being not

31 baptized of him. Whereunto then shall I liken the men of this generation, and to

32 what are they like? They are like unto

KEY.—ᵃ Matthew, ᵇ Mark, ᶜ Luke, ᵈ John.

¹ Gr. *lesser*.   ² Or, *him*.
³ Some ancient authorities omit *to hear*.
⁴ Or, *having been*.   ⁵ Or, *not having been*.

children that sit in the marketplace, and call one to another; who say, We piped unto you, and ye did not dance; we wailed, and ye did not weep. For John 33 the Baptist is come eating no bread nor drinking wine; and ye say, He hath a demon. The Son of man is come eating 34 and drinking; and ye say, Behold, a gluttonous man, and a winebibber, a friend of publicans and sinners! And wisdom ¹ is 35 justified of all her children, ª by her works.

§ 46. Cities Upbraided.

ª Then began he to upbraid the cities 20 wherein most of his ² mighty works were done, because they repented not. Woe 21 unto thee, Chorazin! woe unto thee, Bethsaida! for if the ² mighty works had been done in Tyre and Sidon which were done in you, they would have repented long ago in sackcloth and ashes. Howbeit I 22 say unto you, it shall be more tolerable for Tyre and Sidon in the day of judgment, than for you. And thou, Caperna- 23 um, shalt thou be exalted unto heaven? thou shalt ³ go down unto Hades: for if the ² mighty works had been done in Sodom which were done in thee, it would have remained until this day. Howbeit I 24 say unto you, that it shall be more tolerable for the land of Sodom in the day of judgement, than for thee.

§ 47. Privileges of the Lowly.

ª At that season Jesus answered and said, 25 I ⁴ thank thee, O Father, Lord of heaven and earth, that thou didst hide these things from the wise and understanding, and didst

KEY.—ª Matthew, ᵇ Mark, ᶜ Luke, ᵈ John.

¹ Or, *was.*   ² Gr. *powers.*
³ Many ancient authorities read *be brought down.*
⁴ Or, *praise.*

Matthew 11.

26 reveal them unto babes: yea, Father, [1] for
27 so it was well-pleasing in thy sight. All
things have been delivered unto me of my
Father: and no one knoweth the Son, save
the Father: neither doth any know the
Father, save the Son, and he to whomsoever the Son willeth to reveal *him*.
28 Come unto me, all ye that labour and are
heavy laden, and I will give you rest.
29 Take my yoke upon you, and learn of me;
for I am meek and lowly in heart: and ye
30 shall find rest unto your souls. For my
yoke is easy, and my burden is light.

§ 48.   The Pharisee and the Sinful Woman.

Luke 7.

36   [c]And one of the Pharisees desired him
that he would eat with him. And he
entered into the Pharisee's house, and sat
37 down to meat. And behold, a woman who
was in the city, a sinner; and when she
knew that he was sitting at meat in the
Pharisee's house, she brought [2] an alabaster
38 cruse of ointment, and standing behind at
his feet, weeping, she began to wet his feet
with her tears, and wiped them with the
hair of her head, and [3] kissed his feet, and
39 anointed them with the ointment. Now
when the Pharisee who had bidden him
saw it, he spake within himself, saying,
This man, if he were [4] a prophet, would
have perceived who and what manner of
woman this is that toucheth him, that she
40 is a sinner. And Jesus answering said
unto him, Simon, I have somewhat to say
unto thee. And he saith, [5] Master, say on.
41 A certain lender had two debtors: the one

KEY.—[a] Matthew, [b] Mark, [c] Luke, [d] John.

[1] Or, *that*.   [2] Or, *a flask*.   [3] Gr. *kissed much*.
[4] Some ancient authorities read *the prophet*.
[5] Or, *Teacher*.

owed five hundred [1] shillings, and the other
fifty. When they had not *wherewith* to 42
pay, he forgave them both. Which of
them therefore will love him most?
Simon answered and said, He, I suppose, 43
to whom he forgave the most. And he
said unto him, Thou hast rightly judged.
And turning to the woman, he said unto 44
Simon, Seest thou this woman? I entered
into thine house, thou gavest me no water
for my feet: but she hath wetted my feet
with her tears, and wiped them with her
hair. Thou gavest me no kiss: but she, 45
since the time I came in, hath not ceased
to [2] kiss my feet. My head with oil thou 46
didst not anoint: but she hath anointed
my feet with ointment. Wherefore I say 47
unto thee, Her sins, which are many, are
forgiven; for she loved much: but to
whom little is forgiven, *the same* loveth
little. And he said unto her, Thy sins are 48
forgiven. And they that sat at meat with 49
him began to say [3] within themselves, Who
is this that even forgiveth sins? And he 50
said unto the woman, Thy faith hath saved
thee ; go in peace.

And it came to pass soon after Luke 8. 1
wards, that he went about through cities
and villages, preaching and bringing the
[4] good tidings of the kingdom of God, and
with him the twelve, and certain women 2
who had been healed of evil spirits and infirmities, Mary that was called Magdalene,
from whom seven demons had gone out,
and Joanna the wife of Chuza Herod's 3
steward, and Susanna, and many others,
that ministered unto [5] them of their substance.

KEY.—[a] Matthew, [b] Mark, [c] Luke, [d] John.

[1] The word in the Greek denotes a coin worth about
eight pence halfpenny.
[3] Gr. *kiss much.*   [2] Or, *among.*   [4] Or, *gospel.*
[5] Many ancient authorities read *him.*

§ 49. Blasphemy Reproved.

Mark's Account.

Chap. 3.

And the scribes that came down from Jerusalem said, 22
He hath Beelzebub, and, By the prince of the demons
casteth he out the demons. And he called them unto him, 23
and said unto them in parables, How can Satan cast out
Satan? And if a kingdom be divided against itself, that 24
kingdom cannot stand. And if a house be divided against 25
itself, that house will not be able to stand. And if Satan 26
hath risen up against himself, and is divided, he cannot
stand, but hath an end. But no one can enter into the 27
house of the strong *man*, and spoil his goods, except he
first bind the strong *man* ; and then he will spoil his house.
Verily I say unto you, All their sins shall be forgiven unto 28
the sons of men, and their blasphemies wherewith soever
they shall blaspheme : but whosoever shall blaspheme 29
against the Holy Spirit hath never forgiveness, but is guilty
of an eternal sin : because they said, He hath an unclean 30
spirit.

71

§ 49. Blasphemy Reproved.*

[Probably Capernaum.]

Mark 3.

19 ᵇAnd he cometh ¹into a house. And the
20 multitude cometh together again, so that
21 they could not so much as eat bread. And
when his friends heard it, they went out to
lay hold on him : for they said, He is beside
22 **Matthew 12.**   himself. ªThen was brought
unto him ²one possessed with a demon, blind
and dumb : and he healed him, insomuch
23 that the dumb man spake and saw. And all
the multitudes were amazed, and said, Can
24 this be the son of David ? But when the
Pharisees ᵇand the scribes who came
down from Jerusalem, ªheard it, they said,
This man doth not cast out demons, but
²by Beelzebub the prince of the demons.
25 And knowing their thoughts he ᵇcalled
them unto him and ªsaid unto them, ᵇin
parables, How can Satan cast out Satan?
ªEvery kingdom divided against itself is
brought to desolation; and every city or
house divided against itself shall not
26 stand : and if Satan casteth out Satan, he
is divided against himself; how then shall
27 his kingdom stand? And if I ²by Beelzebub cast out demons, ²by whom do your
sons cast them out? therefore shall they
28 be your judges. But if I ²by the Spirit
of God cast out demons then is the king-
29 dom of God come upon you. Or how
can one enter into the house of the strong
man, and spoil his goods, except he first

KEY.—ª Matthew, ᵇ Mark, ᶜ Luke, ᵈ John.

¹ Or, *home*.   ² Or, *a demoniac*.   ³ Or, *in*.

* Similar to Luke xi. 14–36 (§ 81), but probably not identical. To make this section and the following one refer to
the same events that are recorded in Luke throws one third
of the gospel of Luke into great chronological confusion.
The authority of G. W. Clark is here followed in consider-
ing Luke's account as referring to a later discourse; and
generally, where reasons do not seem quite conclusive for
interweaving gospel narratives, they have been kept separate.
See § 81.

bind the strong *man?* and then he will
spoil his house. He that is not with me 30
is against me ; and he that gathereth not
with me scattereth. Therefore I say unto 31
you, Every sin and blasphemy shall be
forgiven unto men; but the blasphemy
against the Spirit shall not be forgiven.
And whosoever shall speak a word against 32
the Son of man, it shall be forgiven him ;
but whosoever shall speak against the
Holy Spirit ᵇ is guilty of an eternal sin:
ᵃ it shall not be forgiven him, neither in this
¹ world, nor in that which is to come;
(ᵇ because they said, He hath an unclean
spirit). ᵃ Either make the tree good, and 33
its fruit good ; or make the tree corrupt,
and its fruit corrupt: for the tree is
known by its fruit. Ye offspring of vipers, 34
how can ye, being evil, speak good things?
for out of the abundance of the heart the
mouth speaketh. The good man out of 35
his good treasure bringeth forth good
things: and the evil man out of his evil
treasure bringeth forth evil things. And 36
I say unto you, that every idle word that
men shall speak, they shall give account
thereof in the day of judgement. For by 37
thy words thou shalt be justified, and by
thy words thou shalt be condemned.

§ 50. A Sign Asked.

Then certain of the scribes and Phari- 38
sees answered him, saying, ² Master, we
would see a sign from thee. But he 39
answered and said unto them, An evil and
adulterous generation seeketh after a sign ;
and there shall no sign be given to it but
the sign of Jonah the prophet: for as 40
Jonah was three days and three nights in

KEY.—ᵃ Matthew, ᵇ Mark, ᶜ Luke, ᵈ John.

¹ Or, *age*.   ² Or, *Teacher*.

§ 50. A Sign Asked.

Mark's Account.

Chap. 3.

31 And there come his mother and his brethren ; and,
32 standing without, they sent unto him, calling him. And
a multitude was sitting about him ; and they say unto him,
Behold, thy mother and thy brethren without seek for thee.
33 And he answereth them, and saith, Who is my mother
34 and my brethren? And looking round on them that sat
round about him, he saith, Behold, my mother and my
35 brethren! For whosoever shall do the will of God, the
same is my brother, and sister, and mother.

Luke's Account.

Chap. 8.

19 And there came to him his mother and brethren, and
20 they could not come at him for the crowd. And it was
told him, Thy mother and thy brethren stand without, de-
21 siring to see thee. But he answered and said unto them,
My mother and my brethren are these who hear the word
of God, and do it.

72

the belly of the [1] whale; so shall the Son
of man be three days and three nights in
41 the heart of the earth. The men of
Nineveh shall stand up in the judgement
with this generation, and shall condemn
it: for they repented at the preaching of
Jonah; and behold, [2] a greater than Jonah
42 is here. The queen of the south shall rise
up in the judgement with this generation,
and shall condemn it: for she came from
the ends of the earth to hear the wisdom
of Solomon; and behold, [2] a greater than
43 Solomon is here. But the unclean spirit,
when [3] he is gone out of the man, passeth
· through waterless places, seeking rest,
44 and findeth it not. Then [3] he saith, I will
return into my house whence I came out;
and when [3] he is come, [3] he findeth it
45 empty, swept, and garnished. Then goeth
[3] he, and taketh with [4] himself seven other
spirits more evil than [4] himself, and they
enter in and dwell there: and the last
state of that man becometh worse than the
first. Even so shall it be also unto this
evil generation.
46 While he was yet speaking to the multitudes, behold, his mother and his brethren
stood without, seeking to speak to him,
[c] and they could not come at him for the
47 crowd. [a5] And one said unto him, Behold,
thy mother and thy brethren stand with-
48 out, seeking to speak to thee. But he answered and said unto him that told him,
Who is my mother? and who are my
49 brethren? And he stretched forth his
hand towards his disciples, and said, Be-
50 hold my mother and my brethren! For
whosoever shall [c] hear the word of God
and [a] do the will of my Father who is in

KEY.—[a] Matthew, [b] Mark, [c] Luke, [d] John.
[1] Gr. sea-monster.   [2] Gr. more than.
[3] Or, it.   [4] Or, itself.
[5] Some ancient authorities omit ver 47.

Matthew 12,

heaven, he is my brother, and sister, and mother.

§ 51. Parables of the Kingdom of Heaven.

[Seaside near Capernaum.]

Matthew 13,

ᵃ On that day went Jesus out of the house, 1 and sat by the sea side, ᵇ and again he began to teach. ᵃAnd there were gathered 2 unto him great multitudes, so that he entered into a boat, and sat; and all the multude stood on the beach. And he spake 3 to them many things in parables, saying, Behold, the sower went forth to sow; and 4 as he sowed, some *seeds* fell by the way side, ᶜand it was trodden under foot; ᵃand the birds ᶜof the heaven ᵃ came and devoured them: and others fell upon the 5 ᴗ rocky places, where they had not much earth: and straightway they sprang up, because they had no deepness of earth: and when the sun was risen, they were 6 scorched; and because they had no root, ᶜ and had no moisture,ᵃ they withered away. And others fell upon the thorns; and the 7 thorns grew up, and choked them, ᵇand [they]* yielded no fruit: ᵃand others fell 8 upon the good ground, and yielded fruit, some a hundredfold, some sixty, some thirty. He that hath ears ᵇto hear, ᵃ let 9 him hear.

And ᵇ when he was alone ᵃ the disciples 10 came, and said unto him, Why speakest thou unto them in parables? And he answered and said unto them, Unto you it is 11 given to know the mysteries of the kingdom of heaven, but to them ᵇ that are without ᵃ it is not given. For whosoever hath, 12 to him shall be given, and he shall have abundance: but whosoever hath not, from him shall be taken away even that which

KEY.—ᵃ Matthew, ᵇ Mark, ᶜ Luke, ᵈ John.

* Word inserted by compiler.

§ 51. Parables of the Kingdom of Heaven.

Mark's Account.

Chap. 4.

1 And again he began to teach by the sea side. And there is gathered unto him a very great multitude, so that he entered into a boat, and sat in the sea ; and all the multi-
2 tude were by the sea on the land. And he taught them many things in parables, and said unto them in his teach-
3 ing, Hearken: Behold, the sower went forth to sow: and
4 it came to pass, as he sowed, some *seed* fell by the way
5 side, and the birds came and devoured it. And other fell on the rocky *ground*, where it had not much earth ; and straightway it sprang up, because it had no deepness of
6 earth: and when the sun was risen, it was scorched ; and
7 because it had no root, it withered away. And other fell among the thorns, and the thorns grew up, and choked it,
8 and it yielded no fruit. And others fell into the good ground, and yielded fruit, growing up and increasing ; and brought forth, thirtyfold, and sixtyfold, and a hundredfold.
9 And he said, Who hath ears to hear, let him hear.
10 And when he was alone, they that were about him with
11 the twelve asked of him the parables. And he said unto them, Unto you is given the mystery of the kingdom of God: but unto them that are without, all things are done
12 in parables; that seeing they may see, and not perceive; and hearing they may hear, and not understand; lest haply they should turn again, and it should be forgiven them.
13 And he saith unto them, Know ye not this parable? and
14 how shall ye know all the parables? The sower soweth
15 the word. And these are they by the way side, where the

Luke's Account.

Chap. 8.

4 And when a great multitude came together, and they of
5 every city resorted unto him, he spake by a parable: The sower went forth to sow his seed: and as he sowed, some fell by the way side; and it was trodden under foot, and
6 the birds of the heaven devoured it. And other fell on the rock ; and as soon as it grew, it withered away, because it
7 had no moisture. And other fell amidst the thorns ; and
8 the thorns grew with it, and choked it. And other fell into the good ground, and grew, and brought forth fruit a hundredfold. As he said these things, he cried, He that hath ears to hear, let him hear.
9 And his disciples asked him what this parable might be.
10 And he said, Unto you it is given to know the mysteries of the kingdom of God ; but to the rest in parables; that seeing they may not see, and hearing they may not
11 understand. Now the parable is this: The seed is the
12 word of God. And those by the way side are they that have

[Continued on duplicate page 75.]

§ 51. Parables of the Kingdom of Heaven.—(*Continued*.)

Mark's Account.

Chap. 4.

word is sown; and when they have heard, straightway cometh Satan, and taketh away the word which hath been
16 sown in them. And these in like manner are they that are sown upon the rocky *places*, who, when they have
17 heard the word, straightway receive it with joy; and they have no root in themselves, but endure for a while; then, when tribulation or persecution ariseth because of the
18 word, straightway they stumble. And others are they that are sown among the thorns; these are they that have
19 heard the word, and the cares of the world, and the deceitfulness of riches, and the lusts of other things entering in,
20 choke the word, and it becometh unfruitful. And those are they that were sown upon the good ground; such as hear the word, and accept it, and bear fruit, thirtyfold, and sixtyfold, and a hundredfold.
30 And he said, How shall we liken the kingdom of God?
31 or in what parable shall we set it forth? It is like a grain of mustard seed, which, when it is sown upon the earth, though it be less than all the seeds that are upon the earth,
32 yet when it is sown, groweth up, and becometh greater than all the herbs, and putteth out great branches; so that the birds of the heaven can lodge under the shadow thereof.
33 And with many such parables spake he the word unto them, as they were able to hear it: and without a parable
34 spake he not unto them: but privately to his own disciples he expounded all things.

Luke's Account.

Chap. 8.

heard; then cometh the devil, and taketh away the word from their heart, that they may not believe and be saved.
13 And those on the rock *are* they who, when they have heard, receive the word with joy; and these have no root, who for a while believe, and in time of temptation fall
14 away. And that which fell among the thorns, these are they that have heard, and as they go on their way they are choked with cares and riches and pleasures of *this* life, and
15 bring no fruit to perfection. And that in the good ground, these are such as in an honest and good heart, having heard the word, hold it fast, and bring forth fruit with patience.
16 And no man, when he hath lighted a lamp, covereth it with a vessel, or putteth it under a bed; but putteth it on
17 a stand, that they that enter in may see the light. For nothing is hid, that shall not be made manifest, nor *anything* secret, that shall not be known and come to light.
18 Take heed therefore how ye hear: for whosoever hath, to him shall be given; and whosoever hath not, from him shall be taken away even that which he thinketh he hath.

Matthew 13.

13 he hath. Therefore speak I to them in parables; because seeing they see not, and hearing they hear not, neither do they
14 understand. And unto them is fulfilled the prophecy of Isaiah, which saith,

By hearing ye shall hear, and shall in no wise understand;
And seeing ye shall see, and shall in no wise perceive:
15 For this people's heart is waxed gross, And their ears are dull of hearing, And their eyes they have closed; Lest haply they should perceive with their eyes, And hear with their ears, And understand with their heart, And should turn again, And I should heal them.

16 But blessed are your eyes, for they see;
17 and your ears, for they hear. For verily I say unto you, that many prophets and righteous men desired to see the things which ye see, and saw them not; and to hear the things which ye hear, and heard them not. ᵇ And he saith unto them, Know ye not this parable? and how shall ye
18 know all the parables? ᵇ Hear then ye the
19 parable of the sower. When any one heareth the word of the kingdom, and understandeth it not, *then* cometh ᵇ Satan, ᵃ the evil *one*, and snatcheth away that which hath been sown in his heart, ᶜ that [he]* may not believe and be saved. ᵃ This is he that
20 was sown by the way side. And he that was sown upon the rocky places, this is he that heareth the word, and straightway
21 with joy receiveth it; yet hath he not root in himself, but endureth for a while; and ᶜ in time of temptation, ᵃ when tribulation or persecution ariseth because of the word,

KEY.—ᵃ Matthew, ᵇ Mark, ᶜ Luke, ᵈ John.

* Word inserted by compiler.

straightway he stumbleth. And he that 22
was sown among the thorns, this is he that
heareth the word; and the care °and
pleasures ª of the ¹world, and the deceitfulness of riches, ᵇ and the lusts of other
things, entering in ª choke the word, and
he becometh unfruitful, °and bringeth no
fruit to perfection. ª And he that was sown 23
upon the good ground, this is he that heareth the word, and understandeth, ᵇ and ac-
cepteth it; ª who verily beareth fruit°with
patience, ª and bringeth forth, some a hundredfold, some sixty, some thirty.

Another parable set he before them, say- 24
ing, The kingdom of heaven is likened unto a man that sowed good seed in his
field : but while men slept, his enemy came 25
and sowed ²tares also among the wheat,
and went away. But when the blade 26
sprang up, and brought forth fruit, then
appeared the tares also. And the ²ser- 23
vants of the householder came and said unto him, Sir, didst thou not sow good seed
in thy field? whence then hath it tares?
And he said unto them, ⁴An enemy hath 28
done this. And the ²servants say unto
him, Wilt thou then that we go and gather
them up? But he saith, Nay; lest haply 29
while ye gather up the tares, ye root up
the wheat with them. Let both grow to- 30
gether until the harvest: and in the time
of the harvest I will say to the reapers,
Gather up first the tares, and bind them in
bundles to burn them : but gather the
wheat into my barn.

Another parable set he before them, say- 31
ing, The kingdom of heaven is like unto a
grain of mustard seed, which a man took,
and sowed in his field : which indeed is less 32

¹ Or, *age*.   ² Or, *darnel*.
³ Gr. *bondservants*.   ⁴ Gr. *A man* that is *an enemy*.

Matthew 13.

than all [b] the seeds that are upon the earth, [a] but when it is grown, it is greater than the herbs, [b] and putteth out great branches, [a] and becometh a tree, so that the birds of the heaven come and lodge in the branches [and in]* [b] the shadow thereof.

33 [a] Another parable spake he unto them; The kingdom of heaven is like unto leaven, which a woman took, and hid in three [1] measures of meal, till it was all leavened.

21 **Mark 4.** [b] And he said unto them, Is the lamp brought to be put under the bushel, or under the bed, *and* not to be put on the stand, [c] that they that enter in may see

22 the light? [b] For there is nothing hid, save that it should be manifested; neither was *anything* made secret, but

23 that it should come to light. If any man

24 hath ears to hear, let him hear. And he said unto them, Take heed what ye hear: with what measure ye mete it shall be measured unto you: and more shall be

25 given unto you. For he that hath, to him shall be given: and he that hath not, from him shall be taken away even that which he hath.

26 And he said, So is the kingdom of God, as if a man should cast seed upon the

27 earth; and should sleep and rise night and day, and the seed should spring up and

28 grow, he knoweth not how. The earth [2] beareth fruit of herself; first the blade, then the ear, then the full corn in the ear.

29 But when the fruit [3] is ripe, straightway he [4] putteth forth the sickle, because the harvest is come.

34 **Matthew 13.** [a] All these things spake Jesus in parables unto the multitudes [b] as they

KEY.—[a] Matthew, [b] Mark, [c] Luke, [d] John.

[1] The word in the Greek denotes the Hebrew seah, a measure containing nearly a peck and a half.
[2] Or, *yieldeth.*   [3] Or, *alloweth.*   [4] Or, *sendeth forth.*
* Words inserted by compiler.

were able to hear it; [a]and without a parable spake he nothing unto them, [b]but privately to his own disciples he expounded all things: [a]that it might be fulfilled which was spoken through the 35 prophet, saying,

> I will open my mouth in parables;
> I will utter things hidden from the foundation [1]of the world.

Then he left the multitudes, and went into the house: and his disciples came unto 36 him, saying, Explain unto us the parable of the tares of the field. And he answered 37 and said, He that soweth the good seed is the Son of man; and the field is the world; 38 and the good seed, these are the sons of the kingdom; and the tares are the sons of the evil *one*; and the enemy that sowed 39 them is the devil: and the harvest is [2]the end of the world; and the reapers are angels. As therefore the tares are gathered 40 up and burned with fire; so shall it be in [2]the end of the world. The Son of man 41 shall send forth his angels, and they shall gather out of his kingdom all things that cause stumbling, and them that do iniquity, and shall cast them into the furnace of fire: 42 there shall be the weeping and gnashing of teeth. Then shall the righteous shine forth 43 as the sun in the kingdom of their Father. He that hath ears, let him hear.

The kingdom of heaven is like unto a 44 treasure hidden in the field; which a man found, and hid; and [3]in his joy he goeth and selleth all that he hath, and buyeth that field.

Again, the kingdom of heaven is like unto 45 a man that is a merchant seeking goodly pearls: and having found one pearl of great 46

KEY.—[a] Matthew, [b] Mark, [c] Luke, [d] John

[1] Many ancient authorities omit *of the world*.
[2] Or, *the consummation of the age*.
[3] Or, *for joy thereof*.

§ 52. Calming the Sea.

Matthew's Account.

Chap. 8.

Now when Jesus saw great multitudes about him, he 18 gave commandment to depart unto the other side.

And when he was entered into a boat, his disciples fol- 23 lowed him. And behold, there arose a great tempest in 24 the sea, insomuch that the boat was covered with the waves: but he was asleep. And they came to him, and 25 awoke him, saying, Save, Lord; we perish. And he saith 26 unto them, Why are ye fearful, O ye of little faith? Then he *arose*, and rebuked the winds and the sea; and there was a great calm. And the men marvelled, saying, What man- 27 ner of man is this, that even the winds and the sea obey him?

Luke's Account.

Chap. 8.

Now it came to pass on one of those days, that he en- 22 tered into a boat, himself and his disciples; and he said unto them, Let us go over unto the other side of the lake: and they launched forth. But as they sailed he fell asleep: 23 and there came down a storm of wind on the lake; and they were filling *with water*, and were in jeopardy. And 24 they came to him, and awoke him, saying, Master, mas- ter, we perish. And he awoke, and rebuked the wind and the raging of the water: and they ceased, and there was a calm. And he said unto them, Where is your faith? And 25 being afraid they marvelled, saying one to another, Who then is this, that he commandeth even the winds and the water, and they obey him?

79

Matthew 13.

price, he went and sold all that he had, and bought it.

47 Again, the kingdom of heaven is like unto a [1] net, that was cast into the sea, and gath-
48 ered of every kind: which, when it was filled, they drew up on the beach; and they sat down, and gathered the good into ves-
49 sels, but the bad they cast away. So shall it be in [2] the end of the world: the angels shall come forth, and sever the wicked from
50 among the righteous, and shall cast them into the furnace of fire: there shall be the weeping and gnashing of teeth.

51 Have ye understood all these things?
52 They said unto him, Yea. And he said unto them, Therefore every scribe who hath been made a disciple to the kingdom of heaven is like unto a man that is a householder, who bringeth forth out of his treasure things new and old.

53 And it came to pass, when Jesus had finished these parables, he departed thence.

§ 52. Calming the Sea.

[The sea of Galilee.]

Mark 4.

35 [b]And on that day, when even was come, he saith unto them, Let us go over unto the
36 other side. And leaving the multitude, they take him with them, even as he was, in the boat, [c]himself and his disciples; and they launched forth. [b]And other boats
37 were with him. And there ariseth a great storm of wind [a]in the sea, [b]and the waves beat into the boat, insomuch that the boat
38 was now filling. And he himself was in the stern, asleep on the cushion: and they [c]come to him, [b]awake him, and say unto him, [a]Master, carest thou not that we

KEY.—[a] Matthew, [b] Mark, [c] Luke, [d] John.

[1] Gr. *drag-net.*
[2] Or, *the consummation of the age.*
[3] Or, *Teacher.*

Mark 4.

perish? And he awoke, [a] and arose, [b] and 39
rebuked the wind, [c] and the raging of the
water, [b] and said unto the sea, Peace, be still.
And the wind ceased, and there was a
great calm. And he said unto them, Why 40
are ye fearful? have ye not yet faith?
And they feared exceedingly, and said one 41
to another, Who then is this, that [c] commandeth [b] even the wind and the sea, [c] and
they [b] obey him?

§ 53. The Unclean Spirit and the Swine.*

Mark 5.

[b] And they came to the other side of the 1
sea, into the country of the Gerasenes,
[c] which is over against Galilee. [b] And 2
when he was come out of the boat, straightway there met him out of the tombs a man
[c] of the city, [b] with an unclean spirit, [a] exceeding fierce, [b] who [c] had demons, and for
a long time had worn no clothes, and abode
not in any house, but [b] had his dwelling in 3
the tombs: and no man could any more
bind him, no, not with a chain; because 4
that he had been often bound with fetters
and chains, and the chains had been rent
asunder by him, and the fetters broken in
pieces: and no man had strength to tame
him. And always, night and day, in the 5
tombs and in the mountains, he was crying
out, and cutting himself with stones. [a] No
man could pass by that way. [b] And when 6
he saw Jesus from afar, he ran [c] and fell
down before him [b] and worshipped him;

KEY.—[a] Matthew, [b] Mark, [c] Luke, [d] John.

* Matthew places this miracle in the country of the Gadarenes; Mark and Luke in the country of the Gerasenes.
Probably the location was between the two cities of Gadara
and Gerasa, and was called sometimes for one and sometimes for the other. Matthew speaks of two demoniacs;
Mark and Luke of but one. This is easily reconciled by
supposing that there were two, of whom one was much
more prominent than the other. The mention of one does
not exclude the presence of the other.

§ 53. The Unclean Spirit and the Swine.

Matthew's Account.

Chap. 8.

28 And when he was come to the other side into the country of the Gadarenes, there met him two possessed with demons, coming forth out of the tombs, exceeding fierce,

29 so that no man could pass by that way. And behold, they cried out, saying, What have we to do with thee, thou Son of God? art thou come hither to torment us be-

30 fore the time? Now there was afar off from them a herd

31 of many swine feeding. And the demons besought him, saying, If thou cast us out, send us away into the herd of

Luke's Account.

Chap. 8.

26 And they arrived at the country of the Gerasenes,

27 which is over against Galilee. And when he was come forth upon the land, there met him a certain man out of the city, who had demons; and for a long time he had worn no clothes, and abode not in *any* house, but in the

28 tombs. And when he saw Jesus, he cried out, and fell down before him, and with a loud voice said, What have I to do with thee, Jesus, thou Son of the Most High

29 God? I beseech thee, torment me not. For he was commanding the unclean spirit to come out from the man. For oftentimes it had seized him: and he was kept under guard, and bound with chains and fetters; and breaking the bands asunder, he was driven of the demon into the

30 deserts. And Jesus asked him, What is thy name? And he said, Legion; for many demons were entered into him.

31 And they entreated him that he would not command them

32 to depart into the abyss. Now there was there a herd of many swine feeding on the mountain: and they intreated him that he would give them leave to enter into them.

33 And he gave them leave. And the demons came out from the man, and entered into the swine: and the herd rushed

34 down the steep into the lake, and were drowned. And when they that fed them saw what had come to pass, they

[*Continued on duplicate page* 81.]

Matthew's Account.

Chap. 8.

swine. And he said unto them, Go. And they came out, 32 and went into the swine: and behold, the whole herd rushed down the steep into the sea, and perished in the waters. And they that fed them fled, and went away 33 into the city, and told everything, and what was befallen to them that were possessed with demons. And behold, 34 all the city came out to meet Jesus: and when they saw him, they besought *him* that he would depart from their borders.

Chap. 9.

And he entered into a boat, and crossed over, and came 1 into his own city.

Luke's Account.

Chap. 8.

fled, and told it in the city and in the country. And they 35 went out to see what had come to pass; and they came to Jesus, and found the man, from whom the demons were gone out, sitting, clothed and in his right mind, at the feet of Jesus: and they were afraid. And they that saw it 36 told them how he that was possessed with demons was made whole. And all the people of the country of the 37 Gerasenes round about asked him to depart from them; for they were holden with great fear: and he entered into a boat, and returned. But the man from whom the de- 38 mons were gone out prayed him that he might be with him: but he sent him away, saying. Return to thy house, and 39 declare how great things God hath done for thee. And he went his way, publishing throughout the whole city how great things Jesus had done for him.

and crying out with a loud voice, he saith,
7 What have I to do with thee, Jesus, thou
   Son of the Most High God? I adjure thee
   by God, torment me not ªbefore the time.
8 ᵇFor he said unto him, Come forth, thou
9 unclean spirit, out of the man. And he
   asked him, What is thy name? And he
   saith unto him, My name is Legion; for
   we are many.   ᶜ(For many demons were
10 entered into him).   ᵇAnd he besought him
   much that he would not send them away
   out of the country ᶜand would not com-
11 mand them to depart into the abyss. ᵇNow
   there was there ªafar off from them ᵇon
   the mountain side a great herd of swine
12 feeding. And they besought him, saying,
   Send us into the swine, that we may enter
13 into them. And he gave them leave. And
   the unclean spirits came out ᶜfrom the
   man, ᵇand entered into the swine: and the
   herd rushed down the steep into the sea,
   in number about two thousand; and they
14 were choked in the sea. And they that fed
   them fled, and told it in the city, and in the
   country. And they came to see what it
15 was that had come to pass. And they
   come to Jesus, and behold ¹him that was
   possessed with demons sitting, clothed and
   in his right mind, ᶜat the feet of Jesus, ᵇ*even*
   him that had the legion: and they were
16 afraid. And they that saw it declared unto them how it befel ¹him that was possessed with demons, and concerning the
17 swine. And ᶜall the people of the country
   ᵇbegan to beseech him to depart from their
   borders; ᶜfor they were holden with great
18 fear.   ᵇAnd as he was entering into the
   boat, he that had been possessed with demons besought him that he might be with
19 him. And he suffered him not, but saith

KEY.—ª Matthew, ᵇ Mark, ᶜ Luke, ᵈ John.

¹ Or, *the demoniac.*

unto him, Go to thy house unto thy friends,
and tell them how great things the Lord
hath done for thee, and *how* he had mercy
on thee. And he went his way, and began 20
to publish in Decapolis how great things
Jesus had done for him: and all men did
marvel.

§ 54. Home Revisited.

[Nazareth.]

Mark 6.

[b]And he went out from thence; and he 1
cometh into his own country; and his disciples follow him. And when the sabbath 2
was come, he began to teach in the synagogue: and [1]many hearing him were astonished, saying, Whence hath this man these
things? and, What is the wisdom that is
given unto this man, and *what mean* such
[2]mighty works wrought by his hands?
Is not this the carpenter, [a]the carpenter's 3
son, [b]the son of Mary, and brother of James,
and Joses, and Judas, and Simon? and are
not his sisters [a]all [b]here with us? And
they were [3]offended in him. And Jesus 4
said unto them, A prophet is not without
honour, save in his own country, and
among his own kin, and in his own house.
And he could there do no [4]mighty work, 5
save that he laid his hands upon a few sick
folk, and healed them. And he marvelled 6
because of their unbelief.

§ 55. The Disciples Sent Forth.

[Galilee.]

Matthew 9.

[a]And Jesus went about all the cities and 35
the villages, teaching in their synagogues,
and preaching the gospel of the kingdom,
and healing all manner of disease and all
manner of sickness. But when he saw the 36

KEY.—[a] Matthew, [b] Mark, [c] Luke, [d] John.

[1] Some ancient authorities insert *the*.
[2] *powers.*   [3] Gr. *caused to stumble.*   [4] Gr. *power.*

§ 54. Home Revisited.

Matthew's Account.

Chap. 13.

53 And it came to pass, when Jesus had finished these par-
54 ables, he departed thence. And coming into his own
country he taught them in their synagogue, insomuch that
they were astonished, and said, Whence hath this man
55 this wisdom, and these mighty works? Is not this the
carpenter's son? is not his mother called Mary? and
his brethren, James, and Joseph, and Simon, and Judas?
56 And his sisters, are they not all with us? Whence then
57 hath this man all these things? And they were offended
in him. But Jesus said unto them, A prophet is not
without honor, save in his own country, and in his own
58 house. And he did not many mighty works there because of their unbelief.

82

§ 55. The Disciples Sent Forth.

Mark's Account.

And he went round about the villages teaching.

And he called unto him the twelve, and <u>began</u> to send 7
<u>them forth by two and two</u>; and he gave them authority
over the unclean spirits; and he charged them that they 8
should take nothing for *their* journey, save a staff only;
no bread, no wallet, no money in their purse; but *to go* 9
shod with sandals: and, *said he*, put not on two coats.

And he said unto them, Wheresoever ye enter into a house, 10
there abide till ye depart thence. And whatsoever place 11
shall not receive you, and they hear you not, as ye go forth
thence, shake off the dust that is under your feet for a testimony unto them. And they went out, and preached that 12
men should repent. And they cast out many demons, and 13
anointed with oil many that were sick, and healed them.

Luke's Account.

And he called the twelve together, and gave them 1
<u>power and</u> authority over all demons, and to cure diseases.
And he sent them forth to <u>preach the kingdom of God</u>, 2
<u>and to heal the sick.</u> And he said unto them, Take noth- 3
ing for your journey, neither staff, nor wallet, nor bread,
nor money; neither have two coats. And into whatsoever 4
house ye enter, there abide, and thence depart. And as 5
many as receive you not, when ye depart from that city,
shake off the dust from your feet <u>for a testimony against</u>
them. And they departed, and <u>went throughout the vil-</u> 6
<u>lages, preaching</u> the gospel, and healing everywhere.

Matthew 9.

multitudes, he was moved with compassion for them, because they were distressed and scattered, as sheep not having a shepherd.
37 Then saith he unto his disciples, The harvest truly is plenteous, but the labourers
38 are few. Pray ye therefore the Lord of the harvest, that he send forth labourers in-
1 **Matthew 10.** to his harvest. ªAnd he called un to him his twelve disciples, ᵇ and began to send them forth by two and two, ª and gave them ᶜpower and ª authority over unclean spirits, to cast them out, and to heal all manner of disease and all manner of sickness.

2 Now the names of the twelve apostles are these: The first, Simon, who is called Peter, and Andrew his brother; James the *son* of Zebedee, and John his brother;
3 Philip, and Bartholomew; Thomas, and Matthew the publican; James the *son* of
4 Alphæus, and Thaddæus; Simon the ¹Cananæan, and Judas Iscariot, who also ² betrayed him.
5 trayed him. These twelve Jesus sent forth ᶜto preach the kingdom of God and to heal the sick, ª and charged them, saying,

Go not into *any* way of the Gentiles, and enter not into any city of the Samaritans:
6 but go rather to the lost sheep of the house
7 of Israel. And as ye go, preach, saying,
8 The kingdom of heaven is at hand. Heal the sick, raise the dead, cleanse the lepers, cast out demons: freely ye received, freely
9 give. Get you no gold, nor silver, nor
10 brass in your ³purses; no wallet for *your* journey, neither two coats, nor shoes, nor staff: for the labourer is worthy of his
11 food: ᵇ but go shod with sandals. ª And into whatsoever city or village ye shall enter, search out who in it is worthy; and
12 there abide till ye go forth. And as ye en-

KEY.—ª Matthew, ᵇ Mark, ᶜ Luke, ᵈ John.

¹ Or, *Zealot.* ² Or, *delivered him up.* ³ Gr. *girdles.*

ter into the house, salute it.   And if the 13
house be worthy, let your peace come upon
it: but if it be not worthy, let your peace
return to you.   And whosoever shall not 14
receive you, nor hear your words, as ye go
forth out of that house or that city, shake
off the dust of your feet ᶜfor a testimony
against them.   ªVerily I say unto you, It 15
shall be more tolerable for the land of
Sodom and Gomorrah in the day of judgement, than for that city.

Behold, I send you forth as sheep in 16
the midst of wolves: be ye therefore wise
as serpents, and ¹harmless as doves.   But 17
beware of men : for they will deliver you up
to councils, and in their synagogues they
will scourge you ; yea and before gover- 18
nors and kings shall ye be brought for my
sake, for a testimony to them and to the
Gentiles.   But when they deliver you up, 19
be not anxious how or what ye shall speak :
for it shall be given you in that hour what
ye shall speak.   For it is not ye that 20
speak, but the Spirit of your Father that
speaketh in you.   And brother shall deliv- 21
er up brother to death, and the father his
child : and children shall rise up against
parents, and ²cause them to be put to death.
And ye shall be hated of all men for my 22
name's sake : but he that endureth to the
end, the same shall be saved.   But when 23
they persecute you in this city, flee into
the next : for verily I say unto you, Ye
shall not have gone through the cities of
Israel, till the Son of man be come.

A disciple is not above his ³master, nor 24
a ⁴servant above his lord.   It is enough for 25
the disciple that he be as his ³master, and
the ⁴servant as his lord.   If they have

KEY.—ª Matthew, ᵇ Mark, ᶜ Luke, ᵈ John.

¹ Or, *simple.*   ² Or, *put them to death.*
³ Or, *teacher.*   ⁴ Gr. *bondservant.*

Matthew 10.

called the master of the house [1]Beelzebub, how much more *shall they call* them of his

26 household! Fear them not therefore: for there is nothing covered, that shall not be revealed; and hid, that shall not be known.

27 What I tell you in the darkness, speak ye in the light: and what ye hear in the ear,

28 proclaim upon the housetops. And be not afraid of them that kill the body, but are not able to kill the soul: but rather fear him who is able to destroy both soul

29 and body in [2]hell. Are not two sparrows sold for a penny? and not one of them shall fall on the ground without your

30 Father: but the very hairs of your head

31 are all numbered. Fear not therefore; ye are of more value than many sparrows.

32 Every one therefore who shall confess [3]me before men, [4]him will I also confess before

33 my Father who is in heaven. But whosoever shall deny me before men, him will I also deny before my Father who is in heaven.

34 Think not that I came to [5]send peace on the earth: I came not to [5]send peace, but

35 a sword. For I came to set a man at variance against his father, and the daughter against her mother, and the daughter in

36 law against her mother in law: and a man's foes *shall be* they of his own household.

37 He that loveth father or mother more than me is not worthy of me: and he that loveth son or daughter more than me is not

38 worthy of me. And he that doth not take his cross and follow after me, is not worthy

39 of me. He that [6]findeth his life shall lose it; and he that [7]loseth his life for my sake shall find it.

KEY.—[a] Matthew, [b] Mark, [c] Luke, [d] John.

[1] Gr. *Beelzebul.*
[3] Gr. *in me.*
[5] Gr. *cast.*
[7] Or, *lost.*

[2] Gr. *Gehenna.*
[4] Gr. *in him.*
[6] Or, *found.*

Matthew 10.

He that receiveth you receiveth me, and 40
he that receiveth me receiveth him that
sent me.   He that receiveth a prophet in 41
the name of a prophet shall receive a prophet's reward; and he that receiveth a
righteous man in the name of a righteous
man shall receive a righteous man's reward.
And whosoever shall give to drink unto 42
one of these little ones a cup of cold water
only, in the name of a disciple, verily I say
unto you, he shall in no wise lose his reward.   **Matthew 11.**

And it came to pass when Jesus had made 1
an end of commanding his twelve disciples,
he departed thence to teach and preach in
their cities.

§ 56. The Death of John the Baptist.

[Peræa.]

Mark 6.

ᵇAnd they went out. and preached that 12
men should repent.   And they cast out 13
many demons, and anointed with oil many
that were sick, and healed them.

And king Herod heard *thereof*; for his 14
name had become known, ᶜand all that was
done; and he was much perplexed.   ᵇ And
¹he said, John ⁹the Baptist is risen from
the dead, and therefore do these powers
work in him.   But others said, It is Elijah. 15
And others said, *It is* a prophet, *even* as one
of the prophets.   But Herod, when he 16
heard *thereof*, said, John, whom I beheaded,
he is risen.   ᶜAnd he sought to see him.

ᵇ For Herod himself had sent forth and 17
laid hold upon John, and bound him in
prison for the sake of Herodias, his brother
Philip's wife: for he had married her.
For John said unto Herod, It is not lawful 18
for thee to have thy brother's wife.   And 19
Herodias set herself against him, and de-

KEY.—ᵃ Matthew, ᵇ Mark, ᶜ Luke, ᵈ John.

¹ Some ancient authorities read *they*.   ⁹ Gr. *the Baptizer.*

§ 56. The Death of John the Baptist.

Matthew's Account.

Chap. 14.

1 At that season Herod the tetrarch heard the report con-
2 cerning Jesus, and said unto his servants, This is John
the Baptist; he is risen from the dead; and therefore do
3 these powers work in him. For Herod had laid hold on
John, and bound him, and put him in prison for the sake
4 of Herodias, his brother Philip's wife. For John said
unto him, It is not lawful for thee to have her. And
when he would have put him to death, he feared the mul-
6 titude, because they counted him as a prophet. But when
Herod's birthday came, the daughter of Herodias danced
7 in the midst, and pleased Herod. Whereupon he prom-
ised with an oath to give her whatsoever she should ask.
8 And she, being put forward by her mother, saith, Give me
9 here in a charger the head of John the Baptist. And the
king was grieved; but for the sake of his oaths, and of
them that sat at meat with him, he commanded it to be
10 given; and he sent, and beheaded John in the prison.
11 And his head was brought in a charger, and given to the
12 damsel: and she brought it to her mother. And his disciples came, and took up the corpse, and buried him; and
they went and told Jesus.

Luke's Account.

Chap. 9.

7 Now Herod the tetrarch heard of all that was done:
and he was much perplexed, because that it was said by
8 some, that John was risen from the dead; and by some,
that Elijah had appeared; and by others, that one of the
9 old prophets was risen again. And Herod said, John I beheaded: but who is this, about whom I hear such things i
And he sought to see him.

Mark 6.

20 sired to kill him; and she could not: for Herod feared John, knowing that he was a righteous man and a holy: [a] and when he would have put him to death, he feared the multitude, because they counted him as a prophet; [b] and kept him safe. And when he heard him, he [1] was much perplexed; and he

21 heard him gladly. And when a convenient day was come, that Herod on his birthday made a supper to his lords, and the [2] high

22 captains, and the chief men of Galilee; and when [3] the daughter of Herodias herself came in and danced, [4] she pleased Herod and them that sat at meat with him; and the king said unto the damsel, Ask of me whatsoever thou wilt, and I will give it thee.

23 And he sware unto her, Whatsoever thou shalt ask of me, I will give it thee, unto the

24 half of my kingdom. And she went out, and said unto her mother, What shall I ask? And she said, The head of John [5] the Bap-

25 tist. And she came in straightway with haste unto the king, and asked, saying, I will that thou forthwith give me in a charger

26 the head of John [5] the Baptist. And the king was exceeding sorry; but for the sake of his oaths, and of them that sat at

27 meat, he would not reject her. And straightway the king sent forth a soldier of his guard, and commanded to bring his head: and he went and beheaded him in

28 the prison, and brought his head in a charger, and gave it to the damsel; and the

29 damsel gave it to her mother. And when his disciples heard *thereof*, they came and took up his corpse, and laid it in a tomb; [a] and they went and told Jesus.

KEY.—[a] Matthew. [b] Mark, [c] Luke, [d] John.

[1] Many ancient authorities read *did many things.*
[2] Or, *military tribunes.* Gr *chiliarchs.*
[3] Some ancient authorities read *his daughter Herodias.*
[4] Or, *it*   [5] Gr. *the Baptizer.*

§ 57. Seeking for Rest.

Mark 6.

[b] And the apostles gather themselves to- 30 gether unto Jesus; and they told him all things, whatsoever they had done, and whatsoever they had taught. And he saith 31 unto them, Come ye yourselves apart into a desert place, and rest awhile. For there were many coming and going, and they had no leisure so much as to eat. [d] Now the passover, the feast of the Jews, was at hand. [b] And they went away in the boat 32 [c] to a city called Bethsaida,* [b] to a desert place apart, [d] [on] † the other side of the sea of Galilee, which is the sea of Tiberias.

[b] And *the people* saw them going, and 33 many knew *them*, and they ran there together [1] on foot from all the cities, and outwent them; [d] because they beheld the signs that he did on them that were sick. [b] And 34 he came forth and saw a great multitude and, he had compassion on them, because they were as sheep not having a shepherd : and he [c] welcomed them, [and] † [b] began to teach them many things, [a] and healed their sick.

§ 58. Five Thousand Fed.

[Near Bethsaida.]

Mark 6.

[b] And when the day was now far spent, 35 [a] and when even was come, [b] his disciples came unto him, and said, The place is desert, and the day is now far spent : send 36 them away, that they may go into the country and villages round about, [c] and lodge, [b] and buy themselves somewhat to eat: [c] for we are here in a desert place. [b] But he answered and said unto them, 37 [a] They have no need to go away; [b] give ye them to eat. [d] And this he said to prove

KEY.—[a] Matthew, [b] Mark, [c] Luke, [d] John.

[1] Or, *by land*.

* Doubtless a desert in the territory of this city.
† Word inserted by compiler.

§ 57. Seeking for Rest.

Matthew's Account.

Chap. 14.

13 Now when Jesus heard *it*, he withdrew from thence in a boat, to a desert place apart : and when the multitudes heard *thereof*, they followed him on foot from the
14 cities. And he came forth, and saw a great multitude, and he had compassion on them, and healed their sick.

Luke's Account.

Chap. 9.

10 And the apostles, when they were returned, declared unto him what things they had done. And he took them,
11 and withdrew apart to a city called Bethsaida. But the multitudes perceiving it followed him : and he welcomed them, and spake to them of the kingdom of God, and them that had need of healing he healed.

John's Account.

Chap. 6.

1 After these things Jesus went away to the other side of
2 the sea of Galilee, which is *the sea* of Tiberias. And a great multitude followed him, because they beheld the signs
3 which he did on them that were sick. And Jesus went up into the mountain, and there he sat with his disciples.

§ 58. Five Thousand Fed.

Matthew's Account.

Chap. 14.

15 And when even was come, the disciples came to him, saying, The place is desert, and the time is already past ; send the multitudes away, that they may go into the
16 villages, and buy themselves food. But Jesus said unto them, They have no need to go away ; give ye them to eat.
17 And they say unto him, We have here but five loaves,
18 and two fishes. And he said, Bring them hither to me.
19 And he commanded the multitudes to sit down on the grass ; and he took the five loaves, and the two fishes, and looking up to heaven, he blessed, and brake and gave the loaves to the disciples, and the disciples to the multitudes.
20 And they did all eat, and were filled : and they took up that which remained over of the broken pieces, twelve
21 baskets full. And they that did eat were about five thousand men, beside women and children.

[*Continued on duplicate page 89.*]

§ 58. Five Thousand Fed.—(*Continued.*)

Luke's Account.

And the day began to wear away ; and the twelve came, 12 and said unto him, Send the multitude away, that they may go into the villages and country round about, and lodge, and get provisions : for we are here in a desert place.   But he said unto them, Give ye them to eat. 13 And they said, We have no more than five loaves and two fishes ; except we should go and buy food for all this people.   For they were about five thousand men. 14 And he said unto his disciples, Make them sit down in companies, about fifty each.   And they did so, and 15 made them all sit down.   And he took the five loaves and 16 the two fishes, and looking up to heaven, he blessed them, and brake ; and gave to the disciples to set before the multitude.   And they did eat, and were all filled : and 17 there was taken up that which remained over to them of broken pieces, twelve baskets.

John's Account.

Now the passover, the feast of the Jews, was at hand.   4 Jesus therefore lifting up his eyes, and seeing that a great 5 multitude cometh unto him, saith unto Philip, Whence are we to buy bread, that these may eat?   And this he 6 said to prove him; for he himself knew what he would do. Philip answered him, Two hundred shillings' worth of 7 bread is not sufficient for them, that every one may take a little.   One of his disciples, Andrew, Simon Peter's 8 brother, saith unto him, There is a lad here, who hath five 9 barley loaves, and two fishes : but what are these among so many?   Jesus said, Make the people sit down.   Now 10 there was much grass in the place.   So the men sat down, in number about five thousand.   Jesus therefore took the 11 loaves ; and having given thanks, he distributed to them that were set down ; likewise also of the fishes as much as they would.   And when they were filled, he saith unto his 12 disciples, Gather up the broken pieces which remain over, that nothing be lost.   So they gathered them up, and filled 13 twelve baskets with broken pieces from the five barley loaves, which remained over unto them that had eaten. When therefore the people saw the sign which he did, 14 they said, This is of a truth the prophet that cometh into the world.

Mark 6.

[them] * : for he himself knew what he would do. ᵇ And they say unto him, Shall we go and buy two hundred shillings' worth of bread, and give them to eat,

38 ᵈ that every one may take a little? ᵇ And he saith unto them, How many loaves have ye? go *and* see. And when they knew, they say, ᵈ There is a lad here who hath five barley loaves and two fishes: ᵇ but what are these among so many? ᵃ And he

39 said, bring them hither to me. ᵇ And he commanded them that all should ¹ sit down by companies upon the green grass. ᵈ Now there was much grass in the place.

40 ᵇ and they sat down in ranks, by hundreds,

41 and by fifties. And he took the five loaves and the two fishes, and looking up to heaven, he blessed, and brake the loaves; and he gave to the disciples to set before them; and the two fishes divided he

42 among them all. And they did all eat, and were filled. ᵈ And when they were all filled, he saith unto his disciples, Gather up the broken pieces that remain over that

43 nothing be lost. ᵇ And they took up broken pieces, twelve basketfuls, and also

44 of the fishes. And they that ate the loaves were five thousand men, ᵃ besides women and children. ᵈ When therefore the people saw the sign which he did, they said, This is of a truth the prophet that cometh into the world.

§ 59. Jesus Walks on the Sea.

Matthew 14.

ᵈ Jesus therefore perceiving that they were about to come and take him by force,

22 to make him king, ᵃ constrained the disciples to enter into the boat, and to go before him unto the other side, till he should

23 send the multitudes away. And after he

KEY.—ᵃ Matthew, ᵇ Mark, ᶜ Luke, ᵈ John.

¹ Gr. *recline.*

* Word inserted by compiler.

had sent the multitudes away, he went up
into the mountain apart to pray : and when
even was come, he was there alone. But 24
the boat ¹ was now in the midst of the sea,
distressed by the waves ; for the wind was
contrary, ᵈ and the sea was rising by reason
of a great wind that blew ; and it was dark,
and Jesus had not come unto them. ª And 25
in the fourth watch of the night, ᵈ when
they had rowed about five and twenty or
thirty furlongs, ª he came unto them, walking upon the sea, ᵈ and drawing nigh unto
the boat ; ᵇ and he would have passed by
them ; ª and when the disciples saw him 26
walking on the sea, they were troubled,
saying, It is an apparition ; and they cried
out for fear : ᵇ for they all saw him and
were troubled. ª But straightway Jesus 27
spake unto them, saying, Be of good cheer ;
it is I ; be not afraid. And Peter answered 28
him and said, Lord, if it be thou, bid me
come unto thee upon the waters. And he 29
said, Come. And Peter went down from
the boat, and walked upon the waters, ² to
come to Jesus. But when he saw the 30
wind,³ he was afraid ; and beginning to
sink, he cried out, saying, Lord, save me.
And immediately Jesus stretched forth his 31
hand, and took hold of him, and saith unto
him, O thou of little faith, wherefore didst
thou doubt? And when they were gone 32
up into the boat, the wind ceased. And 33
they that were in the boat worshipped
him, saying, Of a truth thou art the Son
of God ; ᵇ and they were sore amazed in
themselves : for they understood not concerning the loaves, but their heart was
hardened.

KEY.—ª Matthew, ᵇ Mark, ᵉ Luke, ᵈ John.

¹ Some ancient authorities read *was many furlongs distant
from the land*.
² Some ancient authorities read *and came*.
³ Many ancient authorities add *strong*.

§ 59. Jesus Walks on the Sea.

Mark's Account.

Chap. 6.

45 And straightway he constrained his disciples to enter into the boat, and to go before *him* unto the other side to Bethsaida, while he himself sendeth the multitude away.
46 And after he had taken leave of them, he departed into
47 the mountain to pray. And when even was come, the boat was in the midst of the sea, and he alone on the land.
48 And seeing them distressed in rowing, for the wind was contrary unto them, about the fourth watch of the night he cometh unto them, walking on the sea ; and he would have
49 passed by them : but they, when they saw him walking on the sea, supposed that it was an apparition, and cried out :
50 for they all saw him, and were troubled. But he straightway spake with them, and saith unto them, Be of good
51 cheer : it is I ; be not afraid. And he went up unto them into the boat ; and the wind ceased : and they were sore
52 amazed in themselves ; for they understood not concerning the loaves, but their heart was hardened.

John's Account.

Chap. 6.

15 Jesus therefore perceiving that they were about to come and take him by force, to make him king, withdrew again into the mountain himself alone.
16 And when evening came, his disciples went down unto
17 the sea ; and they entered into a boat, and were going over the sea unto Capernaum. And it was now dark, and
18 Jesus had not yet come to them. And the sea was rising
19 by reason of a great wind that blew. When therefore they had rowed about five and twenty or thirty furlongs, they behold Jesus walking on the sea, and drawing nigh
20 unto the boat : and they were afraid. But he saith unto
21 them, It is I ; be not afraid. They were willing therefore to receive him into the boat : and straightway the boat was at the land whither they were going.

[*Continued on duplicate page 91.*]

§ 59. Jesus Walks on the Sea.—(*Continued.*)

Matthew's Account.

Chap. 14.

And when they had crossed over, they came to the 34 land, unto Gennesaret. And when the men of that place 35 knew him, they sent into all that region round about, and brought unto him all that were sick ; and they besought 36 him that they might only touch the border of his garment: and, as many as touched were made whole.

91

Mark 6.

53 [b] And when they had crossed over they came to the land unto Gennesaret,
54 and moored to the shore.   And when they were come out of the boat, straightway
55 the people knew him, and ran round about that whole region, and began to carry about on their [1] beds those that were sick,
56 where they heard he was.   And wheresoever he entered, into villages, or into cities, or into the country, they laid the sick in the marketplaces, and besought him that they might touch if it were but the border of his garment; and as many as touched [2] him were made whole.

§ 60. Discourse on the Bread of Life.

[Capernaum.]

John 6.

22 [d] On the morrow the multitude that stood on the other side of the sea saw that there was none other [3] boat there, save one, and that Jesus entered not with his disciples into the boat, but *that* his disciples went
23 away alone (howbeit there came [4] boats from Tiberias nigh unto the place where they ate the bread after the Lord had
24 given thanks): when the multitude therefore saw that Jesus was not there, neither his disciples, they themselves got into the [4] boats, and came to Capernaum, seeking
25 Jesus.   And when they found him on the other side of the sea, they said unto him,
26 Rabbi, when camest thou hither?   Jesus answered them and said, Verily, verily, I say unto you, Ye seek me, not because ye saw signs, but because ye ate of the loaves,
27 and were filled.   Work not for the meat which perisheth, but for the meat which abideth unto eternal life, which the Son of man shall give unto you: for him the
28 Father, *even* God, hath sealed.   They said

KEY.— [a] Matthew, [b] Mark, [c] Luke, [d] John.

[1] Or, *pallets.*   [2] Or, *it.*
[3] Gr. *little boat.*   [4] Gr. *little boats.*

therefore unto him, What must we do, that we may work the works of God? Jesus answered and said unto them, This is 29 the work of God, that ye believe on him whom [1] he hath sent. They said therefore 30 unto him, What then doest thou for a sign, that we may see, and believe thee? what workest thou? Our fathers ate the manna 31 in the wilderness; as it is written, He gave them bread out of heaven to eat. Jesus 32 therefore said unto them, Verily, verily, I say unto you, It was not Moses that gave you the bread out of heaven; but my Father giveth you the true bread out of heaven. For the bread of God is that 33 which cometh down out of heaven, and giveth life unto the world. They said 34 therefore unto him, Lord, evermore give us this bread. Jesus said unto them, I am 35 the bread of life: he that cometh to me shall not hunger, and he that believeth on me shall never thirst. But I said unto you, 36 that ye have seen me, and yet believe not. All that which the Father giveth me shall 37 come unto me; and him that cometh to me I will in no wise cast out. For I am 38 come down from heaven, not to do mine own will, but the will of him that sent me. And this is the will of him that sent me, 39 that of all that which he hath given me I should lose nothing, but should raise it up at the last day. For this is the will of my 40 Father, that every one that beholdeth the Son, and believeth on him, should have eternal life; and [2] I will raise him up at the last day.

The Jews therefore murmured concern- 41 ing him, because he said, I am the bread which came down out of heaven. And 42 they said, Is not this Jesus, the son of Jo-

KEY.—[a] Matthew, [b] Mark, [c] Luke, [d] John.

[1] Or, *he sent.*   [2] Or, *that I should raise him up.*

seph, whose father and mother we know?
how doth he now say, I am come down out
43 of heaven?   Jesus answered and said unto
44 them, Murmur not among yourselves.   No
man can come to me, except the Father
that sent me draw him: and I will raise
45 him up in the last day.   It is written in the
prophets, And they shall all be taught of
God.   Every one that hath heard from the
Father, and hath learned, cometh unto me.
46 Not that any man hath seen the Father,
save he that is from God, he hath seen the
47 Father.   Verily, verily, I say unto you, He
48 that believeth hath eternal life.   I am the
49 bread of life.   Your fathers did eat the
manna in the wilderness, and they died.
50 This is the bread which cometh down out of
heaven, that a man may eat thereof, and not
51 die. I am the living bread which came down
out of heaven: if any man eat of this
bread, he shall live for ever: yea and the
bread which I will give is my flesh, for the
life of the world.
52   The Jews therefore strove one with another, saying, How can this man give us
53 his flesh to eat?   Jesus therefore said unto
them, Verily, verily, I say unto you, Except ye eat the flesh of the Son of man and
drink his blood, ye have not life in your-
54 selves.   He that eateth my flesh and drinketh my blood hath eternal life; and I will
55 raise him up at the last day.   For my flesh
is [1] meat indeed, and my blood is [2] drink in-
56 deed.   He that eateth my flesh and drinketh my blood abideth in me, and I in him.
57 As the living Father sent me, and I live
because of the Father; so he that eateth
58 me, he also shall live because of me.   This
is the bread which came down out of
heaven: not as the fathers did eat, and

KEY.—[a] Matthew, [b] Mark, [c] Luke, [d] John.

[1] Gr. *true meat.*   [2] Gr. *true drink.*

John 6.

died: he that eateth this bread shall live
for ever. These things said he in 'the 59
synagogue, as he taught in Capernaum.

Many therefore of his disciples, when 60
they heard *this*, said, This is a hard saying;
who can hear *it? But Jesus knowing in 61
himself that his disciples murmured at this,
said unto them, Doth this cause you to
stumble? *What* then if ye should behold 62
the Son of man ascending where he was
before? It is the spirit that quickeneth; 63
the flesh profiteth nothing: the words that
I have spoken unto you are spirit, and are
life. But there are some of you that be- 64
lieve not. For Jesus knew from the beginning who they were that believed not,
and who it was that should betray him.
And he said, For this cause have I said un- 65
to you, that no man can come unto me, except it be given unto him of the Father.

Upon this many of his disciples went 66
back, and walked no more with him.
Jesus said therefore unto the twelve, 67
Would ye also go away? Simon Peter 68
answered him, Lord, to whom shall we go?
thou *hast the words of eternal life. And 69
we have believed and know that thou art
the Holy One of God. Jesus answered 70
them, Did not I choose you the twelve, and
one of you is a devil? Now he spake of 71
Judas *the son* of Simon Iscariot, for he it
was that should betray him, *being* one of the
twelve.   John 7.

And after these things Jesus walked 1
in Galilee: for he would not walk in
Judæa, because the Jews sought to kill
him.

KEY.—ᵃ Matthew, ᵇ Mark, ᶜ Luke, ᵈ John.

¹ Or, *a synagogue*.   ² Or, *him*.   ³ Or, *hast words*

§ 61. Discourse on Jewish Traditions.

Matthew's Account.

Chap. 15.

Then there come to Jesus from Jerusalem Pharisees 1
and scribes, saying, Why do thy disciples transgress 2
the tradition of the elders? for they wash not their hands
when they eat bread. And he answered and said unto 3
them, Why do ye also transgress the commandment of
God because of your tradition? For God said, Honour 4
thy father and thy mother: and, He that speaketh evil of
father or mother, let him die the death. But ye say, 5
Whosoever shall say to his father or his mother, That
wherewith thou mightest have been profited by me is given
to God; he shall not honour his father. And ye have made 6
void the word of God because of your tradition. Ye hyp- 7
ocrites, well did Isaiah prophesy of you, saying,

This people honoureth me with their lips;   8
But their heart is far from me.
But in vain do they worship me,   9

Teaching *as their* doctrines the precepts of men.
And he called to him the multitude, and said unto them, 10
Hear, and understand: Not that which etnereth into the 11
mouth defileth the man; but that which proceedeth out of
the mouth, this defileth the man. Then came the disci- 12
ples, and said unto him, Knowest thou that the Pharisees
were offended, when they heard this saying? But he an- 13
swered and said, Every plant which my heavenly Father
planted not, shall be rooted up. Let them alone: they 14
are blind guides. And if the blind guide the blind, both
shall fall into a pit. And Peter answered and said unto 15
him, Declare unto us the parable. And he said, Are ye 16
also even yet without understanding? Perceive ye not, 17
that whatsoever goeth into the mouth passeth into the
belly, and is cast out into the draught? But the things 18
which proceed out of the mouth come forth out of the
heart; and they defile the man. For out of the heart come 19
forth evil thoughts, murders, adulteries, fornications,
thefts, false witness, railings: these are the things which 20
defile the man: but to eat with unwashen hands defileth
not the man.

PERIOD IV.

Third Year of Public Ministry.

[From the Third (unvisited) Passover to the beginning of the
Fourth Passover week—almost a year.]

§ 61. Discourse on Jewish Traditions.

[Capernaum.]

Mark 7.

1 ᵇ And there are gathered together unto
him the Pharisees, and certain of the
2 scribes, that had come from Jerusalem, and
had seen that some of his disciples ate their
bread with ¹ defiled, that is, unwashen,
3 hands. For the Pharisees, and all the Jews,
except they wash their hands ² diligently,
eat not, holding the tradition of the elders:
4 and *when they come* from the marketplace,
except they ³ bathe themselves, they eat
not: and many other things there are,
which they have received to hold, ⁴ wash-
ings of cups, and pots, and brazen vessels⁵.
5 And the Pharisees and the scribes ask him,
Why walk not thy disciples according to
the tradition of the elders, but eat their
6 bread with ¹ defiled hands? And he said
unto them, Well did Isaiah prophesy of
you hypocrites, as it is written,
>   This people honoureth me with their
>   lips,
>   But their heart is far from me.
7   But in vain do they worship me,
>   Teaching *as their* doctrines the pre-
>   cepts of men.
8 Ye leave the commandment of God, and
9 hold fast the tradition of men. And he said

KEY.—ᵃ Matthew, ᵇ Mark, ᶜ Luke, ᵈ John.

¹ Or, *common.*
² Or, *up to the elbow.* Gr. *with the fist.*
³ Gr. *baptize.* Some ancient authorities read *sprinkle*
themselves.
⁴ Gr. *baptizings.*
⁵ Many ancient authorities add *and couches.*

unto them, Full well do ye reject the commandment of God, that ye may keep your tradition. For Moses said, Honour thy 10 father and thy mother; and, He that speaketh evil of father or mother, let him [1] die the death: but ye say, If a man shall say to 11 his father or his mother, That wherewith thou mightest have been profited by me is Corban, that is to say, given *to God*; ye 12 no longer suffer him to do aught for his father or his mother; making void the word 13 of God by your tradition, which ye have delivered: and many such like things ye do. And he called to him the multitude again, 14 and said unto them, Hear me all of you, and understand: there is nothing from 15 without the man, that going into him can defile him: but the things which proceed out of the man are those that defile the man.[2] [a] Then came the disciples, and said unto him, Knowest thou that the Pharisees were offended when they heard this saying? But he answered and said, Every plant which my heavenly Father planted not shall be rooted up. Let them alone; they are blind guides. And if the blind guide the blind, both shall fall into a pit. [b] And when he was entered into the house 17 from the multitude, his disciples asked of him the parable. And he saith unto them, 18 Are ye so without understanding also? Perceive ye not, that whatsoever from without goeth into the man, *it* cannot defile him; because it goeth not into his heart, 19 but into his belly, and goeth out into the draught? *This he said*, making all meats clean. And he said, That which proceed- 20 eth out of the man, that defileth the man. For from within, out of the heart of men, 21

KEY.—[a] Matthew, [b] Mark, [c] Luke, [d] John.

[1] Or, *surely die.*
[2] Many ancient authorities insert ver. 16: *If any man hath ears to hear, let him hear.*

PLATE IV.

FROM CAPERNAUM TO THE COASTS OF TYRE AND SIDON,
AND RETURN.

§§ 62–69.

As shown by the blue line, Jesus journeys from Capernaum to the vicinity of Tyre, where he heals the daughter of the Syro-Phœnician woman (§ 62); returning, he comes to the east side of the Sea of Galilee, feeds 4000 (§ 64), and crosses the sea to Bethsaida and Magdala, where a blind man was restored (§§ 65 and 66).

As shown by the red line, Jesus journeyed to Cæsarea Philippi, where Peter confessed him the Son of God (§ 67), and on a mountain (probably Hermon) Jesus was transfigured (§ 68); then an epileptic child was healed (§ 69), and Jesus returned to Capernaum.

(Opposite page 97.)

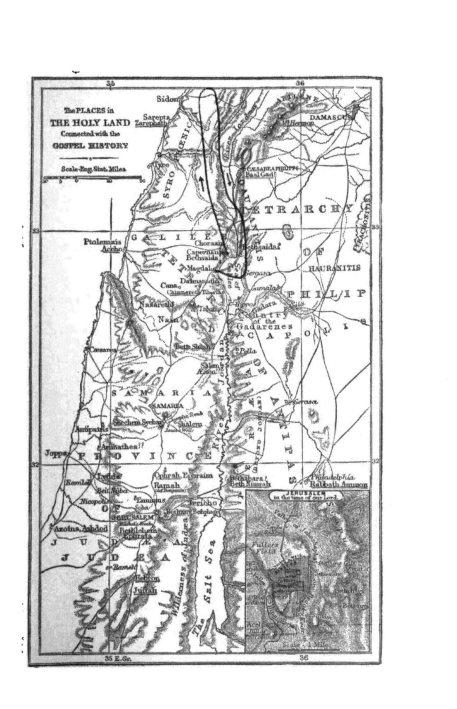

The PLACES in
THE HOLY LAND
Connected with the
GOSPEL HISTORY

Scale-Eng. Stat. Miles.

§ 62. The Syrophœnician Woman.

Matthew's Account.

Chap. 15.

And Jesus went out thence, and withdrew into the parts 21 of Tyre and Sidon. And behold, a Canaanitish woman 22 came out from those borders, and cried, saying, Have mercy on me, O Lord, thou son of David; my daughter is grievously vexed with a demon. But he answered her 23 not a word. And his disciples came and besought him, saying, Send her away; for she crieth after us. But he 24 answered and said, I was not sent but unto the lost sheep of the house of Israel. But she came and worshipped him, 25 saying, Lord, help me. And he answered and said, It is 26 not meet to take the children's bread and cast it to the dogs. But she said, Yea, Lord: for even the dogs eat of 27 the crumbs which fall from their masters' table. Then 28 Jesus answered and said unto her, O woman, great is thy faith: be it done unto thee even as thou wilt. And her daughter was healed from that hour.

Mark 7.

[1] evil thoughts proceed, fornications, thefts,
22 murders, adulteries, [a] false witness, [b] covet-
ings, wickednesses, deceit, lasciviousness,
23 an evil eye, railing, pride, foolishness: all
these evil things proceed from within, and
defile the man : [a] but to eat with unwashed
hands defileth not the man.

§ 62. The Syrophœnician Woman.

[The vicinity of Tyre.]

Mark 7.

24   [b] And from thence he arose, and went
away into the borders of Tyre [a] and Sidon.
And he entered into a house, and would
have no man know it: and he could not
25 be hid.   But   straightway   a woman,
whose little daughter had an unclean
spirit, having heard of him, came and fell
26 down at his feet.   Now the woman was a
[1] Greek, a Syrophœnician—[a] a Canaanitish
woman—[b] by race. And she besought him
that he would cast forth the demon out of
her daughter. [a] But he answered her not
a word.   And his disciples came and besought him, saying, Send her away ; for
she crieth after us.   But he answered and
said, I was not sent but unto the lost sheep
of the house of Israel.   But she came and
worshipped him, saying, Lord, help me.
27 [b] And he said unto her, Let the children
first be filled : for it is not meet to take the
children's [4] bread and cast it to the dogs.
28 But she answered and saith unto him, Yea,
Lord : even the dogs under the table eat of
the children's crumbs, [a] which fall from
29 their master's table. [b] And he said unto her,
[a] O woman, great is thy faith ; [b] for this saying go thy way ; [a] be it done unto thee
even as thou wilt : [b] the demon is gone out
30 of thy daughter.   And she went away un-

KEY.—[a] Matthew, [b] Mark, [c] Luke, [d] John.

[1] Gr. *thoughts that are evil.*
[2] Some ancient authorities omit *and Sidon.*
[3] Or, *Gentile.*   [4] Or, *loaf.*

Mark 7.

to her house, and found the child laid
upon the bed, and the demon gone out.

§ 63. A Dumb and Deaf Man Restored.

[Decapolis.]

Mark 7.

^b And again he went out from the borders 31
of Tyre, and came through Sidon unto the
sea of Galilee, through the midst of the
borders of Decapolis; ^a and he went up
into the mountain, and sat there. ^b And they 32
bring unto him one that was deaf, and had
an impediment in his speech; and they beseech him to lay his hand upon him. And 33
he took him aside from the multitude
privately, and put his fingers into his ears,
and he spat, and touched his tongue; and 34
looking up to heaven, he sighed, and saith
unto him, Ephphatha, that is, Be opened.
And his ears were opened, and the bond 35
of his tongue was loosed, and he spake plain.
And he charged them that they should 36
tell no man: but the more he charged them,
so much the more a great deal they published it. And they were beyond measure 37
astonished, saying, He hath done all things
well: he maketh even the deaf to hear,
and the dumb to speak.

^a And there came unto him great multi-
tudes, having with them the lame, blind,
dumb, maimed, and many others, and they
cast them down at his feet; and he healed
them; insomuch that the multitude wondered, when they saw the dumb speaking,
the maimed whole, and the lame walking,
and the blind seeing: and they glorified
the God of Israel.

§ 64. Four Thousand Fed.

[Decapolis.]

Mark 8.

^b In those days, when there was again a 1
great multitude, and they had nothing to
eat, he called unto him his disciples, and

KEY.—^a Matthew, ^b Mark, ^c Luke, ^d John.

§ 63. A Dumb and Deaf Man Restored.

Matthew's Account.

Chap. 15.

29 And Jesus departed thence, and came nigh unto the sea of Galilee; and he went up into the mountain, and sat
30 there. And there came unto him great multitudes, having with them the lame, dumb, blind, maimed, and many others, and they cast them down at his feet; and he healed
31 them: insomuch that the multitude wondered, when they saw the dumb speaking, the maimed whole, and the lame walking, and the blind seeing: and they glorified the God of Israel.

98

§ 64. Four Thousand Fed.

Matthew's Account.

And Jesus called unto him his disciples and said, I have 32
compassion on the multitude, because they continue with
me now three days and have nothing to eat: and I would
not send them away fasting, lest haply they faint in the
way. And the disciples say unto him, Whence should we 33
have so many loaves in a desert place, as to fill so great a
multitude? And Jesus saith unto them, How many loaves 34
have ye? And they said, Seven, and a few small fishes.
And he commanded the multitude to sit down on the 35
ground; and he took the seven loaves and the fishes; and 36
he gave thanks and brake, and gave to the disciples, and
the disciples to the multitudes. And they did all eat, and 37
were filled: and they took up that which remained over of
the broken pieces, seven baskets full. And they that did 38
eat were four thousand men, beside women and children.

And he sent away the multitudes, and entered into the 39
boat, and came into the borders of Magadan.

Mark 8.

2 saith unto them, I have compassion on
the multitude, because they continue with
me now three days, and have nothing to
3 eat: and if I send them away fasting to
their home, they will faint in the way ; and
4 some of them are come from far. And his
disciples answered him, Whence shall one
be able to fill these men with ¹ bread here
5 in a desert place? And he asked them,
·How many loaves have ye? And· they
6 said, Seven. And he commandeth the
multitude to sit down on the ground: and
he took the seven loaves, and having
given thanks, he brake, and gave to his
disciples, to set before them; and they set
7 them before the multitude. And they had
a few small fishes: and having blessed
them, he commanded to set these also be-
8 fore them. And they did eat, and were
filled: and they took up, of broken pieces
9 that remained over, seven baskets. And
they were about four thousand ᵃ men, beside women and children. ᵇ And he sent
10 them away. And straightway he entered
into the boat with his disciples, and came
into the parts of Dalmanutha.

§ 65. A Sign Refused.

[Sea of Galilee.]

Matthew 16.

1 ᵃ And the Pharisees and Sadducees came,
and trying him asked him to shew them a
2 sign from heaven. But he ᵇ sighed deeply
in his spirit, ᵃ and answered and said unto
them, ᵇ why doth this generation seek a
sign? ᵃ² When it is evening, ye say, *It will be*
3 fair weather: for the heaven is red. And
in the morning, *It will be* foul weather to-
day : for the heaven is red and lowring. Ye
know how to discern the face of the heaven;

KEY.—ᵃ Matthew, ᵇ Mark, ᶜ Luke, ᵈ John.

¹ Gr, *loaves.*
² The following words, to the end of ver. 3, are omitted
by some of the most ancient and other important authorities.

but ye cannot *discern* the signs of the times. An evil and adulterous generation seeketh 4 after a sign; and there shall no sign be given unto it, but the sign of Jonah.　And ᵇagain entering into the boat, ᵃhe left them, and departed.

ᵃAnd the disciples came to the other side 5 and forgot to take ¹ bread; ᵇand they had not with them in the boat more than one loaf.　ᵃAnd Jesus said unto them, Take 6 heed and beware of the leaven of the Pharisees and Sadducees.　And they reasoned 7 among themselves, saying, ²We took no ¹bread.　And Jesus perceiving it said, O 8 ye of little faith, why reason ye among yourselves, because ye have no ¹bread? Do ye not yet perceive, ᵇneither under- 9 stand? have ye your heart hardened? Having eyes, see ye not? and having ears, hear ye not? and do ye not remember ᵃthe five loaves of the five thousand, and how many ³baskets ye took up?　Neither the 10 seven loaves of the four thousand, and how many ³baskets ye took up? How is it that 11 ye do not perceive that I spake not to you concerning ¹bread? But beware of the leaven of the Pharisees and Sadducees. Then understood they how that he bade 12 them not beware of the leaven of ¹ bread, but of the teaching of the Pharisees and Sadducees.

§ 66.　A Blind Man Restored.

[Bethsaida.]

ᵇAnd they come unto Bethsaida.　And 22 they bring to him a blind man, and beseech him to touch him.　And he took hold of 23 the blind man by the hand, and brought him out of the village; and when he had

KEY.—ᵃ Matthew, ᵇ Mark, ᶜ Luke, ᵈ John.

¹ Gr. *loaves.*

² Or, It is *because we took no bread.*

³ *Basket* in ver. 9 and 10 represents different Greek words.

§ 65. A Sign Refused.

Mark's Account.

Chap. 8.

11 And the Pharisees came forth, and began to question with him, seeking of him a sign from heaven, trying him.

12 And he sighed deeply in his spirit, and saith, Why doth this generation seek a sign? verily I say unto you, There

13 shall no sign be given unto this generation. And he left them, and again entering into *the boat* departed to the other side.

14 And they forgot to take bread; and they had not in the

15 boat with them more than one loaf. And he charged them, saying, Take heed, beware of the leaven of the

16 Pharisees and the leaven of Herod. And they reasoned

17 one with another, saying, We have no bread. And Jesus perceiving it saith unto them, Why reason ye, because ye have no bread? do ye not yet perceive, neither under-

18 stand? have ye your heart hardened? Having eyes, see ye not? and having ears, hear ye not? and do ye not remem-

19 ber? When I brake the five loaves among the five thousand, how many baskets full of broken pieces took ye up?

20 They say unto him, Twelve. And when the seven among the four thousand, how many basketfuls of broken pieces

21 took ye up? And they say unto him, Seven. And he said unto them, Do ye not yet understand?

§ 67. Peter's Confession and Rebuke.

Mark's Account.

Chap. 8.

And Jesus went forth, and his disciples, into the vil- 27.
lages of Cæsarea Philippi: and in the way he asked his
disciples, saying unto them, Who do men say that I am?
And they told him, saying, John the Baptist: and others, 28
Elijah; but others, One of the prophets. And he asked 29
them, But who say ye that I am? Peter answereth and
saith unto him, Thou art the Christ. And he charged 30
them that they should tell no man of him.

Matthew's Account.

Chap. 16.

From that time began Jesus to show unto his disciples, 21
how that he must go unto Jerusalem, and suffer many
things of the elders and chief priests and scribes, and be
killed, and the third day be raised up. And Peter took 22
him, and began to rebuke him, saying, Be it far from
thee, Lord: this shall never be unto thee. But he turned, 23
and said unto Peter, Get thee behind me, Satan: thou art
a stumblingblock unto me: for thou mindest not the

Luke's Account.

Chap. 9.

And it came to pass, as he was praying apart, the dis- 18
ciples were with him: and he asked them, saying, Who
do the multitudes say that I am? And they answering 19
said, John the Baptist; but others *say*, Elijah; and others,
that one of the old prophets is risen again. And he said 20
unto them, But who say ye that I am? And Peter
answering said, The Christ of God. But he charged 21
them, and commanded *them* to tell this to no man; say- 22
ing, the Son of man must suffer many things, and be
rejected of the elders and chief priests and scribes, and be
killed, and the third day be raised up. And he said unto 23
all, If any man would come after me, let him deny himself, and take up his cross daily, and follow me. For 24
whosoever would save his life shall lose it; but whosoever
shall lose his life for my sake, the same shall save it. For 25

101

Mark 8.

spit on his eyes, and laid his hands upon
him, he asked him, Seest thou aught?
24 And he looked up, and said, I see men; for
25 I behold *them* as trees, walking. Then
again he laid his hands upon his eyes; and
he looked stedfastly, and was restored, and
26 saw all things clearly. And he sent him
away to his home, saying, Do not even enter into the village.

§ 67. Peter's Confession and Rebuke.

[Near Cæsarea Philippi.]

Matthew 16.

13 ᵃNow when Jesus came into the parts of
Cæsarea Philippi,ᶜ as he was praying apart,
ᵃhe asked his disciples, saying, Who do men
14 say ¹that the Son of man is? And they
said, Some *say* John the Baptist; some,
Elijah: and others, Jeremiah, or one of the
15 ᶜold ᵃprophets ᶜrisen again. ᵃHe saith un-
16 to them, But who say ye that I am? And
Simon Peter answered and said, Thou art
17 the Christ, the Son of the living God. And
Jesus answered and said unto him, Blessed
art thou, Simon Bar-Jonah: for flesh and
blood hath not revealed it unto thee, but
18 my Father who is in heaven. And I also
say unto thee, that thou art ²Peter, and
upon this ³rock I will build my church;
and the gates of Hades shall not prevail
19 against it. I will give unto thee the keys
of the kingdom of heaven: and whatsoever
thou shalt bind on earth shall be bound in
heaven: and whatsoever thou shalt loose
20 on earth shall be loosed in heaven. Then
charged he the disciples that they should
tell no man that he was the Christ.
31 **Mark 8.**   ᵇAnd he began to teach them, that
the Son of man must ᵃgo unto Jerusalem,
and ᵇsuffer many things, and be rejected
by the elders, and the chief priests, and the

Key.—ᵃ Matthew, ᵇ Mark, ᶜ Luke, ᵈ John.

¹ Many ancient authorities read *that I the Son of man am*
² Gr. *Petros*.   ³ Gr. *petra*.

Mark 8.

scribes, and be killed, and after three days
rise again. And he spake the saying open- 32
ly. And Peter took him, and began to rebuke him, ᵃ saying, Be it far from thee,
Lord; this shall never be unto thee. ᵇ But he 33
turning about, and seeing his disciples, rebuked Peter, and saith, Get thee behind
me, Satan: ᵃ thou art a stumblingblock
unto me; ᵇ for thou mindest not the things
of God, but the things of men. And he 34
called unto him the multitude with his disciples, and said unto them, If any man
would come after me, let him deny himself, and take up his cross, and follow me.
For whosoever would save his ¹ life shall 35
lose it; and whosoever shall lose his life
for my sake and the gospel's shall save it.
For what doth it profit a man, to gain the 36
whole world, and forfeit his ¹ life? For 37
what should a man give in exchange for
his ¹ life? For whosoever shall be ashamed 38
of me and of my words in this adulterous
and sinful generation, the Son of man also
shall be ashamed of him, when he cometh
in the glory of his Father with the holy
angels; ᵃ and then shall he render unto
every man according to his deeds.
ᵇ And he said unto them, Verily I Mark 9. 1
say unto you, There are some here of
them that stand *by*, who shall in no wise
taste of death, till they see the kingdom of
God come with power.

§ 68. The Transfiguration.

[Probably Mount Hermon.]

Mark 9.

ᵇ And after six days Jesus taketh with him 2
Peter, and James, and John, and bringeth
them up into a high mountain apart by
themselves, ᶜ to pray : ᵇ and ᶜ as he was praying, the fashion of his countenance was
altered, ᵃ and his face did shine as the sun;

KEY.—ᵃ Matthew, ᵇ Mark, ᶜ Luke, ᵈ John.
¹ Or, *soul.*

§ 67. Peter's Confession and Rebuke.—(*Continued.*)

Matthew's Account.

24 things of God, but the things of men. Then said Jesus unto his disciples, If any man would come after me, let him deny himself, and take up his cross, and follow me.
25 For whosoever would save his life shall lose it: and who-
26 soever shall lose his life for my sake shall find it. For what shall a man be profited, if he shall gain the whole world, and forfeit his life? or what shall a man give in ex-
27 change for his life? For the Son of man shall come in the glory of his Father with his angels; and then shall he ren-
28 der unto every man according to his deeds. Verily I say unto you, there are. some of them that stand here, who shall in no wise taste of death, till they see the Son of man coming in his kingdom.

Luke's Account.

what is a man profited, if he gain the whole world,
26 and lose or forfeit his own self? For whosoever shall be ashamed of me and of my words, of him shall the Son of man be ashamed, when he cometh in his own glory, and
27 *the glory* of the Father, and of the holy angels. But I tell you of a truth, There are some of them that stand here, who shall in no wise taste of death, till they see the kingdom of God.

§ 68. The Transfiguration.

Matthew's Account.

Chap. 17.

And after six days Jesus taketh with him Peter, and 1 James, and John his brother, and bringeth them up into a high mountain apart: and he was transfigured 2 before them: <u>and his face did shine as the sun, and his garments became white as the light.</u> And behold, there 3 appeared unto them Moses and Elijah talking with him. And Peter answered, and said unto Jesus, Lord, it is good 4 for us to be here: <u>if thou wilt, I will make here three tab</u>ernacles; one for thee, and one for Moses, and one for Elijah. <u>While he was yet speaking,</u> behold, a <u>bright</u> 5 cloud overshadowed them: and behold, a voice out of the cloud, saying, This is my beloved Son, <u>in whom I am well pleased;</u> hear ye him. <u>And when the disciples heard it,</u> 6 <u>they fell on their face, and were sore afraid. And Jesus</u> 7 <u>came and touched them and said, Arise, and be not afraid.</u> <u>And lifting up their eyes, they saw no one, save Jesus</u> 8 <u>only.</u>

Mark's Account.

Chap. 9.

And there appeared unto them Elijah with Moses, and 4 they were talking with Jesus. And Peter answereth and 5 saith unto Jesus,

Luke's Account.

Chap. 9.

And it came to pass about eight days after these say- 28 ings, he took with him Peter and John and James, and went up into the mountain to pray. <u>And as he was praying,</u> 29 <u>the fashion of his countenance was altered, and his raiment</u> *became* white *and* dazzling. And behold, there talked 30 with him two men, who were Moses and Elijah; <u>who</u> 31 <u>appeared in glory, and spake of his decease which he was</u> <u>about to accomplish at Jerusalem. Now Peter and they</u> 32 <u>that were with him were heavy with sleep: but when they</u> <u>were fully awake, they saw his glory, and the two men</u>

[*Continued on duplicate page* 104.]

Mark 9.

[and]* ᵇ he was transfigured before them:

3 and his garments became glistering, exceeding white; so as no fuller on earth can

4 whiten them. And there appeared unto them Elijah with Moses, ᶜ in glory, and spake of his decease which he was about to accomplish at Jerusalem. Now Peter and they that were with him were heavy with sleep: but when they were fully awake, they saw his glory, and the two men that stood with him. And it came to pass, as

5 they were parting from him, ᵇ Peter answereth and saith to Jesus, Rabbi, it is good for us to be here: and let us, ᵃ if thou wilt, ᵇmake three ¹ tabernacles; one for thee, and

6 one for Moses, and one for Elijah. For he knew not what to answer; for they became

7 sore afraid. And ᵃ while he was yet speaking, ᵇ there came a ᵃ bright ᵇ cloud overshadowing them, ᶜ and they feared as they entered into the cloud: ᵇ and there came a voice out of the cloud, This is my beloved Son, ᶜ my chosen, ᵃ in whom I am well pleased: ᵇ hear ye him. ᵃ And when the disciples heard it they fell on their face and were sore afraid. And Jesus came and touched them, and said, Arise, and be

8 not afraid. ᵇ And suddenly looking round about, they saw no one any more, save Jesus only with themselves. ᶜ And they held their peace, and told no man in those days any of those things they had seen.

9 ᵇ And as they were coming down from the mountain, he charged them that they should tell no man what things they had seen, save when the Son of man should

10 have risen again from the dead. And they kept the saying, questioning among themselves what the rising again from the dead

KEY.—ᵃ Matthew, ᵇ Mark, ᶜ Luke, ᵈ John.

¹ Or, *booths*.

* Word inserted by compiler.

Mark 9.

should mean.   And they asked him, say- 11
ing, ^a'Why then [do]* ^bthe scribes say that
Elijah must first come?   And he said unto 12
them, Elijah indeed cometh first, and re-
storeth all things: and how is it written
of the Son of man, that he should suffer
many things and be set at naught?   But I 13
say unto you, that Elijah is come, and they
^aknew him not, but ^bhave also done unto
him whatsoever they listed, even as it is
written of him.   ^aThen understood the disciples that he spake unto them of John the
Baptist.

§ 69.   An Epileptic Child.

[Near Cæsarea Philippi.]

Mark 9.

^bAnd when they came to the disciples, 14
^con the next day, when they were come
down from the mountain, ^bthey saw a great
multitude about them, and scribes questioning with them.   And straightway all 15
the multitude, when they saw him, were
greatly amazed, and running to him saluted
him.   And he asked them, What question 16
ye with them?   And one of the multitude 17
answered him, ^aMaster, I brought unto
thee my son, who hath a dumb spirit;
^ahave mercy, ^cfor he is mine only child;
^ahe is epileptic, and suffereth grievously;
^band wheresoever it taketh him, it ^adash- 18
eth him down: and he foameth, and
grindeth his teeth, and pineth away: and
I spake to thy disciples that they should
cast it out; and they were not able.   And 19
he answereth them and saith, O faithless
generation, how long shall I be with you?
how long shall I bear with you? bring
^ahither ^cthy son ^bunto me.   And they 20
brought him unto him: and when he saw
him, straightway the spirit ⁴tare him

KEY.—^a Matthew, ^b Mark, ^c Luke, ^d John.

¹ Or, How is it *that the scribes say . . . come?*
² Or, *Teacher.* · ³ Or, *rendeth him.*   ⁴ Or, *convulsed.*
* Word inserted by compiler.

§ 68. The Transfiguration.—(*Continued.*)

Matthew's Account.

9 And as they were coming down from the mountain, Jesus commanded them, saying, Tell the vision to no man, 10 until the Son of man be risen from the dead. And his disciples asked him, saying, Why then say the scribes 11 that Elijah must first come? And he answered and said, 12 Elijah indeed cometh, and shall restore all things: but I say unto you, that Elijah is come already, and they knew him not, but did unto him whatsoever they listed. Even 13 so shall the Son of man also suffer of them. Then understood the disciples that he spake unto them of John the Baptist.

Luke's Account.

33 that stood with him. And it came to pass, as they were parting from him, Peter said unto Jesus, Master, it is good for us to be here: and let us make three tabernacles; one for thee, and one for Moses, and one for Elijah: not 34 knowing what he said. And while he said these things, there came a cloud, and overshadowed them: and they 35 feared as they entered into the cloud. And a voice came out of the cloud, saying, This is my Son, my chosen: 36 hear ye him. And when the voice came, Jesus was found alone. And they held their peace, and told no man in those days any of the things which they had seen.

§ 69. An Epileptic Child.

Matthew's Account.

Chap. 17.

And when they were come to the multitude, there came 14
to him a man, kneeling to him, and saying, Lord, have 15
mercy on my son: for he is epileptic, and suffereth grievously: for oft-times he falleth into the fire, and oft-times
into the water. And I brought him to thy disciples, and 16
they could not cure him. And Jesus answered and said, 17
O faithless and perverse generation, how long shall I be
with you? how long shall I bear with you? bring him hither
to me. And Jesus rebuked him; and the demon went out 18
from him: and the boy was cured from that hour. Then 19
came the disciples to Jesus apart, and said, Why could not
we cast it out? And he saith unto them, Because of your 20
little faith: for verily I say unto you, If ye have faith as
a grain of mustard seed, ye shall say unto this mountain,
Remove hence to yonder place ; and it shall remove; and
nothing shall be impossible unto you.

Jesus said unto them, The Son of man shall be delivered 22
up into the hands of men; and they shall kill him, and the 23
third day he shall be raised up. And they were exceeding sorry.

Mark's Account.

Chap. 9.

And when he was come into the house, his disciples 28
asked him privately, *saying*, We could not cast it out.

Luke's Account.

Chap. 9.

And it came to pass, on the next day, when they were 37
come down from the mountain, a great multitude met
him. And behold, a man from the multitude cried, say- 38
ing, Master, I beseech thee to look upon my son; for he
is mine only child: and behold, a spirit taketh him, and he 39
suddenly crieth out; and it teareth him, that he foameth,
and it hardly departeth from, him bruising him sorely.
And I besought thy disciples to cast it out; and they could 40
not. And Jesus answered and said, O faithless and per- 41
verse generation how long shall I be with you, and bear
with you? bring hither thy son. And as he was yet a 42
coming, the demon dashed him down, and tare *him* grievously. But Jesus rebuked the unclean spirit, and healed
the boy, and gave him back to his father. And they 43
were all astonished at the majesty of God.

But while all were marvelling at all the things which he
did, he said unto his disciples, Let these words sink into 44
yours ears: for the Son of man shall be delivered into the
hands of men. But they understood not this saying, and 45
it was concealed from them, that they should not perceive
it: and they were afraid to ask him about this saying.

Mark 9.

grievously ; and he fell on the ground, and
21 wallowed foaming. And he asked his
father, How long time is it since this hath
come unto him? And he said, From a
22 child. And oft-times it hath cast him both
into the fire and into the waters, to destroy him : but if thou canst do anything,
23 have compassion on us, and help us. And
Jesus said unto him, If thou canst! All
things are possible to him that believeth.
24 Straightway the father of the child cried
out, and said[1], I believe ; help thou mine
25 unbelief. And when Jesus saw that a
multitude came running together, he rebuked the unclean spirit, saying unto him,
Thou dumb and deaf spirit, I command
thee, come out of him, and enter no more
26 into him. And having cried out, and [2]torn
him much, he came out : and *the child* became as one dead ; insomuch that the
27 more part said, He is dead. But Jesus took
him by the hand, and raised him up ; and
he arose. ^cAnd they were all astonished
19 **Matthew 17.** at the majesty of God. ^aThen
came the disciples to Jesus apart, and said,
20 Why could not we cast it out? And he
saith unto them, Because of your little
faith : for verily I say unto you, If ye have
faith as a grain of mustard seed, ye shall
say unto this mountain, Remove hence to
yonder place ; and it shall remove : and
nothing shall be impossible unto you.
29 **Mark 9.** ^b And he said unto them, This kind
can come out by nothing, save by prayer[3].
30 And they went forth from thence, and
passed through Galilee ; and he would not
31 that any man should know it. For he
taught his disciples, and said unto them,
^c Let these words sink into your ears. ^b The

KEY.—^a Matthew, ^b Mark, ^c Luke, ^d John.
[1] Many ancient authorities add *with tears.*
[2] Or, *convulsed.*
[3] Many ancient authorities add *and fasting.*

Mark 9.

Son of man is delivered up into the hands
of men, and they shall kill him; and when
he is killed, after three days he shall rise
again. ª And they were exceeding sorry.
ᵇ But they understood not the saying, and 32
were afraid to ask him; ᶜ and it was concealed from them that they should not
perceive it.

§ 70.   Tribute Money provided.

[Capernaum.]

Matthew 17.

ª And when they were come to Caper- 24
naum, they that received the ¹ half-shekel
came to Peter, and said, Doth not your
² master pay the ¹ half-shekel?   He saith, 25
Yea.   And when he came into the house,
Jesus spake first to him, saying, What thinkest thou, Simon? the kings of the earth,
from whom do they receive toll or tribute?
from their sons, or from strangers?   And 26
when he said, From strangers, Jesus said
unto him, Therefore the sons are free.   But, 27
lest we cause them to stumble, go thou to
the sea, and cast a hook, and take up the
fish that first cometh up; and when thou
hast opened his mouth, thou shalt find a
³ shekel: that take, and give unto them for
me and thee.

§ 71.   Little Children as Examples.

[Capernaum.]

Mark 9.

ᵇ And when he was in the house he 33
asked them, What were ye reasoning in
the way?   But they held their peace: for 34
they had disputed one with another in the
way, who *was* the ⁴ greatest.   And he sat 35
down, and called the twelve; and he saith
unto them, If any man would be first, he
shall be last of all, and minister of all.   And 36
he took a little child, and set him ᶜ by his

KEY.—ª Matthew, ᵇ Mark, ᶜ Luke, ᵈ John.

¹ Gr. *didrachma*.   ² Or, *teacher*.   ³ Gr. *stater*.
⁴ Gr. *greater*.

§ 71. Little Children as Examples.

Matthew's Account.

Chap. 18.

1 In that hour came the disciples unto Jesus, saying, Who
2 then is greatest in the kingdom of heaven? And he called
to him a little child, and set him in the midst of them,
3 and said, Verily I say unto you, Except ye turn, and become as little children, ye shall in no wise enter into the
4 kingdom of heaven. Whosoever therefore shall humble
himself as this little child, the same is the greatest in the
5 kingdom of heaven. And whoso shall receive one such
6 little child in my name receiveth me: but whoso shall
cause one of these little ones that believe on me to stumble, it is profitable for him that a great millstone should be
hanged about his neck, and *that* he should be sunk in the
7 depth of the sea. Woe unto the world because of occasions
of stumbling! for it must needs be that the occasions
come; but woe to that man through whom the occasion
8 cometh! And if thy hand or thy foot causeth thee to
stumble, cut it off, and cast it from thee : it is good for
thee to enter into life maimed or halt, rather than having
9 two hands or two feet to be cast into the eternal fire. And
if thine eye causeth thee to stumble, pluck it out, and
cast it from thee: it is good for thee to enter into life with
one eye, rather than having two eyes to be cast into the
hell of fire.

Luke's Account.

Chap. 9.

46 And there arose a reasoning among them, which of
47 them was the greatest. But when Jesus saw the reasoning of their heart, he took a little child, and set him by his
48 side, and said unto them, Whosoever shall receive this little child in my name receiveth me: and whosoever shall
receive me receiveth him that sent me: for he that is least
among you all, the same is great.

106

Mark 9.

side [b] in the midst of them, [a] and said, Verily I say unto you, Except ye turn, and become as little children, ye shall in no wise enter into the kingdom of heaven: [b] and taking him in his arms, he said unto them,

37 Whosoever shall receive one of such little children in my name, receiveth me: and whosoever receiveth me, receiveth not me, but him that sent me; [c] for he that is least among you all, the same is great.

38 [b] John said unto him, [1] Master, we saw one casting out demons in thy name: and we forbade him, because he followed not us.

39 But Jesus said, Forbid him not: for there is no man who shall do a [2] mighty work in my name, and be able quickly to speak evil

40 of me. For he that is not against us is for

41 us. For whosoever shall give you a cup of water to drink, [3] because ye are Christ's, verily I say unto you, he shall in no wise

42 lose his reward. And whosoever shall cause one of these little ones that believe [4] on me to stumble, it were better for him if [5] a great millstone were hanged about his neck, and he were cast into the sea. [a] Woe unto the world because of occasions of stumbling, for it must needs be that the occasions come; but woe to that man

43 through whom the occasion cometh! [b] And if thy hand cause thee to stumble, cut it off: it is good for thee to enter into life maimed, rather than having thy two hands to go into [6] hell, into the unquenchable fire.[7]

45 And if thy foot cause thee to stumble, cut it off: it is good for thee to enter into life halt, rather than having thy two feet to be

KEY.—[a] Matthew, [b] Mark, [c] Luke, [d] John.

[1] Or, *Teacher*. [2] Gr. *power*.
[3] Gr. *in name that ye are*.
[4] Many ancient authorities omit *on me*.
[5] Gr. *a millstone turned by an ass*. [6] Gr. *Gehenna*.
[7] Ver. 44 and 46 (which are identical with ver. 48) are omitted by the best ancient authorities.

cast into ¹ hell.   And if thine eye cause 47
thee to stumble, cast it out: it is good for
thee to enter into the kingdom of God
with one eye, rather than having two eyes
to be cast into ¹ hell; where their worm 48
dieth not, and the fire is not quenched.
For every one shall be salted with fire.² 49
Salt is good: but if the salt have lost its 50
saltness, wherewith will ye season it?
Have salt in yourselves, and be at peace
one with another.   ˗   Matthew 18.

ᵃ See that ye despise not one of these little 10
ones; for I say unto you, that in heaven
their angels do always behold the face of
my Father who is in heaven.³   How think 12
ye? if any man have a hundred sheep, and
one of them be gone astray, doth he not
leave the ninety and nine, and go unto the
mountains, and seek that which goeth
astray?   And if so be that he find it, verily 13
I say unto you, he rejoiceth over it more
than over the ninety and nine which have
not gone astray.   Even so it is not ᵃ the 14
will of ⁵ your Father who is in heaven, that
one of these little ones should perish.

§ 72.   Forgiveness of Brothers.
[Capernaum.]

Matthew 18.
ᵃ And if thy brother sin ⁶ against thee, go, 15
shew him his fault between thee and him
alone: if he hear thee, thou hast gained thy
brother.   But if he hear *thee* not, take with 16
thee one or two more, that at the mouth of
two witnesses or three every word may be
established.   And if he refuse to hear them, 17

KEY.—ᵃ Matthew, ᵇ Mark, ᶜ Luke, ᵈ John.

¹ Gr. *Gehenna.*
² Many ancient authorities add *and every sacrifice shall be salted with salt.*
³ Many authorities, some ancient, insert ver. 11 *For the Son of man came to save that which was lost.*
⁴ Gr. *a thing willed before your Father.*
⁵ Some ancient authorities read *my.*
⁶ Some ancient authorities omit *against thee.*

Matthew 18.

tell it unto the 'church: and if he refuse
to hear the ' church also, let him be unto
thee as the Gentile and the publican.

18 Verily I say unto you, What things soever ye shall bind on earth shall be bound
in heaven: and what things soever ye shall
loose on earth shall be loosed in heaven.

19 Again I say unto you, that if two of you
shall agree on earth as touching anything
that they shall ask, it shall be done for
them of my Father who is in heaven.

20 For where two or three are gathered together in my name, there am I in the midst
of them.

21 Then came Peter, and said to him, Lord,
how oft shall my brother sin against me,
and I forgive him? until seven times?

22 Jesus saith unto him, I say not unto thee,
Until seven times; but, Until 'seventy

23 times seven. Therefore is the kingdom of
heaven likened unto a certain king, who
would make a reckoning with his 'ser-

24 vants. And when he had begun to reckon,
one was brought unto him, who owed him

25 ten thousand 'talents. But forasmuch as
he had not *wherewith* to pay, his lord commanded him to be sold, and his wife, and
children, and all that he had, and payment

26 to be made. The 'servant therefore fell
down and worshipped him, saying, Lord,
have patience with me, and I will pay thee

27 all. And the lord of that 'servant, being
moved with compassion, released him, and

28 forgave him the 'debt. But that 'servant
went out, and found one of his fellow-servants, who owed him a hundred ' shillings:
and he laid hold on him, and took *him* by

KEY.—* Matthew, ᵇ Mark, ᶜ Luke, ᵈ John.

¹ Or, *congregation.*　　　　² Or, *seventy times and seven.*
³ Gr. *bondservants.*
⁴ This talent was probably worth about £240.
⁵ Gr. *bondservant.*　　　　⁶ Gr. *loan.*
⁷ The word in the Greek denotes a coin worth about eight
pence half-penny.

the throat, saying, Pay what thou owest.
So his fellow servant fell down and be- 29
sought him, saying, Have patience with
me, and I will pay thee. And he would 30
not : but went and cast him into prison,
till he should pay that which was due. So 31
when his fellow-servants saw what was
done, they were exceeding sorry, and came
and told unto their lord all that was done.
Then his lord called him unto him, and 32
saith to him, Thou wicked 'servant, I forgave thee all that debt, because thou be-
soughtest me : shouldest not thou also 33
have had mercy on thy fellow-servant,
even as I had mercy on thee? And his 34
lord was wroth, and delivered him to the
tormentors, till he should pay all that was
due. So shall also my heavenly Father 35
do unto you, if ye forgive not every one
his brother from your hearts.

§ 73. Journeying to the Feast of Tabernacles.

[Samaria.]

John ".

ᵈ Now the feast of the Jews, the feast of 2
tabernacles, was at hand. His brethren 3
therefore said unto him, Depart hence,
and go into Judæa, that thy disciples also
may behold thy works which thou doest.
For no man doeth anything in secret, 'and 4
himself seeketh to be known openly. If
thou doest these things, manifest thyself
to the world. For even his brethren did 5
not believe on him. Jesus therefore saith 6
unto them, My time is not yet come ; but
your time is alway ready. The world can- 7
not hate you ; but me it hateth, because I
testify of it, that its works are evil. Go 8
ye up unto the feast : I go not up ' unto
this feast ; because my time is not yet ful-

KEY.—ᵃ Matthew, ᵇ Mark, ᶜ Luke, ᵈ John.

¹ Gr. *bondservant.*

² Some ancient authorities read *and seeketh it to be known
openly*   ³ Many ancient authorities add *yet.*

§ 73. Journeying to the Feast of Tabernacles.

Matthew's Account.

Chap. 8.

19 And there came a scribe, and said unto him, Master, I
20 will follow thee whithersoever thou goest.   And Jesus
saith unto him, The foxes have holes, and the birds of the
heaven *have* nests; but the Son of man hath not where to
21 lay his head.   And another of the disciples said unto him,
22 Lord, suffer me first to go and bury my father.   But Jesus
saith unto him, Follow me; and leave the dead to bury
their own dead.

PLATE V.

FROM CAPERNAUM TO JERUSALEM, AND RETURNING TO
GALILEE; AGAIN TO JERUSALEM.

§§ 73–118.

As shown by the blue line, Jesus leaves Capernaum, journeying to the Feast of Tabernacles at Jerusalem, through Samaria, where his disciples wish to burn a village with fire from heaven (§ 73). At Jerusalem he taught in the Temple and in the country round about (§§ 74–90). Then he went away beyond Jordan, into Perea, where he taught and uttered many parables, including that of the Prodigal Son (§§ 91–102).

As shown by the red line, he then returned to Bethany, where Lazarus was raised from the dead (§ 103), and retired to Ephraim (§ 104). He then passed through Samaria and made a final circuit of Galilee (§§ 105–107), and once more entered Perea, where, after much teaching (§§ 108–114) he returned toward Jerusalem. At Jericho a blind man was restored and Zaccheus approved (§§ 115 and 116). Then he triumphantly entered Jerusalem (§ 118). During the Passover-week he went out morning and evening to Bethany, and at the close of the week died upon the Cross, and on the first day of the next week ROSE FROM THE DEAD.

The location of the several appearances of Jesus to the disciples after the Resurrection is sufficiently clear without delineation.

(Opposite page 111.)

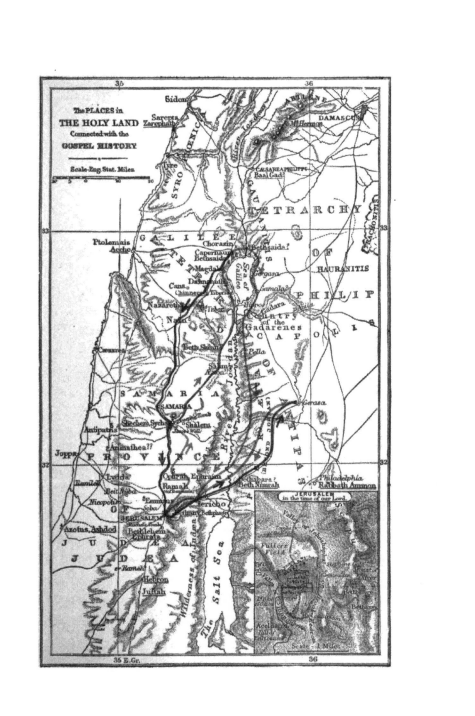

The PLACES in
THE HOLY LAND
Connected with the
GOSPEL HISTORY

Scale—Eng. Stat. Miles.

John 7.

9 filled. And having said these things unto
10 them, he abode *still* in Galilee. But when
his brethren were gone up unto the feast,
then went he also up, not publicly, but as
it were in secret.

51 **Luke 9.** ᶜAnd it came to pass, when the
days ¹ were well-nigh come that he should
be received up, he stedfastly set his face
52 to go to Jerusalem, and sent messengers
before his face: and they went, and entered into a village of the Samaritans, to
53 make ready for him. And they did not
receive him, because his face was *as though*
54 *he were* going to Jerusalem. And when
his disciples James and John saw *this*,
they said, Lord, wilt thou that we bid fire
to come down from heaven, and consume
55 them²? But he turned, and rebuked them³.
56 And they went to another village.
57 And as they went in the way, a certain
man said unto him, I will follow thee
58 whithersoever thou goest. And Jesus
said unto him, The foxes have holes, and
the birds of the heaven *have* ⁴nests; but
the Son of man hath not where to lay his
59 head. And he said unto another, Follow
me. But he said, Lord, suffer me first to
60 go and bury my father. But he said unto
him, Leave the dead to bury their own
dead; but go thou and publish abroad the
61 kingdom of God. And another also said,
I will follow thee, Lord; but first suffer
me to bid farewell to them that are at my
62 house. But Jesus said unto him, No man,
having put his hand to the plough, and
looking back, is fit for the kingdom of God.

Key.—ᵃ Matthew, ᵇ Mark, ᶜ Luke, ᵈ John.

¹ Gr *were being fulfilled*.
² Many ancient authorities add *even as Elijah did*.
³ Some ancient authorities add *and said, Ye know not what
manner of spirit ye are of*. Some, but fewer, add also *For
the Son of man came not to destroy men's lives, but to save* them.
⁴ Gr. *lodging-places*.

§ 74   Teaching in the Temple.

[Jerusalem.]

John 7.

d The Jews therefore sought him at the 11 feast, and said, Where is he? And there 12 was much murmuring among the multitudes concerning him: some said, He is a good man; others said, Not so, but he leadeth the multitude astray. Howbeit no 13 man spake openly of him for fear of the Jews.

But when it was now the midst of the 14 feast Jesus went up into the temple, and taught. The Jews therefore marvelled, 15 saying, How knoweth this man letters, having never learned? Jesus therefore 16 answered them, and said, My teaching is not mine, but his that sent me. If any man 17 willeth to do his will, he shall know of the teaching, whether it be of God, or *whether* I speak from myself. He that speaketh 18 from himself seeketh his own glory: but he that seeketh the glory of him that sent him, the same is true, and no unrighteousness is in him. Did not Moses give you 19 the law, and *yet* none of you doeth the law? Why seek ye to kill me? The mul- 20 titude answered, Thou hast a demon: who seeketh to kill thee? Jesus answered and 21 said unto them, I did one work, and ye all marvel because thereof. Moses hath given 22 you circumcision (not that it is of Moses, but of the fathers); and on the sabbath ye circumcise a man. If a man receiveth cir- 23 cumcision on the sabbath, that the law of Moses may not be broken; are ye wroth with me, because I made ¹ a man every whit whole on the sabbath? Judge not 24 according to appearance, but judge righteous judgement.

Some therefore of them of Jerusalem 25 said, Is not this he whom they seek to kill?

KEY.—ᵃ Matthew, ᵇ Mark, ᶜ Luke, ᵈ John.

¹ Gr. a *whole man sound.*

26 And lo, he speaketh openly, and they say nothing unto him. Can it be that the rulers
27 indeed know that this is the Christ? Howbeit we know this man, whence he is: but when the Christ cometh, no one knoweth
28 whence he is. Jesus therefore cried in the temple, teaching and saying, Ye both know me, and know whence I am; and I am not come of myself, but he that sent me is true,
29 whom ye know not. I know him; because
30 I am from him, and he sent me. They sought therefore to take him: and no man laid his hand on him, because his hour was
31 not yet come. But of the multitude many believed on him; and they said, When the Christ shall come, will he do more signs than those which this man hath done?
32 The Pharisees heard the multitude murmuring these things concerning him; and the chief priests and the Pharisees sent
33 officers to take him. Jesus therefore said, Yet a little while am I with you, and I go
34 unto him that sent me. Ye shall seek me, and shall not find me: and where I am, ye
35 cannot come. The Jews therefore said among themselves, Whither will this man go that we shall not find him? will he go unto the Dispersion ¹among the Greeks,
36 and teach the Greeks? What is this word that he said, Ye shall seek me, and shall not find me: and where I am, ye cannot come?
37 Now on the last day, the great *day* of the feast, Jesus stood and cried, saying, If any man thirst, let him come unto me, and
38 drink. He that believeth on me, as the scripture hath said, ²from within him shall
39 flow rivers of living water. But this spake he of the Spirit, which they that believed on him were to receive: ³for the Spirit was

KEY.—ᵃ Matthew, ᵇ Mark, ᶜ Luke, ᵈ John.

¹ Gr. *of.*   ² Gr. *out of his belly.*
³ Some ancient authorities read *for the Holy Spirit was not yet given.*

not yet *given*; because Jesus was not yet
glorified. *Some* of the multitude therefore, 40
when they heard these words, said, This is
of a truth the prophet.   Others• said, This 41
is the Christ.   But some said, What, doth
the Christ come out of Galilee?   Hath not 42
the scripture said that the Christ cometh
of the seed of David, and from Bethlehem,
the village where David was?   So there 43
arose a division in the multitude because
of him.   And some of them would have 44
taken him; but no man laid hands on him.

The officers therefore came to the chief 45
priests and Pharisees; and they said unto
them, Why did ye not bring him?   The 46
officers answered, Never man so spake.
The Pharisees therefore answered them, 47
Are ye also led astray?   Hath any of the 48
rulers believed on him, or of the Pharisees?
But this multitude who knoweth not the law 49
are accursed.   Nicodemus saith unto them 50
(he that came to him before, being one of
them), Doth our law judge a man, except 51
it first hear from himself and know what
he doeth?   They answered and said unto 52
him, Art thou also of Galilee?   Search,
and ¹see that out of Galilee ariseth no
prophet.

§ 75.   The Woman taken in Adultery.

[Jerusalem.]

ᵈ²[And they went every man unto his 53
own house: but Jesus went unto **John 8.** 1
the mount of Olives. And early in the morn- 2
ing he came again into the temple, and
all the people came unto him; and he sat
down, and taught them. And the scribes and 3
the Pharisees bring a woman taken in adultery; and having set her in the midst, they 4

KEY.—ᵃ Matthew, ᵇ Mark, ᶜ Luke, ᵈ John.

¹ Or, *see ; for out of Galilee &c.*
² Most of the ancient authorities omit John vii. 53—viii.
11.   Those which contain it vary much from each other.

say unto him, ¹ Master, this woman hath been taken in adultery, in the very act.

5 Now in the law Moses commanded us to stone such : what then sayest thou of her?

6 And this they said, trying him, that they might have *whereof* to accuse him. But Jesus stooped down, and with his finger

7 wrote on the ground. But when they continued asking him, he lifted up himself, and said unto them, He that is without sin among you, let him first cast a stone at her.

8 And again he stooped down, and with his

9 finger wrote on the ground. And they, when they heard it, went out one by one, beginning from the eldest, *even* unto the last: and Jesus was left alone, and the

10 woman, where she was, in the midst. And Jesus lifted up himself, and said unto her, Woman, where are they? did no man con-

11 demn thee? And she said, No man, Lord. And Jesus said, Neither do I condemn thee : go thy way ; from henceforth sin no more.]

§ 76. The Light of the World.

[Jerusalem.]

12 ᵈ Again therefore Jesus spake unto them, saying, I am the light of the world : he that followeth me shall not walk in the dark-

13 ness, but shall have the light of life. The Pharisees therefore said unto him, Thou bearest witness of thyself ; thy witness is

14 not true. Jesus answered and said unto them, Even if I bear witness of myself, my witness is true ; for I know whence I came, and whither I go ; but ye know not whence

15 I come, or whither I go. Ye judge after

16 the flesh ; I judge no man. Yea and if I judge, my judgement is true ; for I am not alone, but I and the Father that sent me.

17 Yea and in your law it is written, that the

KEY.—ᵃ Matthew, ᵇ Mark, ᶜ Luke, ᵈ John.

¹ Or, *Teacher.*

witness of two men is true. I am he that 18
beareth witness of myself, and the Father
that sent me beareth witness of me. They 19
said therefore unto him, Where is thy
Father? Jesus answered, Ye know neither
me, nor my Father: if ye knew me, ye
would know my Father also. These words 20
spake he in the treasury, as he taught in
the temple : and no man took him ; because
his hour was not yet come.

He said therefore again unto them, I go 21
away, and ye shall seek me, and shall die
in your sin : whither I go, ye cannot come.
The Jews therefore said, Will he kill him- 22
self, that he saith, Whither I go, ye cannot
come? And he said unto them, Ye are 23
from beneath ; I am from above : ye are of
this world ; I am not of this world. I said 24
therefore unto you, that ye shall die in
your sins : for except ye believe that I am
he, ye shall die in your sins. They said 25
therefore unto him, Who art thou? Jesus
said unto them, [1]Even that which I have
also spoken unto you from the beginning.
I have many things to speak and to judge 26
concerning you : howbeit he that sent me
is true ; and the things which I heard from
him, these speak I unto the world. They 27
perceived not that he spake to them of the
Father. Jesus therefore said, When ye 28
have lifted up the Son of man, then shall
ye know that [2]I am *he*, and *that* I do nothing of myself, but as the Father taught
me, I speak these things. And he that 29
sent me is with me ; he hath not left me
alone ; for I do always the things that are
pleasing to him. As he spake these things, 30
many believed on him.

Jesus therefore said to those Jews who 31
had believed him, If ye abide in my word,

KEY.—[a] Matthew, [b] Mark, [c] Luke, [d] John.

[1] Or, *Altogether that which I also speak unto you.*
[2] Or, *I am* he : *and I do.*

John 8.

32 *then* are ye truly my disciples ; and ye shall

33 know the truth, and the truth shall make you free. They answered unto him, We are Abraham's seed, and have never yet been in bondage to any man : how sayest thou,

34 Ye shall be made free ? Jesus answered them, Verily, verily, I say unto you, Every one that committeth sin is the bondservant

35 of sin. And the bondservant abideth not in the house for ever : the son abideth for ever.

36 If therefore the Son shall make yon free,

37 ye shall be free indeed. I know that ye are Abraham's seed ; yet ye seek to kill me, because my word [1]hath not free course

38 in you. I speak the things which I have seen with [2]*my* Father : and ye also do the things which ye heard from *your* father.

39 They answered and said unto him, Our father is Abraham. Jesus saith unto them, If ye [3]were Abraham's children, [4]ye

40 would do the works of Abraham. But now ye seek to kill me, a man that hath told you the truth, which I heard from

41 God : this did not Abraham. Ye do the works of your father. They said unto him, We were not born of fornication ; we have

42 one Father, *even* God. Jesus said unto them, If God were your Father, ye would love me : for I came forth and am come from God ; for neither have I come of my-

43 self, but he sent me. Why do ye not [5]understand my speech ? *Even* because ye

44 cannot hear my word. Ye are of *your* father the devil, and the lusts of your father it is your will to do. He was a murderer from the beginning, and standeth not in the truth, because there is no truth

KEY.—[a] Matthew, [b] Mark, [c] Luke, [d] John.

[1] Or, *hath no place in you.*
[2] Or. *the Father: do ye also therefore the things which ye heard from the Father.* [3] Gr. *are.*
[4] Some ancient authorities read *ye do the works of Abraham.*
[5] Or, *know.*

in him. ¹ When he speaketh a lie, he speaketh of his own: for he is a liar, and the father thereof.   But because I say the 45 truth, ye believe me not.   Which of you 46 convicteth me of sin?   If I say truth, why do ye not believe me?   He that is of God 47 heareth the words of God: for this cause ye hear *them* not, because ye are not of God.   The Jews answered and said unto 48 him, Say we not well that thou art a Samaritan, and hast a demon?   Jesus an- 49 swered, I have not a demon; but I honour my Father, and ye dishonour me.   But I 50 seek not mine own glory: there is one that seeketh and judgeth.   Verily, verily, 61 I say unto you, If a man keep my word, he shall never see death.   The Jews said unto 52 him, Now we know that thou hast a demon.   Abraham died, and the prophets; and thou sayest, If a man keep my word, he shall never taste of death.   Art thou 53 greater than our father Abraham, who died? and the prophets died: whom makest thou thyself?   Jesus answered, If I 54 glorify myself, my glory is nothing: it is my Father that glorifieth me ; of whom ye say, that he is your God: and ye have not 55 known him: but I know him; and if I should say, I know him not, I shall be like unto you, a liar: but I know him, and keep his word.   Your father Abraham rejoiced 56 ² to see my day; and he saw it, and was glad.   The Jews therefore said unto him, 57 Thou art not yet fifty years old, and hast thou seen Abraham?   Jesus said unto 58 them, Verily, verily, I say unto you, Before Abraham was born, I am.   They took up 59 stones therefore to cast at him : but Jesus

KEY.—ᵃ Matthew, ᵇ Mark, ᶜ Luke, ᵈ John.

¹ Or, *When* one *speaketh a lie, he speaketh of his own : for his father also is a liar.*
² Or, *that he should see.*

John 8.
¹ hid himself, and went out of the temple ².

§ 77. Seventy Disciples sent forth.

[Probably Jerusalem.]

Luke 10.

1   ᶜ Now after these things the Lord appointed seventy ³ others, and sent them
two and two before his face into every
city and place, whither he himself was
2 about to come. And he said unto them,
The harvest is plenteous, but the labourers
are few : pray ye therefore the Lord of
the harvest, that he send forth labourers
3 into his harvest. Go your ways : behold, I
send you forth as lambs in the midst of
4 wolves. Carry no purse, no wallet, no
shoes : and salute no man on the way.
5 And into whatsoever house ye shall ⁴ en-
6 ter, first say, Peace *be* to this house. And
if a son of peace be there, your peace shall
rest upon ⁵ him : but if not, it shall turn to
7 you again. And in that same house remain, eating and drinking such things as
they give : for the labourer is worthy of
his hire. Go not from house to house.
8 And into whatsoever city ye enter, and
they receive you, eat such things as are set
9 before you : and heal the sick that are
therein, and say unto them, The kingdom
10 of God is come nigh unto you. But into
whatsoever city ye shall enter, and they
receive you not, go out into the streets
11 thereof and say, Even the dust from your
city, that cleaveth to our feet, we do wipe
off against you : howbeit know this, that
12 the kingdom of God is come nigh. I say
unto you, It shall be more tolerable in that
13 day for Sodom, than for that city. Woe

KEY.—ᵃ Matthew, ᵇ Mark, ᶜ Luke, ᵈ John.

¹ Or, *was hidden, and went &c.*
² Many ancient authorities add *and going through the midst
of them went his way, and so passed by.*
³ Many ancient authorities add *and two*: and so in ver. 17.
⁴ Or, *enter first, say.*   ⁵ Or, *it.*

unto thee, Chorazin! woe unto thee, Bethsaida! for if the ¹mighty works had been
done in Tyre and Sidon, which were done
in you, they would have repented long
ago, sitting in sackcloth and ashes. How- 14
beit it shall be more tolerable for Tyre and
Sidon in the judgement, than for you. And 15
thou, Capernaum, shalt thou be exalted
unto heaven? thou shalt be brought
down unto Hades. He that heareih you 16
heareth me; and he that rejecteth you rejecteth me; and he that rejecteth me rejecteth him that sent me.

And the seventy returned with joy, say- 17
ing, Lord, even the demons are subject unto us in thy name. And he said unto them, 18
I beheld Satan fallen as lightning from
heaven. Behold, I have given you author- 19
ity to tread upon serpents and scorpions,
and over all the power of the enemy: and
nothing shall in any wise hurt you. How- 20
beit in this rejoice not, that the spirits are
subject unto you; but rejoice that your
names are written in heaven.

In that same hour he rejoiced ³in the 21
Holy Spirit, and said, I ²thank thee, O
Father, Lord of heaven and earth, that
thou didst hide these things from the wise
and understanding, and didst reveal them
unto babes: yea, Father; ⁴for so it was
well-pleasing in thy sight. All things have 22
been delivered unto me of my Father: and
no one knoweth who the Son is, save the
Father; and who the Father is, save the
Son, and he to whomsoever the Son willeth to reveal *him*. And turning to the dis- 23
ciples, he said privately, Blessed *are* the
eyes which see the things that ye see: for I 24
say unto you, that many prophets and kings

KEY.—ᵃ Matthew, ᵇ Mark, ᶜ Luke, ᵈ John.

¹ Gr. *powers*. ³ Or, *by*.
² Or, *praise*. ⁴ Or, *that*.

Luke 10.

desired to see the things which ye see, and saw them not; and to hear the things which ye hear, and heard them not.

§ 78. Parable of the Good Samaritan.

[Judea.]

Luke 10.

25 ᶜAnd behold, a certain lawyer stood up and tried him, saying, ¹Master, what shall

26 I do to inherit eternal life? And he said unto him, What is written in the law?

27 how readest thou? And he answering said, Thou shalt love the Lord thy God ²with all thy heart, and with all thy soul, and with all thy strength, and with all thy

28 mind; and thy neighbour as thyself. And he said unto him, Thou hast answered

29 right: this do, and thou shalt live. But he, desiring to justify himself, said unto Jesus,

30 And who is my neighbour? Jesus made answer and said, A certain man was going down from Jerusalem to Jericho; and he fell among robbers, who both stripped him and beat him, and departed, leaving him

31 half dead. And by chance a certain priest was going down that way: and when he saw him, he passed by on the other side.

32 And in like manner a Levite also, when he came to the place, and saw him, passed by

33 on the other side. But a certain Samaritan, as he journeyed, came where he was: and when he saw him, he was moved with

34 compassion, and came to him, and bound up his wounds, pouring on *them* oil and wine; and he set him on his own beast, and brought him to an inn, and took care

35 of him. And on the morrow he took out two ³shillings, and gave them to the host, and said, Take care of him; and whatsoever thou spendest more, I, when I come

KEY.—ª Matthew, ᵇ Mark, ᶜ Luke, ᵈ John.

¹ Or, *Teacher.*   ² Gr. *from.*

³ The word in the Greek denotes a coin worth about eight pence halfpenny.

Luke 10.

back again, will repay thee. Which of 36
these three, thinkest thou, proved neighbour unto him that fell among the robbers?
And he said, He that shewed mercy on 37
him. And Jesus said unto him, Go, and do
thou likewise.

§ 79. Martha and Mary.

[Bethany.]

Luke 10.

^c Now as they went on their way, he en- 38
tered into a certain village : and a certain
woman named Martha received him into
her house. And she had a sister called 39
Mary, who also sat at the Lord's feet, and
heard his word. But Martha was ¹ cum- 40
bered about much serving : and she came
up to him, and said, Lord, dost thou not
care that my sister did leave me to serve
alone? bid her therefore that she help me.
But the Lord answered and said unto her, 41
² Martha, Martha, thou art anxious and
troubled about many things : ³ but one 42
thing is needful : for Mary hath chosen the
good part, which shall not be taken away
from her.

§ 80. A Lesson on Prayer.

[Judea.]

Luke 11.

^c And it came to pass, as he was praying 1
in a certain place, that when he ceased,
one of his disciples said unto him, Lord,
teach us to pray, even as John also taught
his disciples. Aud he said unto them, 2
When ye pray, say, ' Father, Hallowed be
thy name. Thy kingdom come.' Give us 3

KEY.—^a Matthew, ^b Mark, ^c Luke, ^d John.

¹ Gr. *distracted.*

² A few ancient authorities read *Martha, Martha, thou art troubled: Mary hath chosen &c.*

³ Many ancient authorities read *but few things are needful, or one.*

⁴ Many ancient authorities read *Our Father, who art in heaven.*

⁵ Many ancient authorities add *Thy will be done, as in heaven, so on earth.*

Luke 11.
day by day ¹ our daily bread. And for-
4 give us our sins; for we ourselves also
forgive every one that is indebted to us.
And bring us not into temptation².

5 And he said unto them, Which of you
shall have a friend, and shall go unto him
at midnight, and say to him, Friend, lend
6 me three loaves; for a friend of mine is
come to me from a journey, and I have
7 nothing to set before him; and he from
within shall answer and say, Trouble me
not: the door is now shut, and my children
are with me in bed; I cannot rise and give
8 thee? I say unto you, Though he will not
rise and give him, because he is his friend,
yet because of his importunity he will
arise and give him ³ as many as he needeth.
9 And I say unto you, Ask, and it shall be
given you; seek, and ye shall find; knock,
10 and it shall be opened unto you. For every
one that asketh receiveth; and he that
seeketh findeth; and to him that knocketh
11 it shall be opened. And of which of you
that is a father shall his son ask ⁴ a loaf,
and he give him a stone? or a fish, and he
12 for a fish give him a serpent? Or *if* he
shall ask an egg, will he give him a scor-
13 pion? If ye then, being evil, know how
to give good gifts unto your children, how
much more shall *your* heavenly Father
give the Holy Spirit to them that ask him?

§ 81. A Demon Cast Out.

[Judea.]

Luke 11.
14 ᶜ And he was casting out a demon *which
was* dumb. And it came to pass, when the
demon was gone out, the dumb man spake;

KEY.—ᵃ Matthew, ᵇ Mark, ᶜ Luke, ᵈ John.

¹ Gr. *our bread for the coming day*, or *our needful bread*.
² Many ancient authorities add *but deliver us from the evil
one* (or, *from evil*).
³ Or, *whatsoever things.*
⁴ Some ancient authorities omit *a loaf, and he gave him a
stone? or.*

and the multitudes marvelled.   But some 15
of them said, ¹ By Beelzebub the prince of
the demons casteth he out demons.   And 16
others, trying *him*, sought of him a sign
from heaven.   But he, knowing their 17
thoughts, said unto them, Every kingdom
divided against itself is brought to desolation ; ² and a house *divided* against a house
falleth.   And if Satan also is divided 18
against himself, how shall his kingdom
stand ? because ye say that I cast out
demons ¹ by Beelzebub.   And if I ¹ by 19
Beelzebub cast out demons, by whom do
your sons cast them out ? therefore shall
they be your judges.   But if I by the fin- 20
ger of God cast out demons, then is the
kingdom of God come upon you.   When 21
the strong *man* fully armed guardeth his
own court, his goods are in peace : but 22
when a stronger than he shall come upon
him, and overcome him, he taketh from
him his whole armour wherein he trusted,
and divideth his spoils.   He that is not 23
with me is against me ; and he that gathereth not with me scattereth.   The unclean 24
spirit when ³ he is gone out of the man,
passeth through waterless places, seeking
rest; and finding none, ³ he saith, I will
turn back unto my house whence I came
out.   And when ³ he is come, ³ he findeth it 25
swept and garnished.   Then goeth ⁸ he, and 26
taketh to *him* seven other spirits more evil
than ⁴ himself ; and they enter in and dwell
there : and the last state of that man becometh worse than the first.

And it came to pass, as he said these 27
things, a certain woman out of the multitude lifted up her voice, and said unto him,
Blessed is the womb that bare thee, and
the breasts which thou didst suck.   But 28

KEY.—ᵃ Matthew, ᵇ Mark, ᶜ Luke, ᵈ John.

¹ Or, *In.*   ³ Or, *and house falleth upon house.*
²Or, *it.*   ⁴ Or, *itself.*

L▪ ● 11.

he said, Yea rather, blessed are they that hear the word of God, and keep it.

§ 82. A Sign again Refused.

Luke 11. [Judea.]

.9 °And when the multitudes were gathering together unto him, he began to say, This generation is an evil generation : it seeketh after a sign ; and there shall no sign be given to it but the sign of Jonah.
30 For even as Jonah became a sign unto the Ninevites, so shall also the Son of man
31 be to this generation. The queen of the south shall rise up in the judgement with the men of this generation, and shall condemn them : for she came from the ends of the earth to hear the wisdom of Solomon ; and behold, ¹a greater than
32 Solomon is here. The men of Nineveh shall stand up in the judgement with this generation, and shall condemn it : for they repented at the preaching of Jonah ; and behold, ¹a greater than Jonah is here.
33 No man, when he hath lighted a lamp, putteth it in a cellar, neither under the bushel, but on the stand, that they that
34 enter in may see the light. The lamp of thy body is thine eye : when thine eye is single, thy whole body also is full of light ; but when it is evil, thy body also is full of
35 darkness. Look therefore whether the
36 light that is ín thee be not darkness. If therefore thy whole body be full of light, having no part dark, it shall be wholly full of light, as when the lamp with its bright shining doth give thee light.

§ 83. Woes on Pharisees and Lawyers.

Luke 11. [Judea.]

37 °Now as he spake, a Pharisee asketh him to ²dine with him : and he went in,

Key.—ᵃ Matthew, ᵇ Mark, ᶜ Luke, ᵈ John.

¹ Gr. *more than.*   ² Gr. *breakfast.*

and sat down to meat. And when the 38
Pharisee saw it, he marvelled that he had
not first bathed himself before ¹ dinner.
And the Lord said unto him, Now do ye 39
Pharisees cleanse the outside of the cup
and of the platter; but your inward part
is full of extortion and wickedness. Ye 40
foolish ones, did not he that made the outside make the inside also? Howbeit give 41
for alms those things which ² are within ;
and behold, all things are clean unto you.

But woe unto you Pharisees! for ye 42
tithe mint and rue and every herb, and
pass over justice and the love of God : but
these ought ye to have done, and not to
leave the other undone. Woe unto you 43
Pharisees! for ye love the chief seats in
the synagogues, and the salutations in the
marketplaces. Woe unto you! for ye are 44
as the tombs which appear not, and the
men that walk over *them* know it not.

And one of the lawyers answering saith 45
unto him, ² Master, in saying this thou re-
proachest us also. And he said, Woe unto 46
you lawyers also ! for ye lade men with
burdens grievous to be borne, and ye
yourselves touch not the burdens with one
of your fingers. Woe unto you! for ye 47
build the tombs of the prophets, and your
fathers killed them. So ye are witnesses 48
and consent unto the works of your
fathers : for they killed them, and ye build
their tombs. Therefore also said the wis- 49
dom of God, I will send unto them prophets and apostles; and *some* of them they
shall kill and persecute; that the blood of 50
all the prophets, which was shed from the
foundation of the world, may be required
of this generation; from the blood of Abel 51
unto the blood of Zachariah, who perished

KEY.—ᵃ Matthew, ᵇ Mark, ᶜ Luke, ᵈ John.

¹ Gr. *breakfast.*   ² Or, *ye can.*   ³ Or, *Teacher.*

Luke 11.

between the altar and the [1] sanctuary : yea,
I say unto you, it shall be required of this
52 generation. Woe unto you lawyers! for
ye took away the key of knowledge : ye
entered not in yourselves, and them that
were entering in ye hindered.

53   And when he was come out from thence,
the scribes and the Pharisees began to
[2] press upon *him* vehemently, and to pro-
54 voke him to speak of [3] many things; laying
wait for him, to catch something out of his
mouth.

§ 84. Warning and Encouragement.

Luke 12.   [Judea.]

1   [c] In the mean time, when [4] the many thou-
sands of the multitude were gathered together, insomuch that they trode one upon
another, he began to [5] say unto his disciples first of all, Beware ye of the leaven of
2 the Pharisees, which is hypocrisy. But
there is nothing covered up, that shall not
be revealed : and hid, that shall not be
3 known. Wherefore whatsoever ye have
said in the darkness shall be heard in the
light; and what ye have spoken in the ear
in the inner chambers shall be proclaimed
4 upon the housetops. And I say unto you
my friends, Be not afraid of them that kill
the body, and after that have no more that
5 they can do. But I will warn you whom
ye shall fear : Fear him, who after he hath
killed hath [6] power to cast into [7] hell; yea,
6 I say unto you, Fear him. Are not five
sparrows sold for two pence? and not one
of them is forgotten in the sight of God.
7 But the very hairs of your head are all
numbered. Fear not : ye are of more

KEY.—[a] Matthew, [b] Mark, [c] Luke, [d] John.

[1] Gr. *house.*
[2] Or, *set themselves vehemently against* him.
[3] Or, *more.*   [4] Gr. *the myriads of.*
[5] Or, *say unto his disciples, First of all beware ye.*
[6] Or, *authority.*   [7] Gr. *Gehenna.*

value than many sparrows. And I say 8
unto you, Every one who shall confess [1] me
before men, [2] him shall the Son of man
also confess before the angels of God: but 9
he that denieth me in the presence of men
shall be denied in the presence of the
angels of God. And every one who shall 10
speak a word against the Son of man, it
shall be forgiven him: but unto him that
blasphemeth against the Holy Spirit it
shall not be forgiven. And when they 11
bring you before the synagogues, and the
rulers, and the authorities, be not anxious
how or what ye shall answer, or what ye
shall say: for the Holy Spirit shall teach 12
you in that very hour what ye ought to
say.

§ 85. The Foolish Rich Man.

[Judea..]

[c]And one out of the multitude said unto 13
him, [3]Master, bid my brother divide the inheritance with me. But he said unto him, 14
Man, who made me a judge or a divider
over you? And he said unto them, Take 15
heed, and keep yourselves from all covet-
ousness: [4]for a man's life consisteth not in
the abundance of the things which he
possesseth. And he spake a parable unto 16
them, saying, The ground of a certain rich
man brought forth plentifully: and he rea- 17
soned within himself, saying, What shall I
do, because I have not where to bestow
my fruits? And he said, This will I do: I 18
will pull down my barns, and build greater;
and there will I bestow all my corn and
my goods. And I will say to my [5]soul, 19
[5]Soul, thou hast much goods laid up for
many years; take thine ease, eat, drink, be
merry. But God said unto him, Thou 20

KEY.—[a] Matthew, [b] Mark, [c] Luke, [d] John.

[1] Gr. *in me.*   [2] Gr. *in him.*   [3] Or, *Teacher.*
[4] Gr. *for not in a man's abundance consisteth his life, from
the things which he possesseth.*   [5] Or, *life.*

foolish one, this night [1] is thy [3] soul required of thee; and the things which thou hast
21 prepared, whose shall they be? So is he
that layeth up treasure for himself, and is
not rich toward God.

22   And he said unto his disciples, Therefore
I say unto you, Be not anxious for *your*
[3] life, what ye shall eat; nor yet for your
23 body, what ye shall put on. For the [3] life is
more than the food, and the body than the
24 raiment. Consider the ravens, that they
sow not, neither reap; which have no
store-chamber nor barn; and God feedeth
them: of how much more value are ye
25 than the birds! And which of you by being anxious can add a cubit unto [4] the mea-
26 sure of his life? If then ye are not able to
do even that which is least, why are ye
27 anxious concerning the rest? Consider
the lilies, how they grow: they toil not,
neither do they spin; yet I say unto you,
Even Solomon in all his glory was not ar-
28 rayed like one of these. But if God doth
so clothe the grass in the field, which to-
day is, and to-morrow is cast into the oven;
how much more *shall he clothe* you, O ye
29 of little faith? And seek not ye what ye
shall eat, and what ye shall drink, neither
30 be ye of doubtful mind. For all these
things do the nations of the world seek
after: but your Father knoweth that ye
31 have need of these things. Howbeit seek
ye [5] his kingdom, and these things shall be
32 added unto you. Fear not, little flock;
for it is your Father's good pleasure to
33 give you the kingdom. Sell that ye have,
and give alms; make for yourselves purses
which wax not old, a treasure in the heavens that faileth not, where no thief draw-

Key.—[a] Matthew, [b] Mark, [c] Luke, [d] John.
[1] Gr. *they require thy soul.*   [3] Or, *life.*
[3] Or, *soul.*   [4] Or, *his stature.*
[5] Many ancient authorities read *the kingdom of God.*

eth near, neither moth destroyeth.   For 34
where your treasure is, there will your
heart be also.

Let your loins be girded about, and your 35
lamps burning ; and be ye yourselves like 36
unto men looking for their lord, when he
shall return from the marriage feast; that,
when he cometh and knocketh, they may
straightway open unto him.   Blessed are 37
those [1] servants, whom the lord when he
cometh shall find watching : verily I say
unto you, that he shall gird himself, and
make them sit down to meat, and shall
come and serve them.   And if he shall 38
come in the second watch, and if in the
third, and find *them* so, blessed are those
servants.   [2] But know this, that if the mas- 39
ter of the house had known in what hour
the thief was coming, he would have
watched, and not have left his house to be
[3] broken through.   Be ye also ready : for 40
in an hour that ye think not the Son of
man cometh.

And Peter said, Lord, speakest thou this 41
parable unto us, or even unto all?   And 42
the Lord said, Who then is the [4] faithful
and wise steward, whom his lord shall set
over his household, to give them their portion of food in due season?   Blessed is 43
that [5] servant, whom his lord when he cometh shall find so doing.   Of a truth I say 44
unto you, that he will set him over all that
he hath.   But if that [5] servant shall say in 45
his heart, My lord delayeth his coming;
and shall begin to beat the menservants
and the maidservants, and to eat and drink,
and to be drunken; the lord of that [5] ser- 46
vant shall come in a day when he expect-

KEY.—[a] Matthew, [b] Mark, [c] Luke, [d] John.

[1] Gr. *bondservants.*   [2] Or, *but this ye know.*
[3] Gr. *digged through.*
[4] Or, *the faithful steward, the wise* man *whom &c.*
[5] Gr. *bondservant.*

eth not, and in an hour when he knoweth not, and shall [1] cut him asunder, and ap-

47 point his portion with the unfaithful. And that [2] servant, who knew his lord's will, and made not ready, nor did according to his

48 will, shall be beaten with many *stripes;* but he that knew not, and did things worthy of stripes, shall be beaten with few *stripes.* And to whomsoever much is given, of him shall much be required: and to whom they commit much, of him will they ask the more.

49 I came to cast fire upon the earth; and [3] what do I desire, if it is already kindled?

50 But I have a baptism to be baptized with; and how am I straitened till it be accom-

51 plished! Think ye that I am come to give peace in the earth? I tell you, Nay; but

52 rather division: for there shall be from henceforth five in one house divided, three

53 against two, and two against three. They shall be divided, father against son, and son against father; mother against daughter, and daughter against her mother; mother in law against her daughter in law, and daughter in law against her mother in law.

54 And he said to the multitudes also, When ye see a cloud rising in the west, straightway ye say, There cometh a shower; and

55 so it cometh to pass. And when *ye see* a south wind blowing, ye say, There will be a [4] scorching heat; and it cometh to pass.

56 Ye hypocrites, ye know how to [5] interpret the face of the earth and the heaven; but how is it that ye know not how to [5] inter-

57 pret this time? And why even of your-

58 selves judge ye not what is right? For as thou art going with thine adversary before

KEY.—[a] Matthew, [b] Mark, [c] Luke, [d] John.

[1] Or, *severely scourge him.* [2] Gr. *bondservant.*
[3] Or, *how I would that it were already kindled!*
[4] Or, *hot wind.* [5] Gr. *prove.*

Luke 12.

the magistrate, on the way give diligence to
be quit of him ; lest haply he drag thee unto
the judge, and the judge shall deliver thee
to the [1]officer, and the [1]officer shall cast
thee into prison. I say unto thee, Thou 59
shalt by no means come out thence, till
thou have paid the very last mite.

§ 86. Repentance taught.

[Judea.]

Luke 13.

[c] Now there were some present at that 1
very season who told him of the Galilæans,
whose blood Pilate had mingled with their
sacrifices. And he answered and said un- 2
to them, Think ye that these Galilæans
were sinners above all the Galilæans, because they have suffered these things? I 3
tell you, Nay : but, except ye repent, ye
shall all in like manner perish. Or those 4
eighteen, upon whom the tower in Siloam
fell, and killed them, think ye that they
were [2]offenders above all the men that
dwell in Jerusalem? I tell you, Nay : but, 5
except ye repent, ye shall all likewise perish.

§ 87. The Barren Fig Tree.

[Jerusalem.]

Luke 13.

[c]And he spake this parable; A certain 6
man had a fig tree planted in his vineyard;
and he came seeking fruit thereon, and
found none. And he said unto the vine- 7
dresser, Behold, these three years I come
seeking fruit on this fig tree, and find none :
cut it down; why doth it also cumber the
ground? And he answering saith unto 8
him, Lord, let it alone this year also, till I
shall dig about it, and dung it : and if it 9
bear fruit thenceforth, *well*; but if not, thou
shalt cut it down.

KEY.—[a] Matthew, [b] Mark, [c] Luke, [d] John.

[1] Gr. *exactor*.   [2] Gr. *debtors*.

§ 88. The Blind Man at the Pool of Siloam.

John 9.

1 ᵈAnd as he passed by, he saw a man
2 blind from his birth. And his disciples
asked him, saying, Rabbi, who did sin,
this man, or his parents, that he should be
3 born blind? Jesus answered, Neither did
this man sin, nor his parents: but that the
works of God should be made manifest in
4 him. We must work the works of him
that sent me, while it is day: the night
5 cometh, when no man can work. When I
am in the world, I am the light of the
6 world. When he had thus spoken, he spat
on the ground, and made clay of the spittle,
7 ¹and anointed his eyes with the clay, and
said unto him, Go, wash in the pool of Siloam (which is by interpretation, Sent).
He went away therefore, and washed, and
8 came seeing. The neighbours therefore,
and they who saw him aforetime, that he
was a beggar, said, Is not this he that sat
9 and begged? Others said, It is he: others
said, No, but he is like him. He said, I am
10 *he*. They said therefore unto him, How
11 then were thine eyes opened? He answered, The man that is called Jesus made
clay, and anointed mine eyes, and said unto me, Go to Siloam, and wash: so I went
away and washed, and I received sight.
12 And they said unto him, Where is he? He
saith, I know not.
13 They bring to the Pharisees him that
14 aforetime was blind. Now it was the sabbath on the day when Jesus made the clay,
15 and opened his eyes. Again therefore the
Pharisees also asked him how he received
his sight. And he said unto them, He
put clay upon mine eyes, and I washed,
16 and do see. Some therefore of the Pharisees said, This man is not from God, be-

KEY.—ᵃ Matthew, ᵇ Mark, ᶜ Luke, ᵈ John.

¹ Or, *and with the clay thereof anointed* his *eyes.*

cause he keepeth not the sabbath. But others said, How can a man that is a sin-ner do such signs? And there was a di-vision among them. They say therefore 17 unto the blind man again, What sayest thou of him, in that he opened thine eyes? And he said, He is a prophet. The Jews 18 therefore did not believe concerning him, that he had been blind, and had received his sight, until they called the parents of him that had received ·his sight, and 19 asked them, saying, Is this your son, who ye say was born blind? how then doth he now see? His parents answered and said, 20 We know that this is our son, and that he was born blind: but how he now seeth, 21 we know not; or who opened his eyes, we know not: ask him; he is of age; he shall speak for himself. These things said his 22 parents, because they feared the Jews: for the Jews had agreed already, that if any man should confess him *to be* Christ, he should be put out of the synagogue. Therefore said his parents, He is of age; 23 ask him. So they called a second time the 24 man that was blind, and said unto him, Give glory to God: we know that this man is a sinner. He therefore answered, 25 Whether he be a sinner, I know not: one thing I know, that, whereas I was blind, now I see. They said therefore unto him, 26 What did he to thee? how opened he thine eyes? He answered them, I told you 27 even now, and ye did not hear: wherefore would ye hear it again? would ye also be-come his disciples? And they reviled 28 him, and said, Thou art his disciple; but we are disciples of Moses. We know that 29 God hath spoken unto Moses: but as for this man, we know not whence he is. The man answered and said unto them, 30

KEY.—ᵃ Matthew, ᵇ Mark, ᵉ Luke, ᵈ John.

John 9.

Why, herein is the marvel, that ye know not whence he is, and *yet* he opened mine
31 eyes. We know that God heareth not sin-ners: but if any man be a worshipper of God, and do his will, him he heareth.
32 Since the world began it was never heard that any one opened the eyes of a man
33 born blind. If this man were not from
34 God, he could do nothing. They an-swered and said unto him, Thou wast al-together born in sins, and dost thou teach us? And they cast him out.
35 Jesus heard that they had cast him out; and finding him, he said, Dost thou believe
36 on ¹ the Son of God? He answered and said, And who is he, Lord, that I may be-
37 lieve on him? Jesus said unto him, Thou hast both seen him, and he it is that speak-
38 eth with thee. And he said, Lord, I be-
39 lieve. And he worshipped him. And Jesus said, For judgement came I into this world, that they who see not may see; and that they who see may become blind.
40 Those of the Pharisees that were with him heard these things, and said unto him, Are
41 we also blind? Jesus said unto them, If ye were blind, ye would have no sin: but now ye say, We see: your sin remaineth.

§ 89. The Good Shepherd.

John 10. [Jerusalem.]

1 ᵈ Verily, verily, I say unto you, He that entereth not by the door into the fold of the sheep, but climbeth up some other way, the same is a thief and a robber.
2 But he that entereth in by the door is ² the
3 shepherd of the sheep. To him the porter openeth; and the sheep hear his voice: and he calleth his own sheep hy name, and
4 leadeth them out. When he hath put

KEY.—ᵃ Matthew, ᵇ Mark, ᶜ Luke, ᵈ John.

¹ Many ancient authorities read *the Son of man.*
² Or, *a shepherd.*

forth all his own, and goeth before them,
and the sheep follow him : for they know
his voice.   And a stranger will they not 5
follow, but will flee from him : for they
know not the voice of strangers.   This 6
¹ parable spake Jesus unto them : but they
understood not what things they were
which he spake unto them.

Jesus therefore said unto them again, 7
Verily, verily, I say unto you, I am the
door of the sheep.   All that came ² before 8
me are thieves and robbers : but the sheep
did not hear them.   I am the door : by me 9
if any man enter in, he shall be saved, and
shall go in and go out, and shall find past-
ure.   The thief cometh not, but that he 10
may steal, and kill, and destroy : I came
that they may have life, and may ³ have it
abundantly.   I am the good shepherd : the 11
good shepherd layeth down his life for the
sheep.   He that is a hireling, and not a 12
shepherd, whose own the sheep are not,
beholdeth the wolf coming, and leaveth
the sheep, and fleeth, and the wolf snatcheth them, and scattereth *them* : *he fleeth* 13
because he is a hireling, and careth not for
the sheep.   I am the good shepherd ; and 14
I know mine own, and mine own know me, 15
even as the Father knoweth me, and I know
the Father ; and I lay down my life for
the sheep.   And other sheep I have, which 16
are not of this fold : them also I must
⁴ bring, and they shall hear my voice ; and
⁵ they shall become one flock, one shepherd.
Therefore doth the Father love me, be- 17
cause I lay down my life, that I may take
it again.   No one ⁶ taketh it away from me, 18

KEY.—ᵃ Matthew, ᵇ Mark, ᶜ Luke, ᵈ John.

¹ Or, *proverb.*
² Some ancient authorities omit *before me.*
³ Or, *have abundance.*   ⁴ Or, *lead.*
⁵ Or, *there shall be one flock.*
⁶ Some ancient authorities read *took it away.*

but I lay it down of myself. I have [1] power
to lay it down, and I have [1] power to take
it again. This commandment received I
from my Father.

§ 90. Division among the Jews.

[Jerusalem.]

John 10.

19   [d]There arose a division again among the
20 Jews because of these words. And many
of them said, He hath a demon, and is mad;
21 why hear ye him? Others said, These are
not the sayings of one possessed with a demon. Can a demon open the eyes of the
blind?

22   [2]And it was the feast of the dedication
23 at Jerusalem: it was winter; and Jesus
was walking in the temple in Solomon's
24 porch. The Jews therefore came round
about him, and said unto him, How long
dost thou hold us in suspense? If thou art
25 the Christ, tell us plainly. Jesus answered them, I told you, and ye believe
not: the works that I do in my Father's
26 name, these bear witness of me. But ye
believe not, because ye are not of my
27 sheep. My sheep hear my voice, and I
28 know them, and they follow me: and I
give unto them eternal life; and they shall
never perish, and no one shall snatch them
29 out of my hand. [3]My Father, who hath
given *them* unto me, is greater than all;
and no one is able to snatch [4] *them* out of
30 the Father's hand. I and the Father are
31 one. The Jews took up stones again to
32 stone him. Jesus answered them, Many
good works have I shewed you from the
Father; for which of those works do ye
33 stone me? The Jews answered him, For

KEY.—[a] Matthew, [b] Mark, [c] Luke, [d] John.

[1] Or, *right*.
[2] Some ancient authorities read *At that time was the feast.*
[3] Some ancient authorities read *That which my Father
hath given unto me.*   [4] Or, aught.

a good. work we stone thee not, but for
blasphemy; and because that thou. being
a man, makest thyself God. Jesus an- 34
swered them, Is it not written in your law,
I said, Ye are gods? If he called them 35
gods, unto whom the word of God came
(and the scripture cannot be broken), say 36
ye of him, whom the Father ¹ sanctified
and sent into the world, Thou blasphem-
est; because I said, I am *the* Son of God?
If I do not the works of my Father, be- 37
lieve me not. But if I do them, though 38
ye believe not me, believe the works: that
ye may know and understand that the
Father is in me, and I in the Father.
They sought again to take him: and he 39
went forth out of their hand.

And he went away again beyond Jor- 40
dan into the place where John was at the
first baptizing; and there he abode. And 41
many came unto him; and they said, John
indeed did no sign: but all things whatsoever John spake of this man were true.
And many believed on him there.   42

§ 91. Woman healed in the Synagogue.

[Peræa.]

ᶜAnd he was teaching in one of the syn- 10
agogues on the sabbath day. And behold, 11
a woman who had a spirit of infirmity
eighteen years; and she was bowed together, and could in no wise lift herself up.
And when Jesus saw her, he called her, 12
and said to her, Woman, thou art loosed
from thine infirmity. And he laid his 13
hands upon her: and immediately she was
made straight, and glorified God. And 14
the ruler of the synagogue, being moved
with indignation because Jesus had healed
on the sabbath, answered and said to the
multitude, There are six days in which

KEY.—ᵃ Matthew, ᵇ Mark, ᶜ Luke, ᵈ John,

¹ Or, *consecrated.*

Luke 13.

men ought to work: in them therefore come and be healed, and not on the day of
15 the sabbath. But the Lord answered him, and said, Ye hypocrites, doth not each one of you on the sabbath loose his ox or his ass from the ¹ stall, and lead him away to
16 watering? And ought not this woman, being a daughter of Abraham, whom Satan had bound, lo, *these* eighteen years, to have been loosed from this bond on the day of
17 the sabbath? And as he said these things, all his adversaries were put to shame: and all the multitude rejoiced for all the glorious things that were done by him.

§ 92. Parables of the Kingdom of Heaven.

[Peræa.]

Luke 13.

18 ᶜHe said therefore, Unto what is the kingdom of God like? and whereunto
19 shall I liken it? It is like unto a grain of mustard seed, which a man took, and cast into his own garden; and it grew, and became a tree; and the birds of the heaven
20 lodged in the branches thereof. And again he said, Whereunto shall I liken the
21 kingdom of God? It is like unto leaven, which a woman took and hid in three ² measures of meal, till it was all leavened.
22 And he went on his way through cities and villages, teaching, and journeying on
23 unto Jerusalem. And one said unto him,
24 Lord, are they few that are saved? And he said unto them, Strive to enter in by the narrow door: for many, I say unto you, shall seek to enter in, and shall not be
25 ³ able. When once the master of the house is risen up, and hath shut to the door, and ye begin to stand without, and to knock at

KEY.—ᵃ Matthew, ᵇ Mark, ᶜ Luke, ᵈ John.

¹ Gr. *manger.*
² The word in the Greek denotes the Hebrew *seah*, a measure containing nearly a peck and a half.
³ Or, *able, when once.*

the door, saying, Lord, open to us; and he shall answer and say to you, I know you not whence ye are; then shall ye be- 26 gin to say, We did eat and drink in thy presence, and thou didst teach in our streets; and he shall say, I tell you, I know 27 not whence ye are; depart from me, all ye workers of iniquity. There shall be the 28 weeping and gnashing of teeth, when ye shall see Abraham, and Isaac, and Jacob, and all the prophets, in the kingdom of God, and yourselves cast forth without. And they shall come from the east and 29 west, and from the north and south, and shall [1] sit down in the kingdom of God. And behold, there are last who shall be 30 first, and there are first who shall be last.

§ 93. Lamentation over Jerusalem.

[Peræa.]

[c] In that very hour there came certain 31 Pharisees, saying to him, Get thee out, and go hence: for Herod would fain kill thee. And he said unto them, Go and say 32 to that fox, Behold, I cast out demons and perform cures to-day and to-morrow, and the third *day* [2] I am perfected. Howbeit I 33 must go on my way to-day and to-morrow and the *day* following: for it cannot be that a prophet perish out of Jerusalem. O Jerusalem, Jerusalem, that killeth the 34 prophets, and stoneth them that are sent unto her! how often would I have gather- ed thy children together, even as a hen *gathereth* her own brood under her wings, and ye would not! Behold, your house is 35 left unto you *desolate*: and I say unto you, Ye shall not see me until ye shall say, Blessed *is* he that cometh in the name of the Lord.

KEY.—[a] Matthew, [b] Mark, [c] Luke, [d] John.

[1] Gr. *recline*.   [2] Or, *I end my course*.

§ 94. Dining with a Pharisee.

Luke 14.

1 °And it came to pass, when he went into the house of one of the rulers of the Pharisees on a sabbath to eat bread, that they

2 were watching him. And behold, there was before him a certain man who had the

3 dropsy. And Jesus answering spake unto the lawyers and Pharisees, saying, Is it

4 lawful to heal on the sabbath or not? But they held there peace. And he took him,

5 and healed him, and let him go. And he said unto them, Which of you shall have ¹ an ass or an ox fallen into a well, and will not straightway draw him up on a sabbath

6 day? And they could not answer again unto these things.

§ 95. Supper Parables.

[Peræa.]

Luke 14.

7 °And he spake a parable unto those who were bidden, when he marked how they chose out the chief seats; saying unto

8 them, When thou art bidden of any man to a marriage feast, ² sit not down in the chief seat; lest haply a more honourable man

9 than thou be bidden of him, and he that bade thee and him shall come and say to thee, Give this man place; and then thou shalt begin with shame to take the lowest

10 place. But when thou art bidden, go and sit down in the lowest place; that when he that hath bidden thee cometh, he may say to thee, Friend, go up higher: then shalt thou have glory in the presence of all that

11 sit at meat with thee. For every one that exalteth himself shall be humbled; and he that humbleth himself shall be exalted.

12 And he said to him also that had bidden him, When thou makest a dinner or a supper, call not thy friends, nor thy breth-

KEY.—ª Matthew, ᵇ Mark, ° Luke, ᵈ John.

¹ Many ancient authorities read *a son.*

² Gr. *recline not.*

ren, nor thy kinsmen, nor rich neighbours; lest haply they also bid thee again, and a recompense be made thee.   But when 13 thou makest a feast, bid the poor, the mained, the lame, the blind : and thou shalt 14 be blessed ; because they have not *where-with* to recompense thee : for thou shalt be recompensed in the resurrection of the just.

And when one of them that sat at meat 15 with him heard these things, he said unto him, Blessed is he that shall eat bread in the kingdom of God.   But he said unto 16 him, A certain man made a great supper ; and he bade many : and he sent forth his 17 ¹ servant at supper time to say to them that were bidden, Come ; for *all* things are now ready.   And they all with one *consent* 18 began to make excuse.   The first said unto him, I have bought a field, and I must needs go out and see it ; I pray thee have me excused.   And another said, I have 19 bought five yoke of oxen, and I go to prove them : I pray thee have me excused. And another said, I have married a wife, 20 and therefore I cannot come.   And the 21 ¹ servant came, and told his lord these things.   Then the master of the house be-ing angry said to his ¹ servant, Go out quickly into the streets and lanes of the city, and bring in hither the poor and maimed and blind and lame.   And the ¹ ser- 22 vant said, Lord, what thou didst com-mand is done, and yet there is room. And the Lord said unto the ¹ servant, Go 23 out into the highways and hedges, and constrain *them* to come in, that my house may be filled.   For I say unto you, that 24 none of those men that were bidden shall taste of my supper.

KEY.—ᵃ Matthew, ᵇ Mark, ᶜ Luke, ᵈ John.

¹ Gr. *bondservant.*

§ 96. Cost of Discipleship.

Luke 14. [Peræa.]

25 Now there went with him great multitudes: and he turned, and said unto them,

26 If any man cometh unto me, and hateth
not his own father, and mother, and wife,
and children, and brethren, and sisters, yea,
and his own life also, he cannot be my

27 disciple. Whosoever doth not bear his
own cross, and come after me, cannot be

28 my disciple. For which of you, desiring
to build a tower, doth not first sit down
and count the cost, whether he have *where-*

29 *with* to complete it? Lest haply, when he
hath laid a foundation, and is not able to
finish, all that behold begin to mock him,

30 saying, This man began to build, and was

31 not able to finish. Or what king, as he
goeth to encounter another king in war,
will not sit down first and take counsel
whether he is able with ten thousand to
meet him that cometh against him with

32 twenty thousand? Or else, while the other
is yet a great way off, he sendeth an ambassage, and asketh conditions of peace.

33 So therefore whosoever he be of you that
renounceth not all that he hath, he cannot

34 be my disciple. Salt therefore is good:
but if even the salt have lost its savour,

35 wherewith shall it be seasoned? It is fit
neither for the land nor for the dunghill:
men cast it out. He that hath ears to hear,
let him hear.

§ 97. The Lost Sheep.

Luke 15. [Peræa.]

1 ^cNow all the publicans and sinners were

2 drawing near unto him for to hear him.
And both the Pharisees and the scribes
murmured, saying, This man receiveth sinners, and eateth with them.

3 ^cAnd he spake unto them this parable,

KEY.—ᵃ Matthew, ᵇ Mark, ᶜ Luke, ᵈ John.

Luke 15.

saying, What man of you, having a hun- 4
dred sheep, and having lost one of them,
doth not leave the ninety and nine in the
wilderness, and go after that which is lost,
until he find it? And when he hath found 5
it, he layeth it on his shoulders, rejoicing.
And when he cometh home, he calleth to- 6
gether his friends and his neighbours, saying unto them, Rejoice with me, for I have
found my sheep which was lost. I say un- 7
to you, that even so there shall be joy in
heaven over one sinner that repenteth,
more than over ninety and nine righteous
persons, that need no repentance.

§ 98. The Lost Coin.
[Peræa.]

Luke 15.

cOr what woman having ten ¹pieces of 8
silver, if she lose one piece, doth not light
the lamp, and sweep the house, and seek diligently until she find it? And when she 9
hath found it, she calleth together her
friends and neighbours, saying, Rejoice
with me, for I have found the piece which
I had lost. Even so, I say unto you, there 10
is joy in the presence of the angels of God
over one sinner that repenteth.

§ 99. The Prodigal Son.
[Peræa.]

Luke 15.

cAnd he said, A certain man had two 11
sons: and the younger of them said to his
father, Father, give me the portion of ² *thy* 12
substance that falleth to me. And he divided unto them his living. And not many 13
days after the younger son gathered all together, and took his journey into a far
country; and there he wasted his substance with riotous living. And when he 14
had spent all, there arose a mighty famine

KEY.—ᵃ Matthew, ᵇ Mark, ᶜ Luke, ᵈ John.

¹ Gr. *drachma*, a coin worth about eight pence.
² Gr. *the.*

in that country; and he began to be in
15 want.   And he went and joined himself to
one of the citizens of that country ; and he
16 sent him into his fields to feed swine. And
he would fain ¹have filled his belly with
²the husks that the swine did eat: and no
17 man gave unto him. But when he came to
himself he said, How many hired servants
of my father's have bread enough and to
18 spare, and I perish here with hunger !   I
will arise and go to my father, and will say
unto him, Father, I have sinned against
19 heaven, and in thy sight: I am no more
worthy to be called thy son: make me as
20 one of thy hired servants. And he arose,
and came to his father. But while he was
·yet afar off, his father saw him, and was
moved with compassion, and ran, and fell
21 on his neck, and ²kissed him. And the son
said unto him, Father, I have sinned
against heaven, and in thy sight: I am no
22 more worthy to be called thy son⁴.   But
the father said to his ⁵ servants, Bring forth
quickly the best robe, and put it on him ;
and put a ring on his hand, and shoes on
23 his feet: and bring the fatted calf, *and* kill
24 it, and let us eat, and make merry: for
this my son was dead, and is alive again;
he was lost, and is found. And they be-
25 gan to be merry. Now his elder son was
in the field : and as he came and drew nigh
to the house, he heard music and dancing.
26 And he called to him one of the ⁵servants,
and inquired what these things might be.
27 And he said unto him, Thy brother is
come; and thy father hath killed the fatted calf, because he hath received him

KEY.—ᵃ Matthew, ᵇ Mark, ᶜ Luke, ᵈ John.

¹ Many ancient authorities read *have been filled*.
² Gr. *the pods of the carob tree*.
³ Gr. *kissed him much*.
⁴ Some ancient authorities add *make me as one of thy hired
servants*.   See ver. 19.   ⁵ Gr. *bondservants*.

safe and sound. But he was angry, and 28 would not go in : and his father came out, and intreated him. But he answered and 29 said to his father, Lo, these many years do I serve thee, and I never transgressed a commandment of thine : and *yet* thou never gavest me a kid, that I might make merry with my friends : but when this thy son 30 came, who hath devoured thy living with harlots, thou killedst for him the fatted calf. And he said unto him, ' Son thou art 31 ever with me, and all that is mine is thine. But it was meet to make merry and be 32 glad : for this thy brother was dead, and is alive *again* ; and *was* lost, and is found.

§ 100. The Unjust Steward.

[Peræa.]

ᶜAnd he said also unto the disciples, 1 There was a certain rich man, who had a steward ; and the same was accused unto him that he was wasting his goods. And 2 he called him, and said unto him, What is this that I hear of thee ? render the account of thy stewardship ; for thou canst be no longer steward. And the steward said 3 within himself, What shall I do, seeing that my lord taketh away the stewardship from me ? I have not strength to dig ; to beg I am ashamed. I am resolved what to do, 4 that, when I am put out of the steward-ship, they may receive me into their houses. And calling to him each one of his 5 lord's debtors, he said to the first, How much owest thou unto my lord ? And he 6 said, A hundred ' measures of oil. And he said unto him, Take thy 'bond, and sit down quickly and write fifty. Then said 7 he to another, And how much owest thou ?

KEY.—ᵃ Matthew, ᵇ Mark, ᶜ Luke, ᵈ John.

¹ Gr. *Child.*
² Gr. *baths,* the bath being a Hebrew measure.
³ Gr. *writings.*

And he said, A hundred [1] measures of wheat. He saith unto him, Take thy
8 [2] bond, and write fourscore. And his lord commended [3] the unrighteous steward because he had done wisely: for the sons of this [4] world are for their own generation
9 wiser than the sons of the light. And I say unto you, Make to yourselves friends [5] by means of the mammon of unrighteousness; that, when it shall fail, they may receive you into the eternal tabernacles.
10 He that is faithful in a very little is faithful also in much: and he that is unrighteous in a very little is unrighteous also in much.
11 If therefore ye have not been faithful in the unrighteous mammon, who will commit
12 to your trust the true *riches*? And if ye have not been faithful in that which is another's, who will give you that which is
13 [6] your own? No [7] servant can serve two masters: for either he will hate the one, and love the other; or else he will hold to one, and despise the other. Ye cannot serve God and mammon.
14 And the Pharisees, who were lovers of money, heard all these things; and they
15 scoffed at him. And he said unto them, Ye are they that justify yourselves in the sight of men; but God knoweth your hearts: for that which is exalted among men is an abomination in the sight of God.
16 The law and the prophets *were* until John: from that time the gospel of the kingdom of God is preached, and every man enter-
17 eth violently into it. But it is easier for heaven and earth to pass away, than for

KEY.—[a] Matthew, [b] Mark, [c] Luke, [d] John.

[1] Gr. *cors*, the cor being a Hebrew measure.
[2] Gr. *writings*.
[3] Gr. *the steward of unrighteousness*.
[4] Or, *age*.   [5] Gr. *out of*.
[6] Some ancient authorities read *our own*.
[7] Gr. *household-servant*.

one tittle of the law to fall. Every one that 18
putteth away his wife, and marrieth another, committeth adultery: and he that
marrieth one that is put away from a husband committeth adultery.

§ 101. The Rich Man and Lazarus.

[Peræa.]

⁰Now there was a certain rich man, and 19
he was clothed in purple and fine linen,
¹faring sumptuously every day: and a 20
certain beggar named Lazarus was laid at
his gate, full of sores, and desiring to be 21
fed with the *crumbs* that fell from the rich
man's table; yea, even the dogs came and
licked his sores. And it came to pass, that 22
the beggar died, and that he was carried
away by the angels into Abraham's bosom:
and the rich man also died, and was buried.
And in Hades he lifted up his eyes, being 23
in torments, and seeth Abraham afar off,
and Lazarus in his bosom. And he cried 24
and said, Father Abraham, have mercy on
me, and send Lazarus, that he may dip the
tip of his finger in water, and cool my
tongue; for I am in anguish in this flame.
But Abraham said, ²Son, remember that 25
thou in thy lifetime receivedst thy good
things, and Lazarus in like manner evil
things: but now here he is comforted, and
thou art in anguish. And ³beside all this, 26
between us and you there is a great gulf
fixed, that they who would pass from hence
to you may not be able, and that none may
cross over from thence to us. And he said, 27
I pray thee therefore, father, that thou
wouldest send him to my father's house;
for I have five brethren; that he may testi- 28
fy unto them, lest they also come into this

KEY.—ᵃ Matthew, ᵇ Mark, ᶜ Luke, ᵈ John.
¹ Or, *living in mirth and splendour every day.*
² Gr. *Child.*   ³ Or, *in all these things.*

Luke 16.

29 place of torment.   But Abraham saith,
  They have Moses and the prophets; let
30 them hear them.   And he said, Nay, father
  Abraham : but if one go to them from the
31 dead, they will repent.   And he said unto
  him, If they hear not Moses and the prophets, neither will they be persuaded, if
  one rise from the dead.

§ 102.   Occasions of Stumbling.

[Peræa.]

Luke 17.

1   ᶜAnd he said unto his disciples, It is impossible but that occasions of stumbling
  should come : but woe unto him, through
2 whom they come!   It were well for him
  if a millstone were hanged about his neck,
  and he were thrown into the sea, rather
  than that he should cause one of these little
3 ones to stumble.   Take heed to yourselves :
  if thy brother sin, rebuke him ; and if he
4 repent, forgive him.   And if he sin against
  thee seven times in the day, and seven
  times turn again to thee, saying, I repent ;
  thou shalt forgive him.

5   And the apostles said unto the Lord, In-
6 crease our faith.   And the Lord said, If ye
  had faith as a grain of mustard seed, ye
  would say unto this sycamine tree, Be thou
  rooted up, and be thou planted in the sea ;
7 and it would obey you.   But who is there
  of you, having a ¹servant plowing or keeping sheep, that will say unto him, when he
  is come in from the field, Come straight-
8 way and sit down to meat ; and will not
  rather say unto him, Make ready wherewith I may sup, and gird thyself, and serve
  me, till I have eaten and drunken ; and af-
9 terward thou shalt eat and drink ?   Doth
  he thank the ¹servant because he did the
10 things that were commanded ?   Even so ye

KEY.—ᵃ Matthew, ᵇ Mark, ᶜ Luke, ᵈ John.

¹ Gr. *bondservant.*

Luke 17.

also, when ye shall have done all the things that are commanded you, say, We are unprofitable ¹ servants; we have done that which it was our duty to do.

§ 103.   Resurrection of Lazarus.

[Bethany.]

John 11.

ᵈ Now a certain man was sick, Lazarus of 1 Bethany, of the village of Mary and her sister Martha.   And it was that Mary who 2 anointed the Lord with ointment, and wiped his feet with her hair, whose brother Lazarus was sick.   The sisters therefore 3 sent unto him, saying, Lord, behold, he whom thou lovest is sick.   But when Je- 4 sus heard it, he said, This sickness is not unto death, but for the glory of God, that the Son of God may be glorified thereby. Now Jesus loved Martha, and her sister, 5 and Lazarus.   When therefore he heard 6 that he was sick, he abode at that time two days in the place where he was.   Then af- 7 ter this he saith to the disciples, Let us go into Judæa again.   The disciples say unto 8 him, Rabbi, the Jews were but now seeking to stone thee; and goest thou thither again?   Jesus answered, Are there not 9 twelve hours in the day?   If a man walk in the day, he stumbleth not, because he seeth the light of this world.   But if a man 10 walk in the night, he stumbleth, because the light is not in him.   These things spake 11 he: and after this he saith unto them, Our friend Lazarus is fallen asleep; but I go, that I may awake him out of sleep.   The 12 disciples therefore said unto him, Lord, if he is fallen asleep, he will ² recover.   Now 13 Jesus had spoken of his death: but they thought that he spake of taking rest in sleep.   Then Jesus therefore said unto 14

KEY.—ᵃ Matthew, ᵇ Mark, ᶜ Luke, ᵈ John.

¹ Gr. *bondservants.*   ² Gr. *be saved.*

John 11.

15 them plainly, Lazarus is dead.   And I am
glad for your sakes that I was not there,
to the intent ye may believe ; nevertheless
16 let us go unto him. Thomas therefore, who
is called ¹ Didymus, said unto his fellow-
disciples, Let us also go, that we may die
with him.

17   So when Jesus came, he found that he
had been in the tomb four days already.
18 Now Bethany was nigh unto Jerusalem,
19 about fifteen furlongs off ; and many of the
Jews had come to Martha and Mary, to
console them concerning their brother.
20 Martha therefore, when she heard that Jesus was coming, went and met him : but
21 Mary still sat in the house.   Martha therefore said unto Jesus, Lord, if thou hadst
22 been here, my brother had not died.   And
even now I know that, whatsoever thou
shalt ask of God, God will give thee.
23 Jesus saith unto her, Thy brother shall rise
24 again.   Martha saith unto him, I know that
he shall rise again in the resurrection at
25 the last day.   Jesus said unto her, I am the
resurrection, and the life : he that believeth on me, though he die, yet shall he live :
26 and whosoever liveth and believeth on me
27 shall never die.   Believest thou this ? She
saith unto him, Yea, Lord : I have believed
that thou art the Christ, the Son of God,
28 *even* he that cometh into the world.   And
when she had said this, she went away, and
called Mary ² her sister secretly, saying,
The ³ Master is here, and calleth thee.
29 And she, when she heard it, arose quickly,
30 and went unto him. (Now Jesus was not
yet come into the village, but was still in
31 the place where Martha met him.)   The
Jews then who were with her in the house,
and were comforting her, when they saw

KEY.—ᵃ Matthew, ᵇ Mark. ᶜ Luke, ᵈ John.

¹ That is, *Twin.*   ² Or, *her sister, saying secretly.*
³ Or, *Teacher.*

Mary, that she rose up quickly and went out, followed her, supposing that she was going unto the tomb to [1] weep there. Mary 32 therefore, when she came where Jesus was, and saw him, fell down at his feet, saying unto him, Lord, if thou hadst been here, my brother had not died. When Jesus 33 therefore saw her [2] weeping, and the Jews *also* [2] weeping who came with her, he [3] groaned in the spirit, and [4] was troubled, and said, Where have ye laid him? They 34 say unto him, Lord, come and see. Jesus 35 wept. The Jews therefore said, Behold 36 how he loved him! But some of them 37 said, Could not this man, who opened the eyes of him that was blind, have caused that this man also should not die? Jesus 38 therefore again [5] groaning in himself cometh to the tomb. Now it was a cave, and a stone lay [6] against it. Jesus saith, Take 39 ye away the stone. Martha, the sister of him that was dead, saith unto him, Lord, by this time he stinketh: for he hath been *dead* four days. Jesus saith unto her, Said 40 I not unto thee, that, if thou believedst, thou shouldest see the glory of God? So 41 they took away the stone. And Jesus lifted up his eyes, and said, Father, I thank thee that thou heardest me. And I knew 42 that thou hearest me always: but because of the multitude which standeth around I said it, that they may believe that thou didst send me. And when he had thus 43 spoken, he cried with a loud voice, Lazarus, come forth. He that was dead came forth, 44 bound hand and foot with [7] grave-clothes; and his face was bound about with a nap-

KEY.—[a] Matthew, [b] Mark, [c] Luke, [d] John.

[1] Gr. *wail.*   [2] Gr. *wailing.*
[3] Or, *was moved with indignation in the spirit.*
[4] Gr. *troubled himself.*
[5] Or, *being moved with indignation in himself.*
[6] Or, *upon.*   [7] Or, *grave-bands.*

John 11.

kin. Jesus saith unto them, Loose him, and let him go.

45 Many therefore of the Jews, who came to Mary and beheld [1] that which he did,
46 believed on him. But some of them went away to the Pharisees, and told them the things which Jesus had done.

§ 104. Conspiracy against Jesus.

[Jerusalem.]

John 11.

47 [d] The chief priests therefore and the Pharisees gathered a council, and said, What do we? for this man doeth many
48 signs. If we let him thus alone, all men will believe on him : and the Romans will come and take away both our place and
49 our nation. But a certain one of them, Caiaphas, being high priest that year, said
50 unto them, Ye know nothing at all, nor do ye take account that it is expedient for you that one man should die for the people, and that the whole nation perish not.
51 Now this he said not of himself : but being high priest that year, he prophesied that
52 Jesus should die for the nation ; and not for the nation only, but that he might also gather together into one the children of
53 God that are scattered abroad. So from that day forth they took counsel that they might put him to death.
54 Jesus therefore walked no more openly among the Jews, but departed thence into the country near to the wilderness, into a city called Ephraim : and there he tarried
55 with the disciples. Now the passover of the Jews was at hand : and many went up to Jerusalem out of the country before the
56 passover, to purify themselves. They sought therefore for Jesus, and spake one with another, as they stood in the temple,

KEY.—[a] Matthew, [b] Mark, [c] Luke, [d] John.

[1] Many ancient authorities read *the things which he did.*

What think ye? That he will not come to
the feast? Now the chief priests and the 57
Pharisees had given commandment, that,
if any man knew where he was, he should
shew it, that they might take him.

§ 105. Ten Lepers Cleansed.

[Border of Samaria.]

Luke 17.

ᶜAnd it came to pass, ¹ as they were on 11
the way to Jerusalem, that he was passing
² along the borders of Samaria and Galilee.
And as he entered into a certain village, 12
there met him ten men that were lepers,
who stood afar off : and they lifted up their 13
voices, saying, Jesus, Master, have mercy
on us. And when he saw them, he said 14
unto them, Go and shew yourselves unto
the priests. And it came to pass, as they
went, they were cleansed. And one of 15
them, when he saw that he was healed,
turned back, with a loud voice glorifying
God ; and he fell upon his face at his feet, 16
giving him thanks : and he was a Samaritan. And Jesus answering said, Were not 17
the ten cleansed? but where are the nine?
³ Were there none found that returned to 18
give glory to God, save this ⁴ stranger?
And he said unto him, Arise, and go thy 19
way : thy faith hath ⁵ made thee whole.

§ 106. Coming of the Kingdom of God.

[Galilee.]

Luke 17.

ᶜAnd being asked by the Pharisees, when 20
the kingdom of God cometh, he answered
them and said, The kingdom of God cometh not with observation : neither shall they 21
say, Lo, here! or, There! for lo, the kingdom of God is ⁶ within you.

KEY.—ᵃ Matthew, ᵇ Mark, ᶜ Luke, ᵈ John.

¹ Or, *as he was.*   ² Or, *through the midst of.*
³ Or, *There were none found . . . save this stranger.*
⁴ Or, *alien.*   ⁵ Or, *saved thee.*
⁶ Or, *in the midst of you.*

Luke 17.

22   And he said unto the disciples, The days
will come, when ye shall desire to see one
of the days of the Son of man, and ye shall
23 not see it.   And they shall say to you, Lo,
there! Lo, here! go not away, nor follow
24 after *them*: for as the lightning, when it
lighteneth out of the one part under the
heaven, shineth unto the other part under
heaven; so shall the Son of man be [1] in his
25 day.   But first must he suffer many things
26 and be rejected of this generation.   And
as it came to pass in the days of Noah,
even so shall it be also in the days of the
27 Son of man.   They ate, they drank, they
married, they were given in marriage, until the day that Noah entered into the ark,
and the flood came, and destroyed them all.
28 Likewise even as it came to pass in the
days of Lot; they ate, they drank, they
bought, they sold, they planted, they
29 builded; but in the day that Lot went out
from Sodom it rained fire and brimstone
30 from heaven, and destroyed them all: after
the same manner shall it be in the day that
31 the Son of man is revealed.   In that day,
he who shall be on the housetop, and his
goods in the house, let him not go down
to take them away: and let him that is in
32 the field likewise not return back.   Re-
33 member Lot's wife.   Whosoever shall seek
to gain his life shall lose it: but whosoever
34 shall lose *his life* shall [2] preserve it.   I say
unto you, In that night there shall be two
men on one bed; the one shall be taken,
35 and the other shall be left.   There shall be
two women grinding together; the one
shall be taken, and the other shall be left.

KEY.—[a] Matthew, [b] Mark, [c] Luke, [d] John.

[1] Some ancient authorities omit *in his day*.
[2] Gr. *save it alive*.
[3] Some ancient authorities add ver. 36 *There shall be two
men in the field; the one shall be taken, and the other shall be
left.*

And they answering say unto him, Where, 37
Lord? And he said unto them, Where the
body *is*, thither will the ¹eagles also be
gathered together.

§ 107. The Unjust Judge.

[Galilee.]

ᶜAnd he spake a parable unto them to 1
the end that they ought always to pray,
and not to faint; saying, There was in a 2
city a judge, who feared not God, and re-
garded not man: and there was a widow 3
in that city; and she came oft unto him,
saying, ²Avenge me of mine adversary.
And he would not for a while: but after- 4
ward he said within himself, Though I fear
not God, nor regard man; yet because this 5
widow troubleth me, I will avenge her,
³lest she ⁴wear me out by her continual
coming. And the Lord said, Hear what 6
⁵the unrighteous judge saith. And shall 7
not God avenge his elect, who cry to him
day and night, ⁶and *yet* he is longsuffering
over them? I say unto you, that he will 8
avenge them speedily. Howbeit when the
Son of man cometh, shall he find ⁷faith on
the earth?

§ 108. Pharisee and Publican.

[Galilee.]

ᶜAnd he spake also this parable unto cer- 9
tain who trusted in themselves that they
were righteous, and set ⁸all others at
nought: Two men went up into the tem- 10
ple to pray; the one a Pharisee, and the
other a publican. The Pharisee stood and 11

KEY.—ᵃ Matthew, ᵇ Mark, ᶜ Luke, ᵈ John.

¹ Or, *vultures.*
² Or, *Do me justice of*: and so in ver. 5, 7, 8.
³ Or, *lest at last by her coming she wear me out.*
⁴ Gr. *bruise.*   ⁵ Gr. *the judge of unrighteousness.*
⁶ Or, *and is he slow to punish on their behalf?*
⁷ Or, *the faith.*   ⁸ Or, *the rest.*

§ 109. Divorce.

Mark's Account.

And he arose from thence, and cometh into the borders 1
of Judæa and beyond Jordan: and multitudes came together unto him again; and, as he was wont, he taught
them again.   And there came unto him Pharisees, and 2
asked him, Is it lawful for a man to put away *his* wife?
trying him.   And he answered and said unto them, What 3
did Moses command you? And they said, Moses suffered 4
to write a bill of divorcement, and to put her away.
But Jesus said unto them, For your hardness of heart he 5
wrote you this commandment.   From the beginning of 6
the creation, Male and female made he them.   For this 7
cause shall a man leave his father and mother, and shall
cleave to his wife; and the twain shall become one flesh: 8
so that they are no more twain, but one flesh.   What there- 9
fore God hath joined together, let not man put asunder.
And in the house the disciples asked him again of this 10
matter.   And he saith unto them, Whosoever shall put 11
away his wife, and marry another, committeth adultery
against her: and if she herself shall put away her husband, 12
and marry another, she committeth adultery.

157

Luke 18.

prayed thus with himself, God, I thank
thee, that I am not as the rest of men, ex-
tortioners, unjust, adulterers, or even as
12 this publican. I fast twice in the week; I
13 give tithes of all that I get. But the publican, standing afar off, would not lift up so
much as his eyes unto heaven, but smote
his breast, saying, God, [1] be merciful to me
14 [2] a sinner. I say unto you, This man went
down to his house justified rather than the
other: for every one that exalteth himself
shall be humbled; but he that humbleth
himself shall be exalted.

1 **Matthew 19.** [a]And it came to pass when
Jesus had finished these words, he [b] arose
from thence, and [a] departed from Galilee,
and came into the borders of Judæa be-
2 yond Jordan; and great multitudes followed him; and he healed them there;
[b] and as he was wont, he taught them.

§ 109. Divorce.

Matthew 19. [Peræa.]

3 [a]And there came unto him [2]Pharisees,
trying him, and saying, Is it lawful *for a
man* to put away his wife for every cause?
4 And he answered and said, Have ye not
read, that he who [4] made *them* from the beginning [b] of the creation [a] made them male
5 and female, and said, For this cause shall a
man leave his father and mother, and shall
cleave to his wife; and the twain shall be-
6 come one flesh? So that they are no
more twain, but one flesh. What therefore God hath joined together, let not man
7 put asunder. They say unto him, Why
then did Moses command to give a bill of
8 divorcement, and to put *her* away? He
saith unto them, Moses for your hardness

KEY.—[a] Matthew, [b] Mark, [c] Luke, [d] John.

[1] Or, *be propitiated.* [2] Or, *the sinner.*
[3] Many authorities, some ancient, insert *the.*
[4] Some ancient authorities read *created.*

of heart suffered you to put away your
wives : but from the beginning it hath
not been so. And I say unto you, Whoso- 9
ever shall put away his wife, [1] except for
fornication, and shall marry another, committeth adultery [b] against her : [a] [2] and he
that marrieth her when she is put away
committeth adultery ; [b] and if she herself
shall put away her husband and marry another, she committeth adultery. [a] The dis- 10
ciples say unto him, If the case of the man
is so with his wife, it is not expedient to
marry. But he said unto them, All men 11
cannot receive this saying, but they to
whom it is given. For there are eunuchs, 12
that were so born from their mother's
womb : and there are eunuchs, that were
made eunuchs by men : and there are eunuchs, that made themselves eunuchs for
the kingdom of heaven's sake. He that is
able to receive it, let him receive it.

§ 110. Little Children Received.

[Peraea.]

[a] Then were there brought unto him 13
little children, [c] and also their babes, [a] that
he should lay his hands on them, and pray :
and the disciples rebuked [b] those that
brought [a] them. But [b] when Jesus saw it, 14
he was moved with indignation, and said
unto them, [a] Suffer the little children, and
forbid them not, to come unto me : for [a] to
such belongeth the kingdom of heaven.
[b] Verily I say unto you, Whosoever shall
not receive the kingdom of God as a little
child, he shall in no wise enter therein.
[a] And he [b] took them in his arms and 15

KEY.—[a] Matthew, [b] Mark, [c] Luke, [d] John.

[1] Some ancient authorities read *saving for the cause of fornication, maketh her an adulteress.*

[2] The following words, to the end of the verse, are omitted
by some ancient authorities.

[3] Or, *of such is.*

§ 110. Little Children Received.

Mark's Account.

Chap. 10.

13 And they were bringing unto him little children, that he
14 should teach them: and the disciples rebuked them. But
   when Jesus saw it, he was moved with indignation, and
   said unto them, Suffer the little children to come unto me;
   forbid them not: for to such belongeth the kingdom of God.
15 Verily I say unto you, Whosoever shall not receive the
   kingdom of God as a little child, he shall in no wise enter
16 therein. And he took them in his arms, and blessed them,
   laying his hands upon them.

Luke's Account.

Chap. 18.

15 And they were bringing unto him also their babes, that
   he should touch them: but when the disciples saw it, they
16 rebuked them. But Jesus called them unto him, saying,
   Suffer the little children to come unto me, and forbid them
17 not: for to such belongeth the kingdom of God. Verily
   I say unto you, Whosoever shall not receive the kingdom
   of God as a little child, he shall in no wise enter therein.

§ 111. The Young Ruler.

Mark's Account.

And as he was going forth into the way, there ran one to 17 him, and kneeled to him, and asked him, Good Master, what shall I do that I may inherit eternal life? And 18 Jesus said unto him, Why callest thou me good? none is good save one, *even* God. Thou knowest the com- 19 mandments, Do not kill, Do not commit adultery, Do not steal, Do not bear false witness, Do not defraud, Honour thy father and mother. And he said unto him, Mas- 20 ter, all these things have I observed from my youth. And Jesus looking upon him loved him, and said unto 21 him, One thing thou lackest: go, sell whatsoever thou hast, and give to the poor, and thou shalt have treasure in heaven: and come, follow me. But his countenance 22 fell at the saying, and he went away sorrowful: for he was one that had great possessions.

Luke's Account.

And a certain ruler asked him, saying, Good Master, 18 what shall I do to inherit eternal life? And Jesus said 19 unto him, Why callest thou me good? none is good, save one, *even* God. Thou knowest the commandments, Do 20 not commit adultery, Do not kill, Do not steal, do not bear false witness, Honour thy father and mother. And he 21 said, All these things have I observed from my youth up.

And when Jesus heard it, he said unto him, One thing 22 thou lackest yet: sell all that thou hast, and distribute unto the poor, and thou shalt have treasure in heaven: and come, follow me. But when he heard these things, 23 he became exceeding sorrowful; for he was very rich.

Matthew 19.
blessed them, [and] * ᵃ laid his hands on
them, and departed thence.

§ 111. The Young Ruler.

[Peræa.]

Matthew 19.
16 ᵃAnd ᵇas he was going forth into the
way ᶜa certain ruler ᵇ ran and kneeled to
him, ᵃand said, ᵇGood ᵃ¹ Master, what good
thing shall I do, that I may have eternal
17 life? And he said unto him, ᵃ Why askest
thou me concerning that which is good?
ᵇ Why callest thou me Good? ᵃ One there
is who is good, ᵇ even God : ᵃ but if thou
wouldest enter into life, keep the command-
18 ments. He saith unto him, Which? And
Jesus said, Thou shalt not kill, Thou shalt
not commit adultery, Thou shalt not steal,
19 Thou shalt not bear false witness, Honour
thy father and thy mother : and, Thou
20 shalt love thy neighbour as thyself. The
young man saith unto him, All these things
have I observed ᵇfrom my youth ᶜup;
21 ᵃ what lack I yet? Jesus ᵇlooking upon
him loved him, and ᵃsaid unto him, If
thou wouldest be perfect, go, sell that
thou hast, and give to the poor, and
thou shalt have treasure in heaven :
22 and come, follow me. But when the
young man heard the saying, he went
away sorrowful ; for he was one that had
great possessions.

§ 112. Riches and the Kingdom.

[Peræa.]

Matthew 19.
23 ᵃAnd Jesus ᵇ looked round about and
ᵃ said unto his disciples, Verily I say unto
you, It is hard for a rich man to enter into

KEY.—ᵃ Matthew, ᵇ Mark, ᶜ Luke, ᵈ John.

¹ Or, *Teacher.*

² Some ancient authorities read *Why callest thou me good?*
None is good save one, even *God.*

* Word inserted by compiler.

the kingdom of heaven.   ^bAnd the disciples were amazed at his words.   But Jesus
answereth again, and saith unto them,
Children, how hard is it for them that
trust in riches to enter into the kingdom
of God.   ^aAnd again I say unto you, It is 24
easier for a camel to go through a needle's
eye, than for a rich man to enter into the
kingdom of God.   And when the disciples 25
heard it, they were astonished exceedingly, saying, Who then can be saved?   And 26
Jesus looking upon *them* said to them,
With men this is impossible; but with
God all things are possible.   Then an- 27
swered Peter and said unto him, Lo, we
have left all, and followed thee; what then
shall we have?   And Jesus said unto them, 28
Verily I say unto you, that ye who have
followed me, in the regeneration when the
Son of man shall sit on the throne of his
glory, ye also shall sit upon twelve thrones,
judging the twelve tribes of Israel.   And 29
every one that hath left houses, or brethren,
or sisters, or father, or mother,' or children, or lands, for my name's sake, shall
receive ^a a hundredfold, ^b now in this time
with persecutions; ^a and shall inherit eternal life ^b in the world to come.   ^aBut 30
many shall be last *that are* first; and first
that are last.

§ 113.   Labourers in the Vineyard.
[Peræa.]

^a For the kingdom of heaven is like unto a 1
man that was a householder, who went out
early in the morning to hire labourers into
his vineyard.   And when he had agreed 2
with the labourers for a ^a shilling a day,
he sent them into his vineyard.   And he 3

KEY.—^a Matthew, ^b Mark, ^c Luke, ^d John.

¹ Many ancient authorities add *or wife.*
² Some ancient authorities read *manifold.*
³ About eightpence halfpenny.

§ 112. Riches and the Kingdom.

Mark's Account.

Chap. 10.

23 And Jesus looked round about, and saith unto his disciples, How hardly shall they that have riches enter into
24 the kingdom of God ! And the disciples were amazed at
his words. But Jesus answereth again, and saith unto
them, Children, how hard is it for them that trust in
25 riches to enter into the kingdom of God ! It is easier for
a camel to go through a needle's eye, than for a rich man
26 to enter into the kingdom of God. And they were
astonished exceedingly, saying unto him, Then who can
27 be saved ? Jesus looking upon them saith, With men it
is impossible, but not with God : for all things are possible
28 with God. Peter began to say unto him, Lo, we have left
29 all, and have followed thee. Jesus said, Verily I say unto
you, There is no man that hath left house, or brethren,
or sisters, or mother, or father, or children, or lands, for
30 my sake, and for the gospel's sake, but he shall receive a
hundredfold now in this time, houses, and brethren,
and sisters, and mothers, and children, and lands, with
31 persecutions ; and in the world to come eternal life. But
many *that are* first shall be last ; and the last first.

Luke's Account.

Chap. 18.

24 And Jesus seeing him said, How hardly shall they that
25 have riches enter into the kingdom of God ! For it
is easier for a camel to enter in through a needle's eye,
26 than a rich man to enter into the kingdom of God. And
27 they that heard it said, Then who can be saved ? But he
said, The things which are impossible with men are pos-
28 sible with God. And Peter said, Lo, we have left our
29 own, and followed thee. And he said unto them, Verily
I say unto you, There is no man that hath left house, or
or wife, or brethren, or parents, or children, for the king-
30 dom of God's sake, who shall not receive manifold more
in this time, and in the world to come eternal life.

§ 113. Laborers in the Vineyard.

Mark's Account.

Chap. 10.

And they were in the way, going up to Jerusalem ; and 32 Jesus was going before them : and they were amazed ; and they that followed were afraid. And he took again the twelve, and began to tell them the things that were to happen unto him, *saying*, Behold, we go up to Jerusalem ; 33 and the Son of man shall be delivered unto the chief priests and the scribes ; and they shall condemn him to death, and shall deliver him unto the Gentiles : and they 34 shall mock him, and shall spit upon him, and shall scourge him, and shall kill him ; and after three days he shall rise again.

Luke's Account.

Chap. 18.

And he took unto him the twelve, and said unto them, 31 Behold, we go up to Jerusalem, and all the things that are written through the prophets shall be accomplished unto the Son of man. For he shall be delivered up unto the 32 Gentiles, and shall be mocked, and shamefully entreated, and spit upon : and they shall scourge and kill him: and 33 the third day he shall rise again. And they understood 34 none of these things ; and this saying was hid from them, and they perceived not the things that were said.

Matthew 20.

went out about the third hour, and saw others standing in the marketplace idle;

4 and to them he said, Go ye also into the vineyard, and whatsoever is right I will give you. And they went their way.

5 Again he went out about the sixth and the

6 ninth hour, and did likewise. And about the eleventh *hour* he went out, and found others standing ; and he saith unto them,

7 Why stand ye here all the day idle? They say unto him, Because no man hath hired us. He saith unto them, Go ye also into

8 the vineyard. And when even was come, the lord of the vineyard saith unto his steward, Call the labourers, and pay them their hire, beginning from the last unto

9 the first. And when they came that *were hired* about the eleventh hour, they re-

10 ceived every man a ¹shilling. And when the first came, they supposed that they would receive more; and they likewise re-

11 ceived every man a ¹shilling. And when they received it, they murmured against

12 the householder, saying, These last have spent *but* one hour, and thou hast made them equal unto us, who have borne the burden of the day and the ²scorching heat.

13 But he answered and said to one of them, Friend, I do thee no wrong : didst not thou

14 agree with me for a ¹shilling? Take up that which is thine, and go thy way ; it is my will to give unto this last, even as unto

15 thee. Is it not lawful for me to do what I will with mine own? or is thine eye evil,

16 because I am good? So the last shall be first, and the first last.

17 And as Jesus was going up to Jerusalem, he took the twelve disciples apart ; ᵇand they were amazed : and they that followed were afraid. ᵃAnd in the way he

KEY.—ᵃ Matthew, ᵇ Mark, ᶜ Luke, ᵈ John.

¹ About eightpence halfpenny.   ² Or, *hot wind.*

Matthew 20.

said unto them, Behold, we go up to Jeru- 18
salem, ᶜand all the things that are written
through the prophets shall be accomplished; ᵃand the Son of man shall be delivered unto the chief priests and scribes;
and they shall condemn him to death, and 19
shall deliver him unto the Gentiles to
mock, and to scourge, and to crucify; ᶜand
[he] * shall be mocked, and shamefully entreated, and spit upon; and they shall
scourge and kill him, ᵃand the third day
he shall be raised up. ᶜAnd they understood none of these things; and this saying was hid from them, and they perceived not the things that were said.†

§ 114. Ambition Rebuked.‡

[Peræa.]   **Matthew 20.**

ᵃThen came to him the mother of the 20
sons of Zebedee with her sons, ᵇJames and
John, ᵃworshipping *him*, and asking a certain thing of him. And he said unto her, 21
What wouldest thou? She saith unto
him, Command that these my two sons
may sit, one on thy right hand, and one
on thy left hand, in thy kingdom. But 22
Jesus answered and said, Ye know not
what ye ask. Are ye able to drink the
cup that I am about to drink? They say
unto him, We are able. He saith unto 23
them, My cup indeed ye shall drink : but
to sit on my right hand, and on *my* left
hand, is not mine to give, but *it is for them*
for whom it hath been prepared of my
Father. And when the ten heard it, they 24
were moved with indignation concerning

KEY.—ᵃ Matthew, ᵇ Mark. ᶜ Luke. ᵈ John.

* Word inserted by compiler.

† This warning is very similar in language to one given
soon after the transfiguration   See § 69

‡ Mark speaks of James and John as addressing Jesus.
Doubtless the mother spoke for them, and thus both narratives are correct—the one naming the agent, the other the
principals

§ 114. Ambition Rebuked.

Mark's Account.

Chap. 10.

35 And there come near unto him <u>James and John,</u> the sons of Zebedee, saying unto him, Master, we would that thou shouldest do for us whatsoever we shall ask of thee.
36 And he said unto them, What would ye that I should do
37 for you? And they said unto him, Grant unto us that we may sit, one on thy right hand, and one on *thy* left
38 hand, in thy glory. But Jesus said unto them, Ye know not what ye ask. Are ye able to drink the cup that I drink? or to be baptized with the baptism that I am
39 baptized with? And they said unto him, We are able. And Jesus said unto them, The cup that I drink ye shall drink; and with the baptism that I am baptized withal
40 shall ye be baptized: but to sit on my right hand or on *my* left hand is not mine to give: but *it is for them* for
41 whom it hath been prepared. And when the ten heard it, they began to be moved with indignation concerning <u>James</u>
42 and John. And Jesus called them to him, and saith unto them, Ye know that they who are accounted to rule over the Gentiles lord it over them; and their great ones exer-
43 cise authority over them. But it is not so among you: but whosoever would become great among you, shall be
44 your minister: and whosoever would be first among you,
45 shall be servant of all. For the Son of man also came not to be ministered unto, but to minister, and to give his life a ransom for many.

162

§ 115. The Blind Man at Jericho.

Matthew's Account.

And as they went out from Jericho, a great multitude 29
followed him. And behold, two blind men sitting by the 30
way side, when they heard that Jesus was <u>passing by</u>, cried
out, saying, Lord, have mercy on us, thou son of David.
And the multitude rebuked them, that they should hold 31
their peace: but they cried out the more, saying, <u>Lord,</u>
have mercy on us, thou son of David. And Jesus stood 32
still, and called them, and said, What will ye that I should
do unto you? They say unto him, Lord, that our eyes 33
may be opened. And Jesus, being moved with compas- 34
sion, touched their eyes: and straightway they received
their sight, and followed him.

Luke's Acccount.

And it came to pass, as he drew nigh into Jericho, a cer- 35
tain blind man sat by the way side <u>begging</u> : and hearing a 36
multitude going by, he inquired what this meant. And 37
they told him, that Jesus of Nazareth passeth by. And 38
he cried, saying, Jesus, thou son of David, have mercy on
me. And they <u>that went before</u> rebuked him, that he 39
should hold his peace : but he cried out the more a great
deal, Thou son of David, have mercy on me. And Jesus 40
stood, and commanded him to be brought unto him : and
when he was come near, he asked him, What wilt thou 41
that I should do unto thee? And he said, Lord, that I
may receive my sight. And Jesus said unto him, <u>Receive</u> 42
<u>thy sight</u> : thy faith hath made thee whole. And imme- 43
<u>diately he received his sight, and followed him, glorify-
ing God: and all the people, when they saw it, gave praise
unto God.</u>

Matthew 20.

25 the two brethren, [b] James and John. [a] But
Jesus called them unto him, and said, Ye
know that the rulers of the Gentiles lord it
over them, and their great ones exercise
26 authority over them. Not so shall it be
among you : but whosoever would become
great among you shall be your [1] minister;
27 and whosoever would be first among you
28 shall be your [2] servant : even as the Son of
man came not to be ministered unto, but to
minister, and to give his life a ransom for
many.

§ 115. The Blind Man at Jericho.[*]

Mark 10.

46   [b] And they came to Jericho : and as he
went out from Jericho, with his disciples
and a great multitude, the son of Timæus,
Bartimæus, a blind beggar, was sitting by
47 the way side [c] begging. [b] And when he
heard that it was Jesus of Nazareth [a] passing by, [b] he began to cry out, and say,
Jesus, thou son of David, have mercy on
48 me. And many [c] that went before [b] rebuked him, that he should hold his peace :
but he cried out the more a great deal,
[a] Lord, [b] thou son of David, have mercy
49 on me. And Jesus stood still, and said,
Call ye him. And they call the blind
man, saying unto him, Be of good cheer :
50 rise, he calleth thee. And he, casting
away his garment, sprang up, and came
51 to Jesus. And Jesus answered him, and
said, What wilt thou that I should do unto
thee? And the blind man said unto him,
[2] Rabboni, that I may receive my sight.
52 And Jesus said unto him, [c] Receive thy
sight ; [b] go thy way ; thy faith hath [4] made

KEY.—[a] Matthew, [b] Mark, [c] Luke, [d] John.

[1] Or, *servant.*   [2] Gr. *bondservant.*
[3] Or, *Teacher.*   [4] Or, *saved thee.*

[*] Matthew speaks of two blind men; doubtless Bartimæus
the spokesman, and another less prominent.

thee whole. And straightway he received
his sight, and followed him in the way,
°glorifying God : and all the people when
they saw it, gave praise unto God.

§ 116. Zacchæus.

Luke 19.

°And he entered and was passing through 1
Jericho. And behold, a man called by 2
name Zacchæus; and he was a chief publican, and he was rich. And he sought to 3
see Jesus who he was ; and could not for
the crowd, because he was little of stature.
And he ran on before, and climbed up in- 4
to a sycomore tree to see him : for he was
to pass that way. And when Jesus came 5
to the place, he looked up, and said unto
him, Zacchæus, make haste, and come
down; for to-day I must abide at thy
house. And he made haste, and came down, 6
and received him joyfully. And when 7
they saw it, they all murmured, saying, He
is gone in to lodge with a man that is a
sinner. And Zacchæus stood, and said 8
unto the Lord, Behold, Lord, the half of
my goods I give to the poor; and if I
have wrongfully exacted aught of any
man, I restore fourfold. And Jesus said 9
unto him, To-day is salvation come to this
house, forasmuch as he also is a son of
Abraham. For the Son of man came to 10
seek and to save that which was lost.

§ 117. Parable of the Pounds.

[Jericho.]

Luke 19.

°And as they heard these things, he 11
added and spake a parable, because he was
nigh to Jerusalem, and *because* they supposed that the kingdom of God was immediately to appear. He said therefore, 12
A certain nobleman went into a far country, to receive for himself a kingdom, and

KEY.—ᵃ Matthew, ᵇ Mark, ᶜ Luke, ᵈ John.

13 to return. And he called ten [1] servants of his, and gave them ten [2] pounds, and said unto them, Trade ye *herewith* till I come.

14 But his citizens hated him, and sent an ambassage after him, saying, We will not

15 that this man reign over us. And it came to pass, when he was come back again, having received the kingdom, that he commanded these [1] servants, unto whom he had given the money, to be called to him, that he might know what they had

16 gained by trading. And the first came before him, saying, Lord, thy pound hath

17 made ten pounds more. And he said unto him, Well done, thou good [3] servant: because thou wast found faithful in a very little, have thou authority over ten cities.

18 And the second came, saying, Thy pound,

19 Lord, hath made five pounds. And he said unto him also, Be thou also over five

20 cities. And [4] another came, saying, Lord, behold, *here is* thy pound, which I kept

21 laid up in a napkin: for I feared thee, because thou art an austere man: thou takest up that thou layedst not down, and

22 reapest that thou didst not sow. He saith unto him, Out of thine own mouth will I judge thee, thou wicked [3] servant. Thou knewest that I am an austere man, taking up that I laid not down, and reaping that

23 I did not sow; then wherefore gavest thou not my money into the bank, and [5] I at my coming should have required it with inter-

24 est? And he said unto them that stood by, Take away from him the pound, and give it unto him that hath the ten pounds.

KEY.—[a] Matthew, [b] Mark, [c] Luke, [d] John.

[1] Gr. *bondservants.*
[2] *Mina,* here translated a pound, is equal to one hundred drachmas.
[3] Gr. *bondservant.*   [4] Gr. *the other.*
[5] Or, *I should have gone and required.*

And they said unto him, Lord, he hath ten 25 pounds. I say unto you, that unto every 26 one that hath shall be given ; but from him that hath not, even that which he hath shall be taken away from him. Howbeit these 27 mine enemies, who would not that I should reign over them, bring hither, and slay them before me.

ᶜAnd when he had thus spoken, he went 28 on before, going up to Jerusalem.

KEY.—ᵃ Matthew, ᵇ Mark, ᶜ Luke, ᵈ John.

§ 118. Triumphal Entry into Jerusalem.

Matthew's Account.

Chap. 21.

And when they drew nigh unto Jerusalem, and came 1
unto Bethphage, unto the mount of Olives, then Jesus
sent two disciples, saying unto them, Go into the village 2
that is over against you, and straightway ye shall find an
ass tied, and a colt with her : loose *them*, and bring *them*
unto me. And if any one say aught unto you, ye shall say, 3
The Lord hath need of them ; and straightway he will
send them. Now this is come to pass, that it might be 4
fulfilled which was spoken through the prophet, saying,

Tell ye the daughter of Zion, 5
Behold, thy King cometh unto thee,
Meek, and riding upon an ass,
And upon a colt the foal of an ass.

And the disciples went, and did even as Jesus appointed 6
them, and brought the ass, and the colt, and put on them 7
their garments ; and he sat thereon. And the most part 8
of the multitude spread their garments in the way; and
others cut branches from the trees, and spread them in the
way. And the multitudes that went before him, and that 9
followed, cried, saying, Hosanna to the Son of David :
Blessed *is* he that cometh in the name of the Lord ;
Hosanna in the highest.

Mark's Account.

Chap. 11.

And when they draw nigh unto Jerusalem, unto Beth- 1
phage and Bethany, at the mount of Olives, he sendeth
two of his disciples, and saith unto them, Go your way
into the village that is over against you: and straightway as ye enter into it, ye shall find a colt tied, whereon
no man ever yet sat; loose him, and bring him. And
if any one say unto you, Why do ye this ? say ye, The 3
Lord hath need of him ; and straightway he will send
him back hither. And they went away, and found a 4
colt tied at the door without in the open street ; and
they loose him. And certain of them that stood there 5
said unto them, What do ye, loosing the colt ? And 6

167

PERIOD V.

Tbe Passover Week.

[From the entrance of Jerusalem to the crucifixion.]

---

§ 118. Triumphal Entry of Jerusalem.

John 11.

55 [d]Now the passover of the Jews was at
hand: and many went up to Jerusalem
out of the country before the passover, to
56 purify themselves. They sought therefore
for Jesus, and spake one with another, as
they stood in the temple, What think ye?
57 That he will not come to the feast? Now
the chief priests and the Pharisees had given
commandment, that, if any man knew
where he was, he should shew it, that they
might take him.

1 **John 12.** [d]Jesus therefore six days before the
passover came to Bethany, where Lazarus
was, whom Jesus raised from the dead.
9 The common people therefore of the Jews
learned that he was there: and they came,
not for Jesus' sake only, but that they
might see Lazarus also, whom he had raised
10 from the dead. But the chief priests took
counsel that they might put Lazarus also
11 to death; because that by reason of him
many of the Jews went away, and believed
on Jesus.

29 **Luke 19.** [c]And it came to pass, when he
drew nigh unto Bethphage and Bethany,
at the mount that is called Olivet, he sent
30 two of the disciples, saying, Go your way
into the village over against *you*; in
the which as ye enter ye shall find a

Key.—[a] Matthew, [b] Mark, [c] Luke, [d] John.

colt * tied, whereon no man ever yet sat:
loose him, and bring him. And if any one, 31
ask you Why do ye loose him? thus shall
ye say, The Lord hath need of him, ᵇ and
straightway he will send him back hither.
ᵃNow this is come to pass that it might be
fulfilled which was spoken through the
prophet saying,

 Tell ye the daughter of Zion,
 Behold thy king cometh unto thee
 Meek, and riding upon an ass,
 And upon a colt the foal of an ass.

ᶜAnd they that were sent went away, and 32
found ᵇ a colt tied at the door without in
the open street ᶜ even as he had said unto
them. And as they were loosing the colt, 33
the owners thereof said unto them, Why
loose ye the colt? And they said, The 34
Lord hath need of him: ᵇ and they let
them go. ᶜAnd they brought him to 35
Jesus: and they threw their garments
upon the colt, and set Jesus thereon. And 36
as he went, they spread their garments in
the way; ᵇ and others branches which they
had cut from the fields. ᶜAnd as he was 37
now drawing nigh, *even* at the descent of
the mount of Olives, the whole multitude
of the disciples began to rejoice and praise
God with a loud voice for all the ¹mighty
works which they had seen; [and]† ᵈa
great multitude that had come to the feast,
when they heard that Jesus was coming to
Jerusalem, took the branches of the palm
trees, and went forth to meet him, and cried,
ᶜ saying, Blessed *is* the King that cometh 38
in the name of the Lord: peace in heaven,
and glory in the highest; ᵇ blessed is he

KEY.—ᵃ Matthew, ᵇ Mark, ᶜ Luke, ᵈ John.

¹ Gr. *powers.*

* Matthew, who is always careful to observe agreements
with prophecy, adds the particular that the ass which was
mother of the colt was also brought along.

† Word inserted by compiler.

§ 118. Triumphal Entry into Jerusalem.—(*Continued.*)

Mark's Account.

they said unto them even as Jesus had said: <u>and they</u>
7 <u>let them go.</u>   And they bring the colt unto Jesus, and cast
8 on him their garments; and he sat upon him.   And many
spread their garments upon the <u>way; and others branches,</u>
9 <u>which they had cut from the fields.</u>   And they that went
<u>before, and they that followed, cried, Hosanna; Blessed</u>
10 *is* <u>he that cometh in the name of the Lord : Blessed *is* the</u>
<u>kingdom that cometh, *the kingdom* of our father David :</u>
<u>Hosanna in the highest.</u>

John's Account.

Chap. 12.
12   On the morrow a great multitude that had come unto the
<u>feast, when they heard that Jesus was coming to Jerusa-</u>
13 <u>lem, took the branches of the palm trees, and went forth</u>
<u>to meet him, and cried out, Hosanna: Blessed *is* he that</u>
<u>cometh in the name of the Lord, even the King of Israel.</u>
14 And Jesus, having found a young ass, sat thereon ; as it
15 is written, Fear not, daughter of Zion: behold, thy King
cometh, sitting on an ass's colt.

168

Luke 19.

that cometh in the name of the Lord:
Blessed is the kingdom that cometh, even
the kingdom of our father David: Hosanna
39 in the highest! ᶜAnd some of the Pharisees from the multitude said unto him,
40 ¹ Master, rebuke thy disciples. And he
answered and said, I tell you that, if these
shall hold their peace, the stones will cry
out.

§ 119. Weeping over the City.

Luke 19. [Jerusalem and Bethany.]

41 ᶜAnd when he drew nigh, he saw the
42 city and wept over it, saying, ² If thou hadst
known in this ³ day, even thou, the things
which belong unto ⁴ peace! but now they
43 are hid from thine eyes. For the days
shall come upon thee, when thine enemies
shall cast up a ⁵ bank about thee, and compass thee round, and keep thee in on every
44 side, and shall dash thee to the ground, and
thy children within thee; and they shall
not leave in thee one stone upon another;
because thou knewest not the time of thy
visitation.

16 **John 12.** ᵈThese things understood not
his disciples at the first: but when Jesus
was glorified, then remembered they that
these things were written of him, and that
17 they had done these things unto him. The
multitude therefore that was with him
when he called Lazarus out of the tomb,
and raised him from the dead, bare witness.
18 For this cause also the multitude went and
met him, for that they heard that he had
19 done this sign. The Pharisees therefore
said among themselves, ⁶ Behold how ye
prevail nothing: lo, the world is gone after
him. ᵃAnd when he was come into Jeru-

Key.—ᵃ Matthew, ᵇ Mark, ᶜ Luke, ᵈ John.

¹ Or, *Teacher.*   ² Or, *O that thou hadst known.*
³ Some ancient authorities read *thy day.*
⁴ Some ancient authorities read *thy peace.*
⁵ Gr. *palisade.*   ⁶ Or, *Ye behold.*

Matthew 21.

salem, all the city was stirred, saying, 10
Who is this? And the multitude said, This
is the prophet, Jesus, from Nazareth of
Galilee. ᵃ But when the chief priests and 15
the scribes saw the wonderful things that
he did, and the children that were crying
in the temple and saying, Hosanna to the
Son of David; they were moved with indignation and said unto him, Hearest thou 16
what these are saying? And Jesus saith
unto them, Yea: did ye never read, Out
of the mouth of babes and sucklings thou
hast perfected praise? And he left them, 17
and went forth out of the city to Bethany,
and lodged there.

§ 120. Inquiry of the Greeks.

[Jerusalem.]

John 12.

ᵈ Now there were certain Greeks among 20
those that went up to worship at the feast:
these therefore came to Philip, who was 21
of Bethsaida of Galilee, and asked him,
saying, Sir, we would see Jesus. Philip 22
cometh and telleth Andrew: Andrew cometh, and Philip, and they tell Jesus. And 23
Jesus answereth them, saying, The hour is
come, that the Son of man should be glorified. Verily, verily, I say unto you, Ex- 24
cept a grain of wheat fall into the earth
and die, it abideth by itself alone; but if
it die, it beareth much fruit. He that lov- 25
eth his life loseth it; and he that hateth his
life in this world shall keep it unto life
eternal. If any man serve me, let him fol- 26
low me; and where I am, there shall also
my servant be: if any man serve me, him
will the Father honour. Now is my soul 27
troubled; and what shall I say? Father,
save me from this ¹hour. But for this
cause came I unto this hour. Father, glo- 28

KEY.—ᵃ Matthew, ᵇ Mark, ᶜ Luke, ᵈ John.

¹ Or, *hour?*

John 12.

rify thy name. There came therefore a
voice out of heaven, *saying*, I have both
29 glorified it, and will glorify it again. The
multitude therefore, that stood by, and
heard it, said that it had thundered : others
30 said, An angel hath spoken to him. Jesus
answered and said, This voice hath not
31 come for my sake, but for your sakes. Now
is ¹ the judgement of this world : now
shall the prince of this world be cast out.
32 And I, if I be lifted up ² from the earth, will
33 draw all men unto myself. But this he
said, signifying by what manner of death
34 he should die. The multitude therefore
answered him, We have heard out of the
law that the Christ abideth for ever : and
how sayest thou, The Son of man must be
35 lifted up ? who is this Son of man ? Jesus
therefore said unto them, Yet a little while
is the light ³ among you. Walk while ye
have the light, that darkness overtake you
not : and he that walketh in the darkness
36 knoweth not whither he goeth. While ye
have the light, believe on the light, that ye
may become sons of light.

§ 121. The Wavering of the People.*

John 12.

36 ⁴ These things spake Jesus, and he de-
37 parted and ⁴ hid himself from them. But
though he had done so many signs before
38 them, yet they believed not on him : that
the word of Isaiah the prophet might be
fulfilled, which he spake,
  Lord, who hath believed our report?
  And to whom hath the arm of the
    Lord been revealed?

KEY.—ᵃ Matthew, ᵇ Mark, ᶜ Luke, ᵈ John.

¹ Or, *a judgement.*   ² Or, *out of.*   ³ Or, *in.*
⁴ Or, *was hidden from them.*

* Harmonists usually insert these reflections later. But
John, to whom they are peculiar, gives them this place.

For this cause they could not believe, for 39
that Isaiah said again,

> He hath blinded their eyes, and he 40
> hardened their heart;
> Lest they should see with their eyes,
> and perceive with their heart,
> And should turn,
> And I should heal them.

These things said Isaiah, because he saw 41
his glory; and he spake of him. Never- 42
theless even of the rulers many believed on
him; but because of the Pharisees they
did not confess ¹ *it*, lest they should be put
out of the synagogue: for they loved the 43
glory *that is* of men more than the glory
that is of God.

And Jesus cried and said, He that be- 44
lieveth on me, believeth not on me, but on
him that sent me. And he that beholdeth 45
me beholdeth him that sent me. I am come 46
a light into the world, that whosoever believeth on me may not abide in the darkness. And if any man hear my sayings, 47
and keep them not, I judge him not: for I
came not to judge the world, but to save
the world. He that rejecteth me, and re- 48
ceiveth not my sayings, hath one that
judgeth him: the word that I spake, the
same shall judge him in the last day. For 49
I spake not from myself; but the Father
who sent me, he hath given me a commandment, what I should say, and what I
should speak. And I know that his com- 50
mandment is life eternal: the things therefore which I speak, even as the Father
hath said unto me, so I speak.   **Mark 11.**

ᵇAnd he entered into Jerusalem, into the 11
temple; and when he had looked round
about upon all things, it being now even-

KEY.—ᵃ Matthew, ᵇ Mark, ᶜ Luke, ᵈ John.

¹ Or, him.

§§ 121, 122, 123. Withered Fig Tree and Second Cleansing of the Temple.

Matthew's Account.

Chap. 21.

And when he was come into Jerusalem, all the city was 10 stirred, saying, Who is this? And the multitude said, This 11 is the prophet, Jesus, from Nazareth of Galilee.

And Jesus entered into the temple of God, and cast out 12 all them that sold and bought in the temple, and overthrew the tables of the money-changers, and the seats of them that sold the doves; and he saith unto them, It is written, 13 My house shall be called a house of prayer: but ye make it a den of robbers. And the blind and the lame came to 14 him in the temple: and he healed them. But when the 15 chief priests and the scribes saw the wonderful things that he did, and the children that were crying in the temple and saying, Hosanna to the son of David; they were moved with indignation, and said unto them, Hearest thou what 16 these are saying? And Jesus saith unto them, Yea: did ye never read, Out of the mouth of babes and sucklings thou hast perfected praise? And he left them, and went forth 17 out of the city to Bethany, and lodged there.

Now in the morning as he returned to the city, he hun- 18 gered. And seeing a fig tree by the way side, he came 19 to it, and found nothing thereon, but leaves only; and he saith unto it, Let there be no fruit from thee henceforward for ever. And immediately the fig tree withered away. And when the disciples saw it, they marvelled, saying, 20 How did the fig tree immediately wither away? And Jesus 21 answered and said unto them, Verily I say unto you, If ye have faith, and doubt not, ye shall not only do what is done to the fig tree, but even if ye shall say unto this mountain, Be thou taken up and cast into the sea, it shall be done. And all things, whatsoever ye shall ask in prayer, believ- 22 ing, ye shall receive.

Luke's Account.

Chap. 19.

And he entered into the temple, and began to cast out 45 them that sold, saying unto them, It is written, And my 46 house shall be a house of prayer: but ye have made it a den of robbers.

And he was teaching daily in the temple. But the chief 47 priests and the scribes and the principal men of the people sought to destroy him: and they could not find what they 48 might do; for the people all hung upon him, listening.

Chap. 21.

And every day he was teaching in the temple; and every 37 night he went out, and lodged in the mount that is called Olivet. And all the people came early in the morning to 38 him in the temple, to hear him.

Mark 11.

tide, he went out unto Bethany with the twelve.

§ 122. The Withered Fig Tree.

Mark 11.   [Near Bethany.]

12 ᵇAnd on the morrow, when they were come out from Bethany, ᵃ as he returned to
13 the city, ᵇ he hungered. And seeing a fig tree afar off, ᵃ by the way side, ᵇ having leaves, he came, if haply he might find anything thereon: and when he came to it, he found nothing ᵃ thereon ᵇ but leaves ᵃ only; ᵇ for it was not the season of figs.
14 And he answered and said unto it, No man eat fruit from thee henceforward for ever. And his disciples heard it.*

§ 123. Second Cleansing of the Temple.

Mark 11.   [Jerusalem.]

15 ᵇAnd they come to Jerusalem: and he entered into the temple, and began to cast out them that sold and them that bought in the temple, and overthrew the tables of the money-changers, and the seats of them
16 that sold the doves; and he would not suffer that any man should carry a vessel
17 through the temple. And he taught, and said unto them, Is it not written, My house shall be called a house of prayer for all the nations? but ye have made it a den of
18 robbers.   And the chief priests and the scribes heard it, and sought how they might destroy him: for they feared him, for all the multitude was astonished at his teaching. ᵃAnd the blind and the lame came to him in the temple, and he healed them. ᶜAnd he was teaching daily in the temple. But the chief priests and the scribes and the principal men of the people sought to destroy him: and they could not find what they might do; for the people

KEY.—ᵃ Matthew, ᵇ Mark, ᶜ Luke, ᵈ John.

* See § 123.

all hung upon him, listening. And every day he was teaching in the temple; and every night he went out and lodged in the mount that is called Olivet. And all the people came early in the morning to him in the temple, to hear him.

ᵇAnd ¹every evening ²he went forth out 19 of the city.

ᵇAnd as they passed by in the morning, 20 they saw the fig tree withered away from the roots. And Peter calling to remem- 21 brance saith unto him, Rabbi, behold, the fig tree which thou cursedst is withered away. And Jesus answering saith unto 22 them, Have faith in God : ᵃif ye have faith and doubt not, ye shall not only do what is done unto the fig tree. ᵇ Verily I say unto 23 you, Whosoever shall say unto this moun- tain, Be thou taken up and cast into the sea; and shall not doubt in his heart, but shall believe that what he saith cometh to pass; he shall have it. Therefore I say 24 unto you, All things whatsoever ye pray and ask for, believe that ye ³receive them, and ye shall have them. And whensoever 25 ye stand praying, forgive, if ye have aught against any one; that your Father also who is in heaven may forgive you your trespasses.⁴

§ 124. The Question of Authority.

[Jerusalem.]

ᵇAnd they come again to Jerusalem: and 27 as he was walking in the temple, there come to him the chief priests, and the scribes, and the elders; and they said unto 28

KEY.—ᵃ Matthew, ᵇ Mark, ᶜ Luke, ᵈ John.

¹ Gr. *whenever evening came.*
² Some ancient authorities read *they.*
³ Gr. *received.*
⁴ Many ancient authorities add ver. 26: *But if ye do not forgive, neither will your Father who is in heaven forgive your trespasses.*

§ 124. The Question of Authority.

Matthew's Account.

Chap. 21.

23 And when he was come into the temple, the chief·priests and the elders of the people came unto him as he was teaching, and said, By what authority doest thou these
24 things? and who gave thee this authority? And Jesus answered and said unto them, I also will ask you one question, which if ye tell me, I likewise will tell you by what
25 authority I do these things. The baptism of John, whence was it? from heaven or from men? And they reasoned with themselves, saying, If we shall say, From heaven; he will say unto us, Why then did ye not believe
26 him? But if we shall say, From men; we fear the multi-
27 tude; for all hold John as a prophet. And they answered Jesus, and said, We know not. He also said unto them, Neither tell I you by what authority I do these things.

Luke's Account.

Chap. 20.

1 And it came to pass, on one of the days, as he was teaching the people in the temple, and preaching the gospel, there came upon him the chief priests and the scribes
2 with the elders; and they spake, saying unto him, Tell us: By what authority doest thou these things? or who is
3 he that gave thee this authority? And he answered and said unto them, I also will ask you a question; and tell me:
4 The baptism of John, was it from heaven, or from men?
5 And they reasoned with themselves, saying, If we shall say, From heaven; he will say, Why did ye not believe
6 him? But if we shall say, From men; all the people will stone us: for they are persuaded that John was a prophet.
7 And they answered, that they knew not whence *it was.*
8 And Jesus said unto them, Neither tell I you by what authority I do these things.

Mark 11.

him, By what authority doest thou these things? or who gave thee this authority
29 to do these things? And Jesus said unto them, I will ask of you one [1] question, and answer me, and I will tell you by what au-
30 thority I do these things. The baptism of John, was it from heaven, or from men?
31 answer me. And they reasoned with themselves, saying, If we shall say, From heaven; he will say, Why then did ye not
32 believe him? [2] But should we say, From men—they feared the people: [3] for all
33 verily held John to be a prophet. And they answered Jesus and say, We know not. And Jesus saith unto them, Neither tell I you by what authority I do these things.

§ 125. The Two Sons.

[Jerusalem].

Matthew 21.

28   [a] But what think ye? A man had two sons; and he came to the first, and said, [4] Son, go work to-day in the vineyard.
29 And he answered and said, I will not: but afterward he repented himself, and went.
30 And he came to the second, and said like-wise. And he answered and said, I *go*, sir:
31 and went not. Whether of the twain did the will of his father? They say, The first. Jesus saith unto them, Verily I say unto you, that the publicans and the harlots go
32 into the kingdom of God before you. For John came unto you in the way of right-eousness, and ye believed him not: but the publicans and the harlots believed him: and ye, when ye saw it, did not even re-pent yourselves afterward, that ye might believe him.

KEY.—[a] Matthew, [b] Mark, [c] Luke, [d] John.

[1] Gr. *word.*   [2] Or, *But shall we say, From men?*
[3] Or, *for all held John to be a prophet indeed.*
[4] Gr. *Child.*

§ 126. The Rebel Servants.

ᵃ Hear another parable: There was a 33
man that was a householder, who planted
a vineyard, and set a hedge about it, and
digged a ᵇ pit for the ᵃ winepress in it, and
built a tower, and let it out to husbandmen,
and went into another cuontry ᶜ for a long
time. ᵃ And when the season of the fruits 34
drew near, he sent his ¹ servants to the
husbandmen, to receive ⁴ his fruits. And 35
the husbandmen took his ¹ servants, and
beat one, and killed another, and stoned
another. Again, he sent other ¹ servants 36
more than the first: and they did unto
them in like manner. ᵇ And again he sent
unto them another servant ; and him they
wounded in the head, and handled shamefully. ᵃ But afterward he sent unto them 37
his ᵇ beloved ᵃ son, saying, They will reverence my son. But the husbandmen, when 38
they saw the son, said among themselves,
This is the heir ; come, let us kill him,
and take his inheritance. And they took 39
him, and cast him forth out of the vineyard, and killed him. When therefore the 40
lord of the vineyard shall come, what will
he do unto those husbandmen? They say 41
unto him, He will miserably destroy those
miserable men, and will let out the vineyard unto other husbandmen, that shall
render him the fruits in their seasons. Jesus 42
saith unto them, Did ye never read in the
scriptures,

> The stone which the builders re-
>   jected,
> The same was made the head of the
>   corner :
> This was from the Lord,
> And it is marvellous in our eyes?

KEY.—ᵃ Matthew, ᵇ Mark, ᶜ Luke, ᵈ John.

¹ Gr. *bondservants*.   ² Or, *the fruits of it*.

§ 126. The Rebel Servants.

Mark's Account.

Chap. 12.

1 And he began to speak unto them in parables. A man planted a vineyard, and set a hedge about it, and digged a pit for the winepress, and built a tower, and let it out to

2 husbandmen, and went into another country. And at the season he sent to the husbandmen a servant, that he might receive from the husbandmen of the fruits of the vineyard.

3 And they took him, and beat him, and sent him away

4 empty. And again he sent unto them another servant; and him they wounded in the head, and handled shame-

5 fully. And he sent another; and him they killed: and

6 many others; beating some, and killing some. He had yet one, a beloved son: he sent him last unto them, say-

7 ing, They will reverence my son. But those husbandmen

Luke's Account.

Chap. 20.

9 And he began to speak unto the people this parable: A man planted a vineyard, and let it out to husbandmen, and

10 went into another country for a long time. And at the season he sent unto the husbandmen a servant, that they should give him of the fruit of the vineyard: but the hus-

11 bandmen beat him, and sent him away empty. And he sent yet another servant: and him also they beat, and

12 handled him shamefully, and sent him away empty. And he sent yet a third: and him also they wounded, and cast

13 him forth. And the lord of the vineyard said, What shall I do? I will send my beloved son: it may be they will

14 reverence him. But when the husbandmen saw him, they

[*Continued on duplicate page* 177.]

176

§ 126. The Rebel Servants.—(*Continued*.)

Mark's Account.

said among themselves, This is the heir; come, let us kill
him, and the inheritance shall be ours.   And they took 8
him, and killed him, and cast him forth out of the vineyard.   What therefore will the lord of the vineyard do ? 9
he will come and destroy the husbandmen, and will give
the vineyard unto others.   Have ye not read even this 10
scripture;

> The stone which the builders rejected,
> The same was made the head of the corner:
> This was from the Lord,   11
> And it is marvellous in our eyes?

And they sought to lay hold on him; and they feared 12
the multitude; for they perceived that he spake the parable against them: and they left him, and went away.

Luke's Account.

reasoned one with another, saying, This is the heir: let us
kill him, that the inheritance may be ours.   And they cast 15
him forth out of the vineyard, and killed him.   What
therefore will the lord of the vineyard do unto them ? He 16
will come and destroy these husbandmen, and will give
the vineyard unto others.   And when they heard it, they
said, God forbid.   But he looked upon them, and said, 17
What then is this that is written,

> The stone which the builders rejected,
> The same was made the head of the corner?

Every one that falleth on that stone shall be broken to 18
pieces; but on whomsoever it shall fall, it will scatter him
as dust.

And the scribes and the chief priests sought to lay 19
hands on him in that very hour; and they feared the people: for they perceived that he spake this parable against
them.

Matthew 21.

43 Therefore say I unto you, The kingdom of
God shall be taken away from you, and
shall be given to a nation bringing forth
44 the fruits thereof. ¹And he that falleth on
this stone shall be broken to pieces: but
on whomsoever it shall fall, it will scatter
45 him as dust. And when the chief priests
and the Pharisees heard his parables, they
perceived that he spake of them. ᶜAnd
when they heard it, they said, God forbid.
46 ᵃAnd when they sought to lay hold on him,
they feared the multitudes, because they
took him for a prophet.

§ 127. The King's Supper.

[Jerusalem.]

Matthew 22.

1   ᵃAnd Jesus answered and spake again in
2 parables unto them, saying, The kingdom
of heaven is likened unto a certain king,
3 who made a marriage feast for his son, and
sent forth his ²servants to call them that
were bidden to the marriage feast: and
4 they would not come. Again he sent forth
other ²servants, saying, Tell them that are
bidden, Behold, I have made ready my
dinner: my oxen and my fatlings are
killed, and all things are ready: come to
5 the marriage feast. But they made light
of it, and went their ways, one to his own
6 farm, another to his merchandise: and the
rest laid hold on his ²servants, and entreated them shamefully, and killed them.
7 But the king was wroth; and he sent his
armies, and destroyed those murderers,
8 and burned their city. Then saith he to
his ²servants, The wedding is ready, but
they that were bidden were not worthy.
9 Go ye therefore unto the partings of the
highways, and as many as ye shall find,

KEY.—ᵃ Matthew, ᵇ Mark, ᶜ Luke, ᵈ John.

¹ Some ancient authorities omit ver. 44.
² Gr. *bondservants.*

bid to the marriage feast. And those [1] ser- 10
vants went out into the highways, and
gathered together all as many as they
found, both bad and good: and the wedding
was filled with guests. But when the king 11
came in to behold the guests, he saw there
a man who had not on a wedding-gar-
ment: and he saith unto him, Friend, how 12
camest thou in hither not having a wed-
ding-garment? And he was speechless.
Then the king said to the [2] servants, Bind 13
him hand and foot, and cast him out into
the outer darkness; there shall be the
weeping and gnashing of teeth. For many 14
are called, but few chosen.

§ 128. Question of Tribute.

[Jerusalem.]

[a] Then went the Pharisees, and took 15
counsel how they might ensnare him in *his*
talk. [c] And they watched him, and sent
forth spies, who feigned themselves to be
righteous, that they might take hold of his
speech, so that they might deliver him up
to the rule and to the authority of the
governor. [a] And they send to him their 16
disciples, with the Herodians, saying,
[3] Master, we know that thou art true, and
teachest the way of God in truth, and
carest not for any one: for thou regardest
not the person of men. Tell us therefore, 17
What thinkest thou? Is it lawful to give
tribute unto Cæsar, or not? [b] Shall we give
or not give? [a] But Jesus perceived their 18
wickedness, and said, Why try ye me, ye
hypocrites? Shew me the tribute money.
And they brought unto him a [4] denarius. 19
And he saith unto them, Whose is this 20
image and superscription? They say un- 21

KEY.—[a] Matthew, [b] Mark, [c] Luke, [d] John.

[1] Gr. *bondservants.*   [2] Or, *ministers.*
[3] Or, *Teacher.*   [4] About eightpence halfpenny.

§ 128. Question of Tribute.

Mark's Account.

Chap. 12.

13 And they send unto him certain of the Pharisees and of
14 the Herodians, that they might catch him in talk. And
when they were come, they say unto him, Master, we
know that thou art true, and carest not for any one: for
thou regardest not the person of men, but of a truth
teachest the way of God: Is it lawful to give tribute unto
15 Cæsar, or not? Shall we give, or shall we not give? But
he, knowing their hypocrisy, said unto them, Why try ye
16 me? bring me a denarius, that I may see it. And they
brought it. And he saith unto them, Whose is this image
and superscription? And they said unto him, Cæsar's.
17 And Jesus said unto them, Render unto Cæsar the things
that are Cæsar's, and unto God the things that are God's.
And they marvelled greatly at him.

Luke's Account.

Chap. 20.

20 And they watched him, and sent forth spies, who
feigned themselves to be righteous, that they might take
hold of his speech, so as to deliver him up to the rule and
21 to the authority of the governor. And they asked him,
saying, Master, we know that thou sayest and teachest
rightly, and acceptest not the person *of any*, but of a truth
22 teachest the way of God: Is it lawful for us to give trib-
23 ute unto Cæsar, or not? But he perceived their craftiness,
24 and said unto them, Shew me a denarius. Whose image
25 and superscription hath it? And they said, Cæsar's. And
he said unto them, Then render unto Cæsar the things that
26 are Cæsar's, and unto God the things that are God's. And
they were not able to take hold of the saying before the
people: and they marvelled at his answer, and held their
peace.

§ 129. Marriage and Resurrection.
Mark's Account.

Chap. 12.

And there come unto him Sadducees, who say that 18 there is no resurrection; and they asked him, saying, Master, Moses wrote unto us, If a man's brother die, and 19 leave a wife behind him, and leave no child, that his brother should take his wife, and raise up seed unto his brother. There were seven brethren: and the first took a 20 wife, and dying left no seed; and the second took her, and 21 died, leaving no seed behind him; and the third likewise: and the seven left no seed. Last of all the woman also 22 died. In the resurrection whose wife shall she be of 23 them? for the seven had her to wife. Jesus said unto 24 them, Is it not for this cause that ye err, that ye know not the scriptures, nor the power of God? For when they 25 shall rise from the dead, they neither marry, nor are given in marriage; but are as angels in heaven.

Matthew's Account.

Chap. 22.

But as touching the resurrection of the dead, have ye 31 not read that which was spoken unto you by God, saying, 32 I am the God of Abraham, and the God of Isaac, and the God of Jacob? God is not *the God* of the dead, but of 33 the living. And when the multitudes heard it, they were astonished at his teaching.

Luke's Account.

Chap. 20.

And there came to him certain of the Sadducees, they 27 that say that there is no resurrection; and they asked him, saying, Master, Moses wrote unto us, that if a man's 28 brother die, having a wife, and he be childless, his brother should take the wife, and raise up seed unto his brother. There were therefore seven brethren: and the first took a 29 wife, and died childless; and the second; and the third 30 31 took her; and likewise the seven also left no children, and died. Afterward the woman also died. In the resurrec- 32 33 tion therefore whose wife of them shall she be? for the seven had her to wife. And Jesus said unto them, The 34 sons of this world marry, and are given in marriage: but 35 they that are accounted worthy to attain to that world, and the resurrection from the dead, neither marry, nor are given in marriage: for neither can they die any more: for 36 they are equal unto the angels; and are sons of God, being sons of the resurrection. But that the dead are raised, 37 even Moses shewed, in *the place concerning* the Bush, when he calleth the Lord the God of Abraham, and the God of Isaac, and the God of Jacob. Now he is not the 38 God of the dead, but of the living: for all live unto him. And certain of the scribes answering said, Master, thou 39 hast well said. For they durst not any more ask him any 40 question.

to him, Cæsar's.   Then saith he unto
them, Render therefore unto Cæsar the
things that are Cæsar's; and unto God
the things that are God's.   ᶜAnd they
were not able to take hold of the saying
22 before the people.   ᵃAnd when they
heard it, they marvelled, and left him, and
went their way, ᶜand held their peace.

§ 129.   Marriage and Resurrection.
[Jerusalem.]
Matthew 22.
23   ᵃ On that day there came to him Sadducees, ¹ who say that there is no resurrec-
24 tion : and they asked him, saying, ²Master, Moses said, If a man die, having no
children, his brother ³ shall marry his wife,
25 and raise up seed unto his brother.   Now
there were with us seven brethren : and
the first married and deceased, and having
26 no seed left his wife unto his brother ; in
like manner the second also, and the third,
27 unto the ⁴ seventh.   And after them all the
28 woman died.   In the resurrection therefore whose wife shall she be of the seven?
29 for they all had her.   But Jesus answered
and said unto them, ᵇ Is it not for this
cause that ye err, that ye know not the
scriptures nor the power of God?   ᶜThe
sons of this world marry and are given in
marriage ; but they that are accounted
worthy to attain to that world, and the
resurrection from the dead, neither marry
nor are given in marriage : for neither can
they die any more: for they are equal unto the angels ; and are sons of God, being
sons of the resurrection.
26   Mark 12. ᵇ But as touching the dead, that
they are raised ; have ye not read in the

KEY.—ᵃ Matthew, ᵇ Mark, ᶜ Luke, ᵈ John.
¹ Many ancient authorities read *saying*.
² Or, *Teachor*.
³ Gr. *shall perform the duty of a husband's brother to his
wife*.   ⁴ Gr. *seven*.

book of Moses, in the place concerning
the Bush, how God spake unto him, saying,
I am the God of Abraham, and the God of
Isaac, and the God of Jacob? He is not 27
the God of the dead, but of the living; ye
do greatly err; ^cfor all live unto him.

§ 130. The Greatest Commandment.

[Jerusalem.]

^a But the Pharisees, when they heard that
he had put the Sadducees to silence,
gathered themselves together. ^bAnd one 28
of the scribes came, and heard them questioning together, and knowing that he had
answered them well, asked him, ^atrying
him, ^bWhat commandment is the first of
all? Jesus answered, The first is, Hear, O 29
Israel; ¹The Lord our God, the Lord is
one: and thou shalt love the Lord thy 30
God ²with all thy heart, and ²with all thy
soul, and ²with all thy mind, and ²with all
thy strength. The second ^alike unto it 31
^bis this, Thou shalt love thy neighbour as
thyself. There is none other command-
ment greater than these. ^aOn these two
commandments hangeth the whole law, and
the prophets. ^bAnd the scribe said unto 32
him, Of a truth, ³Master, thou hast well
said that he is one; and there is none other
but he: and to love him with all the heart, 33
and with all the understanding, and with
all the strength, and to love his neighbour
as himself, is much more than all whole
burnt offerings and sacrifices. And when 34
Jesus saw that he answered discreetly, he
said unto him, Thou art not far from the
kingdom of God. And no man after that
durst ask him any question.

^a Now while the Pharisees **Matthew 22.** 41

KEY.—^a Matthew, ^b Mark, ^c Luke, ^d John.

¹ Or, *The Lord is our God; the Lord is one.*
² Gr. *from.*   ³ Or, *Teacher.*

§ 130. The Greatest Commandment.

Matthew's Account.

Chap. 22.

34 But the Pharisees, when they heard that he had put the
35 Sadducees to silence, gathered themselves together. And
one of them, a lawyer, asked him a question, trying him,
36 Master, which is the great commandment in the law?
37 And he said unto him, Thou shalt love the Lord thy God
with all thy heart, and with all thy soul, and with all thy
38 mind. This is the great and first commandment. And a
second like *unto it* is this, Thou shalt love thy neighbour
40 as thyself. On these two commandments hangeth the
whole law, and the prophets.

Mark's Account.

Chap. 12.

35 And Jesus answered and said, as he taught in the temple,
How say the scribes that the Christ is the son of David?
36 David himself said in the Holy Spirit,

The Lord said unto my Lord,
Sit thou on my right hand,
Till I make thine enemies the footstool of thy feet.

37 David himself calleth him Lord; and whence is he his
son? And the common people heard him gladly.

Luke's Account.

Chap. 20.

41 And he said unto them, How say they that the Christ
42 is David's son? For David himself saith in the book of
Psalms,

The Lord said unto my Lord,
Sit thou on my right hand,
43 Till I make thine enemies the footstool of thy feet.
44 David therefore calleth him Lord, and how is he his son?

§ 131. Woes upon Scribes and Pharisees.

Mark's Account.

Chap. 12.

And in his teaching he said, Beware of the scribes, who 38 desire to walk in long robes, and *tò have* salutations in the marketplaces, and chief seats in the synagogues, and chief 39 places at feasts: they who devour widows' houses, and for 40 a pretence make long prayers; these shall receive greater condemnation.

Luke's Account.

Chap. 20.

And in the hearing of all the people he said unto his 45 disciples, Beware of the scribes, who desire to walk in 46 long robes, and love salutations in the marketplaces, and chief seats in the synagogues, and chief places at feasts; who devour widows' houses, and for a pretence make long 47 prayers: these shall receive greater condemnation.

Matthew 22.

were gathered together, Jesus asked them a question, [b] as he taught in the temple,
42 [a] saying, What think ye of the Christ? whose son is he? They say unto him,
43 *The son* of David. He saith unto them, How then doth David in the Spirit call him Lord, saying, [c] in the book of Psalms,
44   [a] The Lord said unto my Lord,
    Sit thou on my right hand,
    Till I put thine enemies underneath
      thy feet?
45 If David then calleth him Lord, how is
46 he his son? And no one was able to answer him a word, neither durst any man from that day forth ask him any more questions: [b] and the common people heard him gladly.

§ 131. Woes upon Scribes and Pharisees.

[In the temple at Jerusalem.]

Matthew 23.

1   [a] Then spake Jesus to the multitudes and to his disciples, saying, [b] in his teaching,
2 [a] The scribes and the Pharisees sit on
3 Moses' seat: all things therefore whatsoever they bid you, *these* do and observe: but do not ye after their works; for they
4 say, and do not. Yea, they bind heavy burdens [1] and grievous to be borne, and lay them on men's shoulders; but they themselves will not move them with their
5 finger. But all their works they do for to be seen of men: for they make broad their phylacteries, and enlarge the borders *of their garments,* [b] and desire to walk in
6 long robes, [a] and love the chief place at feasts, and the chief seats in the syna-
7 gogues, and the salutations in the market-places, and to be called of men, Rabbi; [b] they who devour widows' houses, and for a pretence make long prayers! these

KEY.—[a] Matthew, [b] Mark, [c] Luke, [d] John.

[1] Many ancient authorities omit *and grievous to be borne.*

shall receive greater condemnation. [a] But 8
be not ye called Rabbi: for one is your
teacher, and all ye are brethren. And call 9
no man your father on the earth: for one
is your Father, [1] *even* he who is in heaven.
Neither be ye called masters: for one is 10
your master, *even* the Christ. But he that 11
is [2] greatest among you shall be your [3] servant. And whosoever shall exalt himself 12
shall be humbled; and whosoever shall
humble himself shall be exalted.

But **woe unto you, scribes** and Phari- 13
sees, hypocrites! because ye shut the kingdom of heaven [4] against men: for ye enter
not in yourselves, neither suffer ye them
that are entering in to enter.[5]

Woe unto you, scribes and Pharisees, 15
hypocrites! for ye compass sea and land
to make one proselyte; and when he is
become so, ye make him twofold more a
son of [6] hell than yourselves.

Woe unto you, ye blind guides, who 16
say, Whosoever shall swear by the [7] temple, it is nothing; but whosoever shall
swear by the gold of the [7] temple, he is [8] a
debtor. Ye fools and blind: for whether 17
is greater, the gold, or the [7] temple that
hath sanctified the gold? And, Whoso- 18
ever shall swear by the altar, it is nothing;
but whosoever shall swear by the gift that
is upon it, he is [8] a debtor. Ye blind: for 19
whether is greater, the gift, or the altar
that sanctifieth the gift? He therefore 20
that sweareth by the altar, sweareth by it,
and by all things thereon. And he that 21

KEY.—[a] Matthew, [b] Mark, [c] Luke, [d] John.

[1] Gr. *the heavenly.*   [3] Gr. *greater.*
[2] Or, *minister.*   [4] Gr. *before.*
[5] Some authorities insert here, or after ver. 12, ver.
14: *Woe unto you, scribes and Pharisees, hypocrites! for ye
devour widows' houses, even while for a pretence ye make long
prayers: therefore ye shall receive greater condemnation.*
[6] Gr. *Gehenna.*   [7] Or, *sanctuary.*
[8] Or, *bound* by his oath.

Matthew 23.

sweareth by the 'temple, sweareth by it,
22 and by him that dwelleth therein. And
he that sweareth by the heaven, sweareth
by the throne of God, and by him that sitteth thereon,

23   Woe unto you, scribes and Pharisees,
hypocrites! for ye tithe mint and 'anise
and cummin, and have left undone the
weightier matters of the law, justice, and
mercy, and faith: but these ye ought to
have done, and not to have left the other
24 undone. Ye blind guides, who strain out
the gnat, and swallow the camel.

25   Woe unto you, scribes and Pharisees,
hypocrites! for ye cleanse the outside of
the cup and of the platter, but within they
26 are full from extortion and excess. Thou
blind Pharisee, cleanse first the inside of
the cup and of the platter, that the outside
thereof may become clean also.

27   Woe unto you, scribes and Pharisees,
hypocrites! for ye are like unto whited
sepulchres, which outwardly appear beau-
tiful, but inwardly are full of dead men's
28 bones, and of all uncleanness. Even so ye
also outwardly appear righteous unto men,
but inwardly ye are full of hypocrisy and
iniquity.

29   Woe unto you, scribes and Pharisees,
hypocrites! for ye build the sepulchres of
the prophets, and garnish the tombs of
30 the righteous, and say, If we had been in
the days of our fathers, we should not have
been partakers with them in the blood of
31 the prophets. Wherefore ye witness to
yourselves, that ye are sons of them that
32 slew the prophets. Fill ye up then the
33 measure of your fathers. Ye serpents, ye
offspring of vipers, how shall ye escape the
34 judgement of 'hell? Therefore, behold, I

KEY.—ᵃ Matthew, ᵇ Mark, ᶜ Luke, ᵈ John.

¹ Or, *sanctuary*.   ² Or, *dill*.   ³ Gr. *Gehenna*.

send unto you prophets, and wise men, and
scribes: some of them shall ye kill and
crucify ; and some of them shall ye scourge
in your synagogues, and persecute from
city to city: that upon you may come all 35
the righteous blood shed on the earth, from
the blood of Abel the righteous unto the
blood of Zachariah son of Barachiah, whom
ye slew between the sanctuary and the
altar. Verily I say unto you, All these 36
things shall come upon this generation.

§ 132. Lamentation Repeated.

ᵃO Jerusalem, Jerusalem, that killeth 37
the prophets, and stoneth them that are
sent unto her! how often would I have
gathered thy children together, even as a
hen gathereth her chickens under her
wings, and ye would not! Behold, your 38
house is left unto you ¹ desolate. For I 39
say unto you, Ye shall not see me henceforth, till ye shall say, Blessed *is* he that
cometh in the name of the Lord.

§ 133. The Widow's Mite.

ᵇAnd he sat down over against the treas- 41
ury, and ᶜlooked up [and]* ᵇbeheld how the
multitude cast ²money [and]* ᶜgifts ᵇinto the
treasury : and many that were rich cast in
much. And there came ²a poor widow, 42
and she cast in two mites, which make a
farthing. And he called unto him his dis- 43
ciples, and said unto them, Verily I say unto you, This poor widow cast in more than
all they that are casting into the treasury :
for they all did cast in of their superfluity 44

KEY.—ᵃ Matthew, ᵇ Mark, ᶜ Luke, ᵈ John.

¹ Some ancient authorities omit *desolate.*
² Gr. *brass.*   ³ Gr. *one*
* Word inserted by compiler.

§ 133. The Widow's Mite.

Luke's Account.

Chap. 21.

1 And he looked up, and saw the rich men that were cast-
2 ing their gifts into the treasury. And he saw a certain
3 poor widow casting in thither two mites. And he said,
   Of a truth I say unto you, This poor widow cast in more
4 than they all: for all these did of their superfluity cast in
   unto the gifts: but she of her want did cast in all the living that she had.

§ 134. Destruction of the Temple Foretold.

Mark's Account.

And as he went forth out of the temple, one of his dis- 1
ciples saith unto him, Master, behold, what manner of
stones and what manner of buildings! And Jesus said 2
unto him, Seest thou these great buildings? there shall
not be left here one stone upon another, which shall not
be thrown down.

And as he sat on the mount of Olives over against the 3
temple, Peter and James and John and Andrew asked him
privately, Tell us, when shall these things be? and what 4
shall be the sign when these things are all about to be accomplished? And Jesus began to say unto them, Take 5
heed that no man lead you astray. Many shall come in 6
my name, saying, I am *he*; and shall lead many astray.
And when ye shall hear of wars and rumours of wars, be 7
not troubled: *these things* must needs come to pass; but
the end is not yet. For nation shall rise against nation, 8
and kingdom against kingdom: there shall be earthquakes
in divers places; there shall be famines: these things are
the beginning of travail.

But take ye heed to yourselves: for they shall deliver 9
you up to councils; and in synagogues shall ye be beaten;
and before governors and kings shall ye stand for my

Luke's Account.

And as some spake of the temple, how it was adorned 5
with goodly stones and offerings, he said, As for these 6
things which ye behold, the days will come, in which there
shall not be left here one stone upon another, that shall
not be thrown down. And they asked him, saying, Mas- 7
ter, when therefore shall these things be? and what *shall
be* the sign when these things are about to come to pass?
And he said, Take heed that ye be not led astray: for 8
many shall come in my name, saying, I am *he;* and, The
time is at hand: go ye not after them. And when 9
ye shall hear of wars and tumults, be not terrified: for
these things must needs come to pass first; but the end is
not immediately.

Then said he unto them, Nation shall rise against nation, 10
and kingdom against kingdom: and there shall be great 11
earthquakes, and in divers places famines and pestilences;
and there shall be terrors and great signs from heaven.
But before all these things— [See standard text, page 12
186, verse 12.]
But when ye see Jerusalem compassed with armies, 20
then know that her desolation is at hand. Then let them 21
that are in Judea flee unto the mountains; and let them that
are in the midst of her depart out; and let not them that

[*Continued on duplicate page* 186.]

Mark 12.

^cunto the gifts; ^bbut she of her want did cast in all that she had, *even* all her living.

§ 134. Destruction of the Temple Foretold.

Matthew 24.

1   ^aAnd Jesus went out from the temple, and was going on his way; and his disciples came to him to shew him the buildings of the temple: ^chow it was adorned with goodly stones and offerings; ^band one of his disciples saith unto him, Master, behold, what manner of stones and what

2 manner of buildings! ^aBut he answered and said unto them, See ye not all these ^bgreat buildings? ^averily I say unto you, There shall not be left here one stone upon another, that shall not be thrown down.

3   And as he sat on the mount of Olives, ^bover against the temple, ^athe disciples ^bPeter and James and John and Andrew ^acame unto him privately, saying, Tell us, when shall these things be? and what *shall be* the sign ^bthat these things are all about to be accomplished, [and]* ^aof thy ¹coming, and of ²the end of the world?

4 And Jesus answered and said unto them, Take heed that no man lead you astray.

5 For many shall come in my name, saying, I am the Christ; and shall lead many

6 astray. And ye shall hear of wars and rumours of wars ^cand tumults; ^asee that ye be not troubled: for *these things* must needs come to pass; but the end is not

7 yet. For nation shall rise against nation, and kingdom against kingdom: and there shall be famines and earthquakes in divers places, ^cand there shall be terrors and

8 great signs from heaven. ^aBut all these

9 things are the beginning of travail. Then shall they deliver you up unto tribulation

KEY.—^a Matthew, ^b Mark, ^c Luke, ^d John.

¹ Gr. *presence.*   ² Or, *the consummation of the age.*

* Word inserted by compiler.

and shall kill you : and ye shall be hated of
all the nations for my name's sake. ᶜThey 12
shall lay their hands upon you, and shall
persecute you, delivering you up to the
synagogues and prisons, bringing you before kings and governors for my name's
sake. It shall turn unto you for a testi- 13
mony. Settle it therefore in your hearts 14
not to meditate beforehand how to answer : for I will give you a mouth and 15
wisdom, which all your adversaries shall
not be able to withstand or gainsay : ᵇfor
it is not ye that speak, but the Holy Spirit.
ᶜBut ye shall be delivered up by parents, 16
and brethren, and kinsfolk, and friends;
and some of you shall they cause to be put
to death. And ye shall be hated of all 17
men for my name's sake. And not a hair 18
of your head shall perish. In your patience 19
ye shall win your souls.

ᵃAnd many false prophets　Matthew 24. 11
shall arise, and shall lead many astray.
And because iniquity shall be multiplied, 12
the love of the many shall wax cold. But 13
he that endureth to the end, the same shall
be saved. And ¹this gospel of the king- 14
dom shall be preached in the whole ²world
for a testimony unto all the nations; and
then shall the end come.

When therefore ye see the abomina- 15
tion of desolation, which was spoken of
through Daniel the prophet, standing in
³the holy place (let him that readeth understand) ; ᶜwhen ye shall see Jerusalem
compassed with armies; then know that
her desolation is at hand : ᵃthen let them 16
that are in Judæa flee unto the mountains :
let him that is on the housetop not go 17
down to take out the things that are in his
house : and let him that is in the field not 18
return back to take his cloke. ᶜAnd let them

KEY.—ᵃ Matthew, ᵇ Mark, ᶜ Luke, ᵈ John.

¹ Or, *these good tidings.*　　² Gr. *inhabited earth.*
³ Or, *a holy plac·*

§ 134. Destruction of the Temple Foretold.—(*Continued.*)

Mark's Account.

Chap. 13.

10 sake, for a testimony unto them. And the gospel must
11 first be preached unto all the nations. And when they
lead you *to judgement*, and deliver you up, be not anxious
beforehand what ye shall speak: but whatsoever shall be
given you in that hour, that speak ye: for it is not ye that
12 speak, but the Holy Spirit. And brother shall deliver up
brother to death, and the father his child; and children
shall rise up against parents, and cause them to be put to
13 death. And ye shall be hated of all men for my name's
sake: but he that endureth to the end, the same shall be
saved.
14 But when ye see the abomination of desolation standing
where he ought not (let him that readeth understand),
then let them that are in Judea flee unto the mountains:
15 and let him that is on the housetop not go down, nor en-
16 ter in, to take anything out of his house: and let him
17 that is in the field not return back to take his cloke. But
woe unto them that are with child and to them that give
18 suck in those days! And pray ye that it be not in the
19 winter. For those days shall be tribulation, such as there
hath not been the like from the beginning of the creation
20 which God created until now, and never shall be. And
except the Lord had shortened the days, no flesh would
have been saved: but for the elect's sake, whom he chose,
21 he shortened the days. And then if any man shall say
unto you, Lo, here is the Christ; or, Lo, there; believe *it*
22 not: for there shall arise false Christs and false prophets,
and shall shew signs and wonders, that they may lead
23 astray, if possible, the elect. But take ye heed: behold,
I have told you all things beforehand.

Luke's Account.

Chap. 21.

22 are in the country enter therein. For these are days of
vengeance, that all things which are written may be ful-
23 filled. Woe unto them that are with child and to them
that give suck in those days! for there shall be great dis-
24 tress upon the land, and wrath unto this people. And
they shall fall by the edge of the sword, and shall be led
captive into all the nations: and Jerusalem shall be trodden down of the Gentiles, until the times of the Gentiles be
25 fulfilled. And there shall be signs in sun and moon and
stars; and upon the earth distress of nations, in perplex-
26 ity for the roaring of the sea and the billows; men fainting for fear, and for expectation of the things which are
coming on the world: for the powers of the heavens shall
be shaken.

Matthew's Account.

Chap. 24.

10 And then shall many stumble, and shall deliver up one
another, and shall hate one another.

that are in the midst of Jerusalem depart out; and let not them that are in the
19 country enter therein. ᵃBut woe unto them that are with child and to them that give suck in those days! ᶜfor there shall be great distress upon the land, and wrath upon this people. For these are days of vengeance, that all things that are written
20 may be fulfilled. ᵃAnd pray ye that your flight be not in the winter, neither on a
21 sabbath: for then shall be great tribulation, such as hath not been from the beginning of the world ᵇ which God created, ᵃuntil now, no, nor ever shall be. ᶜAnd they shall fall by the edge of the sword, and shall be led captive into all the nations; and Jerusalem shall be trodden down of the Gentiles till the times of the
22 Gentiles shall be fulfilled. ᵃAnd except those days had been shortened, no flesh would have been saved: but for the elect's
23 sake those days shall be shortened. Then if any man shall say unto you, Lo, here is
24 the Christ, or, Here; believe ¹ *it* not. For there shall arise false Christs, and false prophets, and shall shew great signs and wonders; so as to lead astray, if possible,
25 even the elect. Behold, I have told you
26 beforehand. If therefore they shall say unto you, Behold, he is in the wilderness; go not forth: Behold, he is in the inner
27 chambers; believe ² *it* not. For as the lightning cometh forth from the east, and is seen even unto the west; so shall be the
28 ³coming of the Son of man. Wheresoever the carcase is, there will the ⁴eagles be gathered together.

KEY.—ᵃ Matthew, ᵇ Mark, ᶜ Luke, ᵈ John.

¹ Or, him.   ² Or, them.
³ Gr. *presence.*   ⁴ Or, *vultures.*

§ 135. Coming of the Son Foretold.

Matthew 24.

[a] But immediately, after the tribulation 29 of those days, the sun shall be darkened, and the moon shall not give her light, and the stars shall fall from heaven, and the powers of the heavens shall be shaken: [c] and upon the earth, distress of nations in perplexity for the roaring of the sea and the billows; men fainting for fear and for expectation of the things which are coming upon the world; [a] and then shall appear 31 the sign of the Son of man in heaven: and then shall all the tribes of the earth mourn, and they shall see the Son of man coming on the clouds of heaven with power and great glory. And he shall send forth his 31 angels [1] with [2] a great sound of a trumpet, and they shall gather together his elect from the four winds, [b] from the uttermost part of the earth, [and]* [a] from one end of heaven to the other.

Now from the fig tree [c] (and all the trees) [a] learn her parable: when her 32 branch is now become tender, and putteth forth its leaves, ye know that the summer is nigh; even so ye also, when ye see all 33 these things, know ye that [3] he is nigh, *even* at the doors. Verily I say unto you, 34 This generation shall not pass away, till all these things be accomplished. Heaven 35 and earth shall pass away, but my words shall not pass away. But of that day and 36 hour knoweth no one, not even the angels of heaven, [4] neither the Son, but the Father only. And as *were* the days of Noah, so 37 shall be the [5] coming of the Son of man.

KEY.—[a] Matthew, [b] Mark, [c] Luke, [d] John.

[1] Many ancient authorities read *with a great trumpet, and they shall gather &c.*

[2] Or, *a trumpet of great sound.*　　　[3] Or, *it.*

[4] Many authorities, some ancient, omit *neither the Son.*

[5] Gr. *presence.*

* Word inserted by compiler.

§ 135. Coming of the Son Foretold.

Mark's Account.

Chap. 13.

24 But in those days, after that tribulation, the sun shall
25 be darkened, and the moon shall not give her light, and
the stars shall be falling from heaven, and the powers that
26 are in the heavens shall be shaken. And then shall they
see the Son of man coming in clouds with great power
27 and glory. And then shall he send forth the angels, and
shall gather together his elect from the four winds, from
the uttermost part of the earth to the uttermost part of
heaven.

28 Now from the fig tree learn her parable: when her
branch is now become tender, and putteth forth its leaves,
29 ye know that the summer is nigh; even so ye also, when
ye see these things coming to pass, know ye that he is nigh,
30 *even* at the doors. Verily I say unto you, This generation
shall not pass away, until all these things be accomplished.
31 Heaven and earth shall pass away: but my words shall
32 not pass away. But of that day or that hour knoweth no
one, not even the angels in heaven, neither the Son, but
the Father.

Luke's Account.

Chap. 21.

27 And then shall they see the Son of man coming in a
28 cloud with power and great glory. But when these things
begin to come to pass, look up, and lift up your heads; because your redemption draweth nigh.

29 And he spake to them a parable: Behold the fig tree,
30 and all the trees: when they now shoot forth, ye see it
and know of your own selves that the summer is now
31 nigh. Even so ye also, when ye see these things coming to pass, know ye that the kingdom of God is nigh.
32 Verily I say unto you, This generation shall not pass
away, till all things be accomplished. Heaven and earth
shall pass away: but my words shall not pass away.

33 But take heed to yourselves, lest haply your hearts be
overcharged with surfeiting, and drunkenness, and cares'
of this life, and that day come on you suddenly as a snare:
35 for *so* shall it come upon all them that dwell on the face
36 of all the earth. But watch ye at every season, making
supplication, that ye may prevail to escape all these things
that shall come to pass, and to stand before the Son of
man.

188

Matthew 24.

38 For as in those days which were before
the flood they were eating and drinking,
marrying and giving in marriage, until
the day that Noah entered into the ark,

39 and they knew not until the flood came,
and took them all away ; so shall be the

40 [1]coming of the Son of man. Then shall
two men be in the field; one is taken, and

41 one is left: two women *shall be* grinding
at the mill; one is taken, and one is left.

42 Watch therefore : for ye know not on what

43 day your Lord cometh. [2]But know this,
that if the master of the house had known
in what watch the thief was coming, he
would have watched, and would not have
suffered his house to be [3]broken through.

44 Therefore be ye also ready : for in an hour
that ye think not the Son of man cometh.

45 Who then is the faithful and wise [4]ser-
vant, whom his lord hath set over his
household, to give them their food in due

46 season ? Blessed is that [4]servant, whom
nis lord when he cometh shall find so do-

47 ing. Verily I say unto you, that he will

48 set him over all that he hath. But if that
evil [4]servant shall say in his heart, My

49 lord tarrieth; and shall begin to beat his
fellow-servants, and shall eat and drink

50 with the drunken; the lord of that [4]ser-
vant shall come in a day when he expect-
eth not, and in an hour when he knoweth

51 not, and shall [5]cut him asunder, and appoint his portion with the hypocrites :
there shall be the weeping and **gnashing**

Mark 18. of teeth.

33   [b]Take ye heed, watch [6]and pray : for ye
know not when the time is : [c]take heed to
yourselves, lest haply your hearts be over-

KEY.—[a] Matthew, [b] Mark, [c] Luke, [d] John.

[1] Gr. *presence.*
[2] Or, *But this ye know.*
[3] Gr. *digged through.*
[4] Gr. *bondservant.*
[5] Or, *severely scourge him.*
[6] Some ancient authorities omit *and pray.*

charged with surfeiting, and drunkenness, and cares of this life, and that day come on you suddenly as a snare : for *so* shall it come upon all them that dwell on the face of all the earth. But watch ye at every season, making supplication, that ye may prevail to escape all these things that shall come to pass, and to stand before the Son of man. ᵇ*It is* as *when* a man, sojourning in 34 another country, having left his house, and given authority to his ¹ servants, to each one his work, commanded also the porter to watch. Watch therefore : for ye know 35 not when the lord of the house cometh, whether at even, or at midnight, or at cockcrowing, or in the morning ; lest com- 36 ing suddenly he find you sleeping. And 37 what I say unto you I say unto all, Watch.

§ 136. The Ten Virgins.

Matthew 25.

ᵃ Then shall the kingdom of heaven be 1 likened unto ten virgins, that took their ² lamps, and went forth to meet the bride-groom. And five of them were foolish, and 2 five were wise. For the foolish, when they 3 took their ² lamps, took no oil with them : but the wise took oil in their vessels with 4 their ² lamps. Now while the bridegroom 5 tarried, they all slumbered and slept. But 6 at midnight there is a cry, Behold, the bridegroom ! Come ye forth to meet him. Then all those virgins arose, and trimmed 7 their ² lamps. And the foolish said unto 8 the wise, Give us of your oil ; for our ² lamps are going out. But the wise an- 9 swered, saying, Peradventure there will not be enough for us and you : go ye rather to them that sell, and buy for yourselves. And while they went away to buy, the 10

Key.—ᵃ Matthew, ᵇ Mark, ᶜ Luke, ᵈ John.

¹ Gr. *bondservants*.　　　　² Or, *torches*.

Matthew 25.

bridegroom came; and they that were
ready went in with him to the marriage
11 feast: and the door was shut. Afterward
come also the other virgins, saying, Lord,
12 Lord, open to us. But he answered and
said, Verily I say unto you, I know you
13 not. Watch therefore, for ye know not the
day nor the hour.

§ 137. Parable of the Talents.

Matthew 25.

14   ^aFor *it is* as *when* a man, going into another country, called his own ¹servants,
15 and delivered unto them his goods. And
unto one he gave five talents, to another
two, to another one; to each according to
his several ability; and he went on his
16 journey. Straightway he that received
the five talents went and traded with them,
17 and made other five talents. In like manner he also that *received* the two gained
18 other two. But he that received the one
went away and digged in the earth, and
19 hid his lord's money. Now after a long
time the lord of those ¹servants cometh,
20 and maketh a reckoning with them. And
he that received the five talents came and
brought other five talents, saying, Lord,
thou deliveredst unto me five talents: lo,
21 I have gained other five talents. His lord
said unto him, Well done, good and faithful ²servant: thou hast been faithful over
a few things, I will set thee over many
things: enter thou into the joy of thy lord.
22 And he also that *received* the two talents
came and said, Lord, thou deliveredst unto
me two talents: lo, I have gained other
23 two talents. His lord said unto him, Well
done, good and faithful ²servant; thou
hast been faithful over a few things, I will

KEY.—^a Matthew, ^b Mark, ^c Luke, ^d John.

¹ Gr. *bondservants.*   ² Gr. *bondservant.*

set thee over many things: enter thou into
the joy of thy lord. And he also that had 24
received the one talent came and said,
Lord, I knew thee that thou art a hard
man, reaping where thou didst not sow,
and gathering where thou didst not scatter: and I was afraid, and went away and 25
hid thy talent in the earth: lo, thou hast
thine own. But his lord answered and 26
said unto him, Thou wicked and slothful
¹ servant, thou knewest that I reap where
I sowed not, and gather where I did not
scatter; thou oughtest therefore to have 27
put my money to the bankers, and at my
coming I should have received back mine
own with interest. Take ye away there- 28
fore the talent from him, and give it unto
him that hath the ten talents. For unto 29
every one that hath shall be given, and he
shall have abundance: but from him that
hath not, even that which he hath shall be
taken away. And cast ye out the unprofit- 30
able ¹ servant into the outer darkness:
there shall be the weeping and gnashing of
teeth.

§ 138. The Judgement Depicted.

ᵃ But when the Son of man shall come 31
in his glory, and all the angels with him,
then shall he sit on the throne of his
glory: and before him shall be gathered all 32
the nations: and he shall separate them
one from another, as the shepherd separat-
eth the sheep from the ² goats: and he 33
shall set the sheep on his right hand, but
the ² goats on the left. Then shall the 34
King say unto them on his right hand,
Come, ye blessed of my Father, inherit
the kingdom prepared for you from the
foundation of the world: for I was an 35

KEY.—ᵃ Matthew, ᵇ Mark, ᶜ Luke, ᵈ John.

¹ Gr. *bondservant*.   ² Gr. *kids*.

§ 139. The Supper at Bethany.

Mark's Account.

Chap. 14.

And while he was in Bethany in the house of Simon the 3 leper, as he sat at meat, there came a woman having an alabaster cruse of ointment of pure nard very costly ; *and* she brake the cruse, and poured it over his head. But 4 there were some that had indignation among themselves, *saying*, To what purpose hath this waste of the ointment been made ? For this ointment might have been 5 sold for above three hundred shillings, and given to the poor. And they murmured against her.

John's Account.

Chap. 12.

So they made him a supper there : and Martha served, 2 but Lazarus was one of them that sat at meat with him. Mary therefore took a pound of ointment of pure nard, 3 very precious, and anointed the feet of Jesus, and wiped his feet with her hair : and the house was filled with the odour of the ointment. But Judas Iscariot, one of his 4 disciples, who should betray him, saith, Why was not this 5 ointment sold for three hundred shillings, and given to the poor ? Now this he said, not because cared for the poor ; 6 but because he was a thief, and having the bag took away what was put therein. Jesus therefore said, Suffer her to 7 keep it against the day of my burying. For the poor ye 8 have always with you ; but me ye have not always.

Matthew's Account.

Chap. 26.

But Jesus perceiving it said unto them, Why trouble ye 10 the woman ? for she hath wrought a good work upon me. For ye have the poor always with you ; but me ye have 11 not always. For in that she poured this ointment upon 12 my body, she did it to prepare me for burial. Verily I say 13 unto you, Wheresoever this gospel shall be preached in the whole world, that also which this woman hath done shall be spoken of for a memorial of her.

Matthew 25.

hungred, and ye gave me meat: I was
thirsty, and ye gave me drink: I was a
stranger, and ye took me in; naked, and
36 ye clothed me: I was sick, and ye visited
me ﹕ I was in prison, and ye came unto me.
37 Then shall the righteous answer him, saying, Lord, when saw we thee an hungred,
and fed thee? or athirst, and gave thee
38 drink? And when saw we thee a stranger,
and took thee in? or naked, and clothed
39 thee? And when saw we thee sick, or in
40 prison, and came unto thee? And the
King shall answer and say unto them,
Verily I say unto you, Inasmuch as ye did
it unto one of these my brethren, *even*
41 these least, ye did it unto me. Then shall
he say also unto them on the left hand, ·
¹Depart from me, ye cursed, into the
eternal fire which is prepared for the devil
42 and his angels: for I was an hungred, and
ye gave me no meat: I was thirsty, and ye
43 gave me no drink: I was a stranger, and
ye took me not in; naked, and ye clothed
me not; sick, and in prison, and ye visited
44 me not. Then shall they also answer,
saying, Lord, when saw we thee an hungred, or athirst, or a stranger, or naked, or
sick, or in prison, and did not minister un-
45 to thee? Then shall he answer them, saying, Verily I say unto you, Inasmuch as ye
did it not unto one of these least, ye did it
46 not unto me. And these shall go away
into eternal punishment: but the righteous
into eternal life.

§ 139. The Supper at Bethany.*

Matthew 26.

6   ªNow when Jesus was in Bethany, in the
7 house of Simon the leper, there came un-

KEY.—ª Matthew, ᵇ Mark, ᶜ Luke, ᵈ John.

¹ Or, *Depart from me under a curse.*

* John seems to place the supper at Bethany some days
earlier, when Jesus arrived at that town on his first coming

to him a woman having an alabaster cruse of exceeding precious ointment, and she poured it upon his head, as he sat at meat, [for]* [d] they made him a supper there: and Martha served; but Lazarus was one of them that sat at meat with him. Mary therefore took a pound of [1] pure nard, very precious, and anointed the feet of Jesus, and wiped his feet with her hair: and the house was filled with the odor of the ointment. [a] But when the disciples saw it, they 8 had indignation, saying, To what purpose is this waste? For this ointment might have 9 been sold for much, and given to the poor. [And]* [d] Judas Iscariot, one of his disciples, who should betray him, saith, why was not this ointment sold for three hundred shillings and given to the poor? Now this he said, not because he cared for the poor; but because he was a thief, and having the [2] bag [3] took away what was put therein. **Mark 14.**

[b] But Jesus said, Let her alone; why 6 trouble ye her? She hath wrought a good work on me. For ye have the 7 poor always with you, and whensoever ye will ye can do them good: But me ye have not always. She hath done what 8 she could: she hath anointed my body aforehand for the burying. And verily I 9 say unto you, Wheresoever the gospel shall be preached throughout the whole world, that also which this woman hath done shall be spoken of for a memorial of her.

§ 140. The Traitor.

[a] And it came to pass, when Jesus had 1 finished all these words, he said unto his

KEY.—[a] Matthew, [b] Mark, [c] Luke, [d] John.

[1] Or, *liquid nard.*   [2] Or, *box.*
[3] Or, *carried what was put therein.*

up to the passover. Matthew and Mark place it here in connection with the treason of Judas. We prefer this for internal reasons. Harmonists are divided.

* Word inserted by compiler.

§ 140. The Traitor.

Matthew's Account.

Chap. 26.

14 Then one of the twelve, who was called Judas Iscariot,
15 went unto the chief priests, and said, What are ye willing ·
   to give me, and I will deliver him unto you? And they
   weighed unto him thirty pieces of silver. And from that
16 time he sought opportunity to deliver him *unto them*.

Mark's Account.

Chap. 14.

 1 Now after two days was *the feast of* the passover and
   the unleavened bread : and the chief priests and the scribes
   sought how they might take him with subtilty, and kill
 2 him : for they said, Not during the feast, lest haply there
   shall be a tumult of the people.
10 And Judas Iscariot, he that was one of the twelve, went
   away unto the chief priests, that he might deliver him unto
11 them. And they, when they heard it, were glad, and prom-
   ised to give him money. And he sought how he might
   conveniently deliver him *unto them*.

Luke's Account.

Chap. 22.

 1 Now the feast of unleavened bread drew nigh, which is
 2 called the Passover. And the chief priests and the scribes
   sought how they might put him to death ; for they feared
   the people.

§ 141. The Passover Prepared.

Matthew's Account.

Now on the first *day* of unleavened bread the disciples 17 came to Jesus, saying, Where wilt thou that we make ready for thee to eat the passover? And he said, Go into the 18 city to such a man, and say unto him, The Master saith, My time is at hand ; I keep the passover at thy house with my disciples. And the disciples did as Jesus appointed 19 them ; and they made ready the passover. Now when 20 even was come, he was sitting at meat with the twelve disciples.

Mark's Account.

And on the first day of unleavened bread, when they 12 sacrificed the passover, his disciples say unto him, Where wilt thou that we go and make ready that thou mayest eat the passover? And he sendeth two of his disciples, and 13 saith unto them, Go into the city, and there shall meet you a man bearing a pitcher of water : follow him ; and 14 wheresoever he shall enter in, say to the goodman of the house, The Master saith, Where is my guest-chamber, where I shall eat the passover with my disciples? And 15 he will himself shew you a large upper room furnished *and* ready : and there make ready for us. And the dis- 16 ciples went forth, and came into the city, and found as he had said unto them : and they made ready the passover.

And when it was evening he cometh with the twelve. 17

Matthew 26.

2 disciples, Ye know that after two days the
  passover cometh, and the Son of man is de-
3 livered up to be crucified.   Then were
  gathered together the chief priests, and the
  elders of the people, unto the court of the
4 high priest, who was called Caiaphas ; and
  they took counsel together that they might
5 take Jesus by subtilty, and kill him.   But
  they said, Not during the feast, lest a
Luke 22.   tumult arise among the people.

3   cAnd Satan entered into Judas who was
  called Iscariot, being of the number of the
4 twelve. And he went away, and communed
  with the chief priests and captains, a and
  said, What are ye willing to give me, and I
5 will deliver him unto you ? cAnd they were
  glad, and covenanted to give him money ;
  a and they weighed unto him thirty pieces
6 of silver. cAnd he consented, and sought
  opportunity to deliver him unto them [1] in
  the absence of the multitude.

§ 141. The Passover Prepared.

Luke 22.

7   cAnd the day of unleavened bread came,
  on which the passover must be sacrificed.
8 And he sent Peter and John, saying, Go
  and make ready for us the passover, that
9 we may eat.   And they said unto him,
10 Where wilt thou that we make ready ? And
  he said unto them, Behold, when ye are
  entered into the city, there shall meet you
  a man bearing a pitcher of water ; follow
  him into the house whereinto he goeth.
11 And ye shall say unto the goodman of the
  house, The [2] Master saith unto thee, Where
  is the guest-chamber, where I shall eat the
12 passover with my disciples?   And he will
  b himself cshew you a large upper room
13 furnished: there make ready.   And they

KEY.—a Matthew, b Mark, c Luke, d John.

[1] Or, *without tumult*.   [2] Or, *Teacher*.

went, and found as he had said unto them:
and they made ready the passover.

And when ^b it was evening, [and]* ^cthe 14
hour was come, he sat down, and the apos-
tles with him. And he said unto them, 15
With desire I have desired to eat this passover with you before I suffer: for I say 16
unto you, I shall not eat it, until it be fulfilled in the kingdom of God. And he re- 17
ceived a cup,and when he had given thanks,
he said, Take this, and divide it among 18
yourselves: for I say unto you, I shall not
drink from henceforth of the fruit of the
vine, until the kingdom of God shall
come.

§ 142. Washing the Disciples' Feet.

^cAnd there arose also a contention among 24
them, which of them was accounted to be
¹ greatest. And he said unto them, The 25
kings of the Gentiles have lordship over
them; and they that have authority over
them are called Benefactors. But ye *shall* 26
not *be* so: but he that is the greater among
you, let him become as the younger; and
he that is chief, as he that doth serve. For 27
whether is greater, he that ³ sitteth at meat,
or he that serveth? is not he that ³ sitteth
at meat? but I am in the midst of you as
he that serveth. But ye are they that have 28
continued with me in my trials; and ⁵ I 29
appoint unto you a kingdom, even as my
Father appointed unto me, that ye may 30
eat and drink at my table in my kingdom;
and ye shall sit on thrones judging the
twelve tribes of Israel.

^d Now before the feast of the **John 13.** 1

KEY.—^a Matthew, ^b Mark, ^c Luke, ^d John.

³ Gr. *greater*.   ⁴ Gr. *reclineth*.
⁵ Or, *I appoint unto you, even as my Father appointed unto
me a kingdom, that ye may eat and drink &c.*

* Word inserted by compiler.

John 13.

passover, Jesus knowing that his hour was come that he should depart out of this world unto the Father, having loved his own who were in the world, he loved them

2 [1]unto the end. And during supper, the devil having already put into the heart of Judas Iscariot, Simon's *son*, to betray him,

3 *Jesus*, knowing that the Father had given all things into his hands, and that he came

4 forth from God, and goeth unto God, riseth from supper, and layeth aside his garments; and he took a towel, and girded himself.

5 Then he poureth water into the bason, and began to wash the disciples' feet, and to wipe them with the towel wherewith he

6 was girded. So he cometh to Simon Peter. He saith unto him, Lord, dost thou

7 wash my feet? Jesus answered and said unto him, What I do thou knowest not now;

8 but thou shalt understand hereafter. Peter saith unto him, Thou shalt never wash my feet. Jesus answered him, If I wash thee

9 not, thou hast no part with me. Simon Peter saith unto him, Lord, not my fect only, but also my hands and my head.

10 Jesus saith to him, He that is bathed need-eth not [2]save to wash his feet, but is clean every whit: and ye are clean, but not all. For he knew him that should betray him ; therefore said he, ye are not all clean.

12   So when he had washed their feet, and taken his garments, and [3]sat down again,

13 he said unto them, Know ye what I have done to you? Ye call me 'Master, and,

14 Lord: and ye say well; for so I am. If I then, the Lord and the 'Master, have washed your feet, ye also ought to wash

15 one another's feet. For I have given you an example, that ye also should do as I

KEY.—[a] Matthew, [b] Mark, [c] Luke, [d] John.

[1] Or, *to the uttermost.*
[2] Some ancient authorities omit *save,* and *his feet.*
[3] Gr. *reclined.*   [4] Or, *Teacher.*

have done to you. Verily, verily, I say 16
unto you, A ¹servant is not greater than
his lord; neither ²one that is sent greater
than he that sent him. If ye know these 17
things, blessed are ye if ye do them. I 18
speak not of you all: I know whom I ³have
chosen: but that the scripture may be fulfilled, He that eateth ⁴my bread lifted up
his heel against me. From henceforth I 19
tell you before it come to pass, that, when
it is come to pass, ye may believe that I
am *he*. Verily, verily, I say unto you, He 20
that receiveth whomsoever I send receiveth me; and he that receiveth me receiveth him that sent me.

§ 143. The Traitor Revealed.

ᵈ When Jesus had thus said, he was 21
troubled in the spirit, and testified, and
said, Verily, verily, I say unto you, that
one of you shall betray me. The disciples 22
looked one on another, doubting of whom
he spake. ᵇ They began to be sorrowful,
and to say unto him, one by one, Is it I?
And he said unto them, It is one of the
twelve, he that dippeth with me in the
dish. For the Son of man goeth ᶜ as it
hath been determined, ᵇ even as it is written of him: but woe unto that man
through whom the Son of man is betrayed! Good were it for that man if he
had not been born. ᵈ There was at the table 23
reclining in Jesus' bosom one of his disciples, whom Jesus loved. Simon Peter 24
therefore beckoneth to him, and saith unto
him, Tell *us* who it is of whom he speaketh. He leaning back, as he was, on Jesus' 25
breast saith unto him, Lord, who is it?
Jesus therefore answereth, He it is, for 26

KEY.—ᵃ Matthew, ᵇ Mark, ᶜ Luke, ᵈ John.

¹ Gr. *bondservant.*　　² Gr. *an apostle.*　　³ Or, *chose.*
⁴ Many ancient authorities read *his bread with me.*

§ 143. The Traitor Revealed.

Matthew's Account.

Chap. 26.

21 And as they were eating, he said, Verily I say unto
22 you, that one of you shall betray me. And they were
exceeding sorrowful, and began to say unto him every one,
23 Is it I, Lord? And he answered and said, He that dipped
his hand with me in the dish, the same shall betray me.
24 The Son of man goeth, even as it is written of him : but
woe unto that man through whom the Son of man is
betrayed ! good were it for that man if he had not been
25 born. And Judas, who betrayed him, answered and said,
Is it I, Rabbi? He saith unto him, Thou hast said.

Mark's Account.

Chap. 14.

18 And as they sat and were eating, Jesus said, Verily I
say unto you, One of you shall betray me, *even* he that
19 eateth with me. They began to be sorrowful, and to say
20 unto him one by one, Is it I? And he said unto them, *It is*
one of the twelve, he that dippeth with me in the dish.
21 For the Son of man goeth, even as it is written of him :
but woe unto that man through whom the Son of man is
betrayed ! good were it for that man if he had not been
born.

Luke's Account.

Chap. 22.

21 But behold, the hand of him that betrayeth me is with
22 me on the table. For the Son of man indeed goeth, as it
hath been determined : but woe unto that man through
23 whom he is betrayed ! And they began to question
among themselves, which of them it was that should do
this thing.

198

whom I shall dip the sop, and give it him. So when he had dipped the sop, he taketh and giveth it to Judas, *the son* of Simon Iscariot. ᵃAnd Judas, which betrayed him, said, Is it I, Rabbi? He saith unto
27 him, Thou hast said. ᵈAnd after the sop, then entered Satan into him. Jesus therefore saith unto him, That thou doest, do
28 quickly. Now no man at the table knew for what intent he spake this unto him.
29 For some thought, because Judas had the ¹bag, that Jesus said unto him, Buy what things we have need of for the feast; or, that he should give something to the
30 poor. He then having received the sop went out straightway: and it was night.

§ 144. Several Predictions.

31 ᵈWhen therefore he was gone out, Jesus ⟩ saith, Now ²is the Son of man glorified,
32 and God ²is glorified in him; and God shall glorify him in himself, and straightway
33 shall he glorify him. Little children, yet a little while I am with you. Ye shall seek me: and as I said unto the Jews, Whither I go, ye cannot come; so now I say unto
34 you. A new commandment I give unto you, that ye love one another; ³even as I have loved you, that ye also love one
35 another. By this shall all men know that ye are my disciples, if ye have love one to another.
36 Simon Peter saith unto him, Lord, whither goest thou? Jesus answered, Whither I go, thou canst not follow me now; but thou shalt follow afterwards.
37 Peter saith unto him, Lord, why cannot I follow thee even now? I will lay

KEY.—ᵃ Matthew, ᵇ Mark, ᶜ Luke, ᵈ John.

¹ Or, *box*. ² Or, *was*.
³ Or, *even as I loved you, that ye also may love one another*.

down my life for thee.   ᵇAnd in like manner also said they all.   ᵈJesus answereth, 38
Wilt thou lay down thy life for me?   Verily, verily, I say unto thee, the cock shall
not crow, till thou hast denied me thrice.

ᶜSimon, Simon, behold, Satan **Luke 22.** 31
¹asked to have you, that he might sift you
as wheat: but I made supplication for thee, 32
that thy faith fail not: and do thou, when
once thou hast turned again, stablish thy
brethren.   And he said unto him, Lord, 33
with thee I am ready to go both to prison
and to death.   And he said, I tell thee, 34
Peter, the cock shall not crow this day,
until thou shalt thrice deny that thou
knowest me.

And he said unto them, When I sent 35
you forth without purse, and wallet, and
shoes, lacked ye anything?   And they
said, Nothing.   And he said unto them, 36
But now, he that hath a purse, let him
take it, and likewise a wallet: ²and he
that hath none, let him sell his cloke, and
buy a sword.   For I say unto you, that 37
this which is written must be fulfilled in
me, And he was reckoned with trans-
gressors: for that which concerneth me
hath ³fulfilment.   And they said, Lord, 38
behold, here are two swords.   And he
said unto them, It is enough.

§ 145.   The Lord's Supper Instituted.

Matthew 26.

ᵃAnd as they were eating, Jesus took 26
⁴bread, and blessed, and brake it; and he
gave to the disciples, and said, Take, eat;
this is my body; ᶜthis do in remembrance

KEY.—ᵃ Matthew, ᵇ Mark, ᶜ Luke, ᵈ John.

¹ Or, *obtained you by asking.*
² Or, *and he that hath no sword, let him sell his cloke, and
buy one.*
³ Gr. *end.*   ⁴ Or, *a loaf.*

§ 144. Several Predictions.

Matthew's Account.

Chap. 26.

33 But Peter answered and said unto him, If all shall be
34 offended in thee, I will never be offended. Jesus said
unto him, Verily I say unto thee, that this night, before
35 the cock crow, thou shalt deny me thrice. Peter saith
unto him, Even if I must die with thee, *yet* will I not deny
thee. Likewise also said all the disciples.

Mark's Account.

Chap. 14.

29 But Peter said unto him, Although all men shall be of-
30 fended, yet will not I. And Jesus saith unto him, Verily
I say unto thee, that thou to-day, *even* this night, before
31 the cock crow twice, shalt deny me thrice. But he spake
exceeding vehemently, If I must die with thee, I will not
deny thee. And in like manner also said they all.

Luke's Account.

Chap. 22.

33 And he said unto him, Lord, with thee I am ready to go
34 both to prison and to death. And he said, I tell thee,
Peter, the cock shall not crow this day, until thou shalt
thrice deny that thou knowest me.

§ 145. The Lord's Supper Instituted.

Mark's Account.

Chap. 14.

And as they were eating, he took bread, and when he 22
had blessed, he brake it, and gave to them, and said,
Take ye : this is my body. And he took a cup, and when 23
he had given thanks, he gave to them : <u>and they all drank</u>
<u>of it.</u> And he said unto them, This is my blood of the 24
covenant, which is shed for many. Verily I say unto 25
you, I shall no more drink of the fruit of the vine, until
that day when I drink it new in the kingdom of God.

Luke's Account.

Chap. 22.

And he took bread, and when he had given thanks, he 19
brake it, and gave to them, saying, This is my body
which is given for you : <u>this do in remembrance of me.</u>
And the cup in like manner after supper, saying, This 20
cup is the new covenant in my blood, *even* that which is
<u>poured out for you.</u> I say unto you, I shall not drink
from henceforth of the fruit of the vine, until the kingdom
of God shall come.

Matthew 26.

27 of me. [a]And he took [1]a cup, and gave
thanks, and gave to them, saying, Drink
28 ye all of it; for this is my blood of the
[2]covenant, which is shed for many unto
remission of sins, [c]even that which is
29 poured out for you. [a]But I say unto you,
I shall not drink henceforth of this fruit of
the vine, until that day when I drink it
new with you in my Father's kingdom.
[b]And they all drank of it.

§ 146. The Sermon before the Cross.

John 14.

1 [And Jesus said,]* [d]Let not your heart be
troubled: [3]believe in God, believe also in
2 me. In my Father's house are many [4]man-
sions; if it were not so, I would have told
you; for I go to prepare a place for you.
3 And if I go and prepare a place for you,
I come again, and will receive you unto
myself; that where I am, *there* ye may be
4 also. [5]And whither I go, ye know the
5 way. Thomas saith unto him, Lord, we
know not whither thou goest; how know
6 we the way? Jesus saith unto him, I am
the way, and the truth, and the life:
no one cometh unto the Father, but [6]by
7 me. If ye had known me, ye would have
known my Father also: from henceforth
8 ye know him, and have seen him. Philip
saith unto him, Lord, shew us the Father,
9 and it sufficeth us. Jesus saith unto him,
Have I been so long time with you, and
dost thou not know me, Philip? he that
hath seen me hath seen the Father; how
10 sayest thou, Shew us the Father? Be-

KEY.—[a] Matthew, [b] Mark, [c] Luke, [d] John.

[1] Some ancient authorities read *the cup.*
[2] Many ancient authorities insert *new.*
[3] Or, *ye believe in God.*   [4] Or, *abiding-places.*
[5] Many ancient authorities read *And whither I go ye know,
and the way ye know.*   [6] Or, *through.*

* Words inserted by compiler.

lievest thou not that I am in the Father, and the Father in me? the words that I say unto you I speak not from myself: but the Father abiding in me doeth his works. Believe me that I am in the 11 Father, and the Father in me: or else believe me for the very works' sake. Verily, verily, I say unto you, He that 12 believeth on me, the works that I do shall he do also; and greater *works* than these shall he do; because I go unto the Father. And whatsoever ye shall ask in my name, 13 that will I do, that the Father may he glorified in the Son. If ye shall ' ask any 14 thing in my name, that will I do. If ye 15 love me, ye will keep my commandments. And I will ' pray the Father, and he shall 16 give you another ' Comforter, that he may be with you for ever, *even* the Spirit of 17 truth: whom the world cannot receive; for it beholdeth him not, neither knoweth him: ye know him; for he abideth with you, and shall be in you. I will not leave 18 you ' desolate: I come unto you. Yet a 19 little while, and the world beholdeth me no more; but ye behold me: because I live, ' ye shall live also. In that day ye 20 shall know that I am in my Father, and ye in me, and I in you. He that hath my 21 commandments, and keepeth them, he it is that loveth me: and he that loveth me shall be loved of my Father, and I will love him, and will manifest myself unto him. Judas (not Iscariot) saith unto him, 22 Lord, what is come to pass that thou wilt manifest thyself unto us, and not unto the world? Jesus answered and said unto 23 him, If a man love me, he will keep my

KEY.—ᵃ Matthew, ᵇ Mark, ᶜ Luke, ᵈ John.

¹ Many ancient authorities add *me.*
² Gr. *make request of.*
⁸ Or, *Advocate.* Or, *Helper.* Gr. *Paraclete.*
⁴ Or, *orphans.*   ⁵ Or, *and ye shall live.*

John 14.

word: and my Father will love him, and we will come unto him, and make our
24 abode with him. He that loveth me not keepeth not my words: and the word which ye hear is not mine, but the Father's who sent me.

25 These things have I spoken unto you,
26 while *yet* abiding with you. But the Comforter, *even* the Holy Spirit, whom the Father will send in my name, he shall teach you all things, and bring to your remembrance all that I said unto you. Peace I leave with you; my peace I give
27 unto you: not as the world giveth, give I unto you. Let not your heart be troubled,
28 neither let it be fearful. Ye heard how I said to you, I go away, and I come unto you. If ye loved me, ye would have rejoiced, because I go unto the Father: for the
29 Father is greater than I. And now I have told you before it come to pass, that, when
30 it is come to pass, ye may believe. I will no more speak much with you, for the prince of the world cometh: and he hath nothing
31 in me; but that the world may know that I love the Father, and as the Father gave me commandment, even so I do. Arise, let us go hence.

1 **John 15.** I am the true vine, and my father
2 is the husbandman. Every branch in me that beareth not fruit, he taketh it away: and every *branch* that beareth fruit, he
3 cleanseth it, that it may bear more fruit. Already ye are clean because of the word
4 which I have spoken unto you. Abide in me, and I in you. As the branch cannot bear fruit of itself, except it abide in the vine; so neither can ye, except ye
5 abide in me. I am the vine, ye are the branches: He that abideth in me, and I in him, the same beareth much fruit: for apart

KEY.—ᵃ Matthew, ᵇ Mark, ᶜ Luke, ᵈ John.

from me ye can do nothing. If a man 6
abide not in me, he is cast forth as a branch,
and is withered; and they gather them,
and cast them into the fire, and they are
burned. If ye abide in me, and my words 7
abide in you, ask whatsoever ye will, and it
shall be done unto you. Herein [1] is my 8
Father glorified, [2] that ye bear much fruit;
and *so* shall ye be my disciples. Even as 9
the Father hath loved me, I also have loved
you: abide ye in my love. If ye keep my 10
commandments, ye shall abide in my love;
even as I have kept my Father's commandments, and abide in his love. These things 11
have I spoken unto you, that my joy may
be in you, and *that* your joy may be made
full. This is my commandment, that ye 12
love one another, even as I have loved
you. Greater love hath no man than this, 13
that a man lay down his life for his
friends. Ye are my friends, if ye do the 14
things which I command you. No longer 15
do I call you [3] servants; for the servant
knoweth not what his lord doeth: but I
have called you friends; for all things that
I heard from my Father I have made
known unto you. Ye did not choose me, 16
but I chose you, and appointed you, that
ye should go and bear fruit, and *that* your
fruit should abide: that whatsoever ye
shall ask of the Father in my name, he may
give it you. These things I command you, 17
that ye may love one another. If the 18
world hateth you, [4] ye know that it hath
hated me before *it hated* you. If ye were 19
of the world, the world would love its
own: but because ye are not of the world,
but I chose you out of the world, there-

KEY.—[a] Matthew, [b] Mark, [c] Luke, [d] John.

[1] Or, *was.*
[2] Many ancient authorities read *that ye bear much fruit,
and be my disciples.*
[3] Gr. *bondservants.*   [4] Or, *know ye.*

John 15.

20 fore the world hateth you. Remember
the word that I said unto you, A ¹ servant
is not greater than his lord. If they persecuted me, they will also persecute you;
if they kept my word, they will keep

21 yours also. But all these things will they
do unto you for my name's sake, because

22 they know not him that sent me. If I had
not come and spoken unto them, they had
not had sin: but now they have no excuse

23 for their sin. He that hateth me hateth

24 my Father also. If I had not done
among them the works which none other
did, they had not had sin: but now have
they both seen and hated both me and my

25 Father. But *this cometh to pass*, that the
word may be fulfilled that is written in
their law, They hated me without a cause.

26 But when the Comforter is come, whom I
will send unto you from the Father, *even*
the Spirit of truth, which ² proceedeth
from the Father, he shall bear witness of

27 me: ³ and ye also bear witness, because ye
have been with me from the beginning.

1 **John 16.** These things have I spoken unto
you, that ye should not be made to

2 stumble. They shall put you out of the
synagogues: yea, the hour cometh, that
whosoever killeth you shall think that he

3 offereth service unto God. And these
things will they do, because they have not

4 known the Father, nor me. But these
things have I spoken unto you, that when
their hour is come, ye may remember
them, how that I told you. And these
things I said not unto you from the begin-

5 ning, because I was with you. But now
I go unto him that sent me: and none of

6 you asketh me, Whither goest thou? But
because I have spoken these things unto

KEY.—ᵃ Matthew, ᵇ Mark, ᶜ Luke, ᵈ John.

¹ Gr. *bondservant.*　　² Or, *goeth forth from.*
³ Or, *and bear ye also witness.*

John 16.

you, sorrow hath filled your heart.
Nevertheless I tell you the truth; It is 7
expedient for you that I go away: for if I
go not away, the Comforter will not come
unto you; but if I go, I will send him
unto you. And he, when he is come, will 8
convict the world in respect of sin, and of
righteousness, and of judgement: of sin, 9
because they believe not on me; of right- 10
eousness, because I go to the Father, and 11
ye behold me no more; of judgement,
because the prince of this world hath been
judged. I have yet many things to say 12
unto you, but ye cannot bear them now.
Howbeit when he, the Spirit of truth, is 13
come, he shall guide you into all the truth;
for he shall not speak from himself; but
what things soever he shall hear, *these* shall
he speak: and he shall declare unto you
the things that are to come. He shall 14
glorify me: for he shall take of mine, and
shall declare *it* unto you. All things 15
whatsoever the Father hath are mine:
therefore said I, that he taketh of mine, and
shall declare *it* unto you. A little while, 16
and ye behold me no more; and again a
little while, and ye shall see me. *Some* of 17
his disciples therefore said one to another,
What is this that he saith unto us, A little
while, and ye behold me not; and again a
little while and ye shall see me: and,
Because I go to the Father? They said 18
therefore, What is this that he saith, A
little while? We know not what he saith.
Jesus perceived that they were desirous 19
to ask him, and he said unto them, Do ye
inquire among yourselves concerning this,
that I said, A little while, and ye behold
me not, and again a little while, and ye shall
see me? Verily, verily, I say unto you, 20
that ye shall weep and lament, but the

KEY.—ᵃ Matthew, ᵇ Mark, ᶜ Luke, ᵈ John.

John 16.

world shall rejoice: ye shall be sorrowful, but your sorrow shall be turned into
21 joy. A woman when she is in travail hath
sorrow, because her hour is come: but
when she is delivered of the child, she
remembereth no more the anguish, for the
joy that a man is born into the world.
22 And ye therefore now have sorrow: but I
will see you again, and your heart shall
rejoice, and your joy no one taketh away
23 from you. And in that day ye shall ¹ask
me nothing. Verily, verily, I say unto you,
If ye shall ask anything of the Father, he
24 will give it you in my name. Hitherto have ye asked nothing in my name:
ask, and ye shall receive, that your joy
may be made full.
25 These things have I spoken unto you in
²dark sayings: the hour cometh, when I
shall no more speak unto you in ²dark sayings, but shall tell you plainly of the
26 Father. In that day ye shall ask in my
name: and I say not unto you, that I will
27 ³pray the Father for you; for the Father
himself loveth you, because ye have loved
me, and and have believed that I came
28 forth from the Father. I came out from the
Father, and am come into the world: again,
I leave the world, and go unto the Father.
29 His disciples say, Lo, now speakest thou
plainly, and speakest no ⁴dark saying.
30 Now know we that thou knowest all
things, and needest not that any man
should ask thee: by this we believe that
31 thou camest forth from God. Jesus
32 answered them, Do ye now believe? Behold, the hour cometh, yea, is come, that
ye shall be scattered, every man to his
own, and shall leave me alone: and *yet* I
am not alone, because the Father is with

KEY.—ᵃ Matthew, ᵇ Mark, ᶜ Luke, ᵈ John.

¹ Or, *ask me no questions.*   ² Or, *parables.*
³ Gr. *make request of.*   ⁴ Or. *parable.*

me. These things have I spoken unto you, 33 that in me ye may have peace. In the world ye have tribulation: but be of good cheer; I have overcome the world.

§ 147. The Passover Prayer.

ᵈ These things spake Jesus; and lifting 1 up his eyes to heaven, he said, Father, the hour is come; glorify thy Son, that the Son may glorify thee: even as thou gav- 2 est him authority over all flesh, that whatsoever thou hast given him, to them he should give eternal life. And this is life 3 eternal, that they should know thee the only true God, and him whom thou didst send, *even* Jesus Christ. I glorified thee on 4 the earth, having accomplished the work which thou hast given me to do. And 5 now, O Father, glorify thou me with thine own self with the glory which I had with thee before the world was. I manifested 6 thy name unto the men whom thou gavest me out of the world; thine they were, and thou gavest them to me; and they have kept thy word. Now they know that 7 all things whatsoever thou hast given me are from thee: for the words which thou 8 gavest me I have given unto them; and they received *them,* and knew of a truth that I came forth from thee, and they believed that thou didst send me. I ¹pray 9 for them: I ¹pray not for the world, but for those whom thou hast given me; for they are thine: and all things that are 10 mine are thine, and thine are mine: and I am glorified in them. And I am no more 11 in the world, and these are in the world, and I come to thee. Holy Father, keep them in thy name which thou hast given

KEY.—ᵃ Matthew, ᵇ Mark, ᶜ Luke, ᵈ John.

¹ Gr. *make request.*

§ 147. The Passover Prayer.

Mark's Account.

Chap. 14.

And when they had sung a hymn, they went out unto 26
the mount of Olives.

Luke's Account.

Chap. 22.

And he came out, and went, as his custom was, unto 39
the mount of Olives ; and the disciples also followed
him.

me, that they may be one, even as we *are*.

12 While,I was with them, I kept them in thy
name which thou hast given me: and I
guarded them, and not one of them perished, but the son of perdition; that the

13 scripture might be fulfilled. But now I
come to thee; and these things I speak in
the world, that they may have my joy

14 made full in themselves. I have given
them thy word; and the world hated them,
because they are not of the world, even as

15 I am not of the world. I [1] pray not that
thou shouldest take them [2] from the world,
but that thou shouldest keep them [2] from

16 [3] the evil *one*. They are not of the world,

17 even as I am not of the world. [4] Sanctify

18 them in the truth: thy word is truth. As
thou didst send me into the world, even so

19 sent I them into the world. And for their
sakes I sanctify myself, that they themselves also may be sanctified in truth.

20 Neither for these only do I pray, but for
them also that believe on me through their

21 word; that they may all be one; even as
thou, Father, *art* in me, and I in thee, that
they also may be in us: that the world

22 may believe that thou didst send me. And
the glory which thou hast given me I have
given unto them; that they may be one,

23 even as we *are* one; I in them and thou in
me, that they may be perfected into
one; that the world may know that thou
didst send me, and lovedst them, even as

24 thou lovedst me. Father, [5] that which
thou hast given me, I desire that, where I
am, they also may be with me; that they
may behold my glory, which thou
hast given me: for thou lovedst me be-

25 fore the foundation of the world. O right-

KEY.—[a] Matthew, [b] Mark, [c] Luke, [d] John.

[1] Gr. *make request*   [2] Gr. *out of.*
[3] Or, *evil.*   [4] Or, *Consecrate.*
[5] **Many** ancient authorities read *those whom.*

John 17.

eous Father, the world knew thee not, but
I knew thee; and these knew that thou
didst send me; and I made known unto 26
them thy name, and will make it known;
that the love wherewith thou lovedst me
may be in them, and I in them.   **Matthew 26.**

ᵃAnd when they had sung a hymn, they 30
went out ᵈover the brook Kidron ᵃunto
the mount of Olives, ᶜas his custom was.

§ 148. Gethsemane.

Matthew 26.

ᵃThen saith Jesus unto them, All ye shall 31
be ¹offended in me this night: for it is
written, I will smite the shepherd, and
the sheep of the flock shall be scattered
abroad.   But after I am raised up, I will 32
go before you into Galilee.

Then cometh Jesus with them unto ²a 36
place called Gethsemane, and saith unto
his disciples, Sit ye here, while I go yonder
and pray.   ᶜPray that ye enter not into
temptation.   ᵃAnd he took with him Peter 37
and the two sons of Zebedee, and began to
be sorrowful, ᵇgreatly amazed, ᵃand sore
troubled.   Then saith he unto them, My 38
soul is exceeding sorrowful, even unto
death: abide ye here, and watch with me.
And he went forward a little, ᶜabout a 39
stone's cast, ᵃand fell ᵇon the ground ᵃon
his face, and prayed ᵇthat, if it were possible, the hour might pass away from him,
ᵃsaying, O my Father, if it be possible, let
this cup pass away from me: nevertheless,
not as I will, but as thou wilt.   And he 40
cometh unto the, disciples, and findeth
them sleeping, and saith unto Peter, What,
could ye not watch with me one hour?
³Watch and pray, that ye enter not into 41

KEY.—ᵃ Matthew, ᵇ Mark, ᶜ Luke, ᵈ John.

¹ Gr. *caused to stumble.*
² Gr. *an enclosed piece of ground.*
³ Or, *Watch ye, and pray that ye enter not.*

§ 148. Gethsemane.

Mark's Account.

Chap. 14.

32 And they come unto a place which was named Gethsemane : and he saith unto his disciples, Sit ye here, while
33 I pray. And he taketh with him Peter and James and John,
and began to be greatly amazed, and sore troubled. And
34 he saith unto them My soul is exceeding sorrowful even
35 unto death ; abide ye here, and watch. And he went forward a little, and fell on the ground, and prayed that, if it
36 were possible, the hour might pass away from him. And
he said, Abba, Father, all things are possible unto thee ; remove this cup from me : howbeit not what I will, but what
37 thou wilt. And he cometh, and findeth them sleeping, and
saith unto Peter, Simon, sleepest thou ? couldst thou not
38 watch one hour ? Watch and pray, that ye enter not into temptation : the spirit indeed is willing, but the flesh is
39 weak. And again he went away, and prayed, saying the
40 same words. And again he came, and found them sleeping, for their eyes were very heavy ; and they knew not
41 what to answer him. And he cometh the third time, and
saith unto them, Sleep on now, and take your rest : it is
enough ; the hour is come ; behold, the Son of man is
42 betrayed into the hands of sinners. Arise, let us be going : behold, he that betrayeth me is at hand.

John's Account.

Chap. 18.

1 When Jesus had spoken these words, he went forth
with his disciples over the brook Kidron, where was a
garden, into the which he entered, himself and his disciples.

Luke's Account.

Chap. 22.

40 And when he was at the place, he said unto them, Pray
41 that ye enter not into temptation. And he was parted
from them about a stone's cast ; and he kneeled down
42 and prayed, saying, Father, if thou be willing, remove
this cup from me : nevertheless not my will, but thine, be
43 done. And there appeared unto him an angel from
44 heaven, strengthening him. And being in an agony he
prayed more earnestly : and his sweat became as it were
45 great drops of blood falling down upon the ground. And
when he rose up from his prayer, he came unto the disciples, and found them sleeping for sorrow, and said unto
46 them, Why sleep ye ? rise and pray, that ye enter not into temptation.

§ 149. Jesus Arrested.

Matthew's Account.

Chap. 26.

And while he yet spake, lo, Judas, one of the twelve, 47 came, and with him a great multitude with swords and staves, from the chief priests and elders of the people. And behold, one of them that were with Jesus stretched 51 out his hand, and drew his sword, and smote the servant of the high priest, and struck off his ear. Then saith Jesus 52 unto him, Put up again thy sword into its place.

Mark's Account.

Chap. 14.

And straightaway, while he yet spake, cometh Judas, 43 one of the twelve, and with him a multitude with swords and staves, from the chief priests and the scribes and the elders. Now he that betrayed him had given them a 44 token, saying, Whomsoever I shall kiss, that is he ; take him, and lead him away safely. And when he was come, 45 straightway he came to him, and saith, Rabbi ; and kissed him. And they laid hands on him, and took him. 46 But a certain one of them that stood by drew his sword, 47 and smote the servant of the high priest, and struck off his ear. And Jesus answered and said unto them, Are ye 48 come out, as against a robber, with swords and staves to seize me ? I was daily with you in the temple teaching, 49 and ye took me not : but *this is done* that the scriptures might be fulfilled. And they all left him, and fled. 50 And a certain young man followed with him, having a 51 linen cloth cast about him, over *his* naked *body* : and they lay hold on him ; but he left the linen cloth, and fled 52 naked.

Luke's Account.

Chap. 22.

While he yet spake, behold, a multitude, and he that 47 was called Judas, one of the twelve, went before them ; and he drew near unto Jesus to kiss him. But Jesus said 48 unto him, Judas, betrayest thou the Son of man with a kiss? And when they that were about him saw what 49 would follow, they said, Lord, shall we smite with the sword? And a certain one of them smote the servant of 50

[Continued on duplicate page 212.]

211

Matthew 26.

temptation: the spirit indeed is willing,
42 but the flesh is weak. Again a second
time he went away, and prayed, saying,
O my Father, if this cannot pass away,
43 except I drink it, thy will be done. And
he came again and found them sleeping,
for their eyes were heavy; ᵇand they
44 knew not what to answer him. ᵃAnd he
left them again, and went away, and prayed
a third time, saying again the same words.
ᶜAnd there appeared unto him an angel
from heaven strengthening him. And being in an agony he prayed more earnestly;
and his sweat became as it were great
drops of blood falling down upon the
ground. And when he rose up from his
45 prayer, ᵃthen cometh he to the disciples,
and saith unto them, Sleep on now, and
take your rest: ᵇit is enough: ᵃbehold, the
hour is at hand, and the Son of man is be-
46 trayed unto the hands of sinners. Arise,
let us be going; behold, he is at hand that
betrayeth me.

§ 149. Jesus Arrested.

John 18.

2 ᵈNow Judas also, ᶜone of the twelve, ᵈwho
betrayed him, knew the place: for Jesus
oft-times resorted thither with his disciples.
3 Judas then, having received the ¹band *of
soldiers*, and officers from the chief priests
and the Pharisees, ᵇand the elders, ᵈcometh
thither, ᵃwhile he yet spake, ᵈwith lanterns
and torches and ᵇwith swords and staves.
4 ᵈJesus therefore, knowing all the things
that were coming upon him, went forth,
and saith unto them, Whom seek ye?
5 They answered him, Jesus of Nazareth.
Jesus saith unto them, I am *he*. And Judas
also, who betrayed him, was standing with
6 them. When therefore he said unto them,

KEY.—ᵃ Matthew, ᵇ Mark, ᶜ Luke, ᵈ John.
¹ Or, *cohort.*

John 18.

I am *he*, they went backward, and fell to
the ground. Again therefore he asked 7
them, Whom seek ye? And they said,
Jesus of Nazareth. Jesus answered, I told 8
you that I am *he*: if therefore ye seek me,
let these go their way: that the word 9
might be fulfilled which he spake, Of those
whom thou hast given me I lost not one.

ᵃNow he that betrayed him **Matthew 26.** 48
gave them a sign, saying, Whomsoever I
shall kiss, that is he: take him ᵇand lead
him away safely. ᵃAnd straightway he 49
came to Jesus, and said, Hail, Rabbi; and
¹kissed him. And Jesus said unto him, 50
Friend, *do* that for which thou art come.
ᶜBetrayest thou the Son of man with a kiss?
ᵃThen they came and laid hands on Jesus,
and took him. ᶜAnd when they that were 51
about him saw what would follow, they
said, Lord, shall we smite with the sword?
ᵈSimon Peter therefore having a **John 18.** 10
sword drew it, and struck the high priest's
¹servant, and cut off his right ear. ᶜBut
Jesus answered and said, Suffer ye thus far.
And he touched his ear and healed him.
ᵈNow the ¹servant's name was Malchus.
Jesus therefore said unto Peter, Put up the 11
sword into the sheath: the cup which the
Father hath given me, shall I not drink it?
ᵃAll they that take the sword **Matthew 26.** 52
shall perish with the sword. Or thinkest 53
thou that I cannot beseech my Father, and
he shall even now send me more than
twelve legions of angels? How then 54
should the scriptures be fulfilled, that thus
it must be? In that hour said Jesus to the 55
multitudes, ᶜunto the chief priests, and captains of the temple, and elders that were
come against him, ᵇAre ye come out as
against a robber with swords and staves

KEY.—ᵃ Matthew, ᵇ Mark, ᶜLuke, ᵈ John.

¹ Gr. *kissed him much.*   ² Gr. *bondservant,*

§ 149. Jesus Arrested.—(*Continued.*)

Matthew's Account.

Chap. 26.

57 And they that had taken Jesus led him away to *the house of* Caiaphas the high priest, where the scribes and
58 the elders were gathered together. And Peter followed him afar off, unto the court of the high priest, and entered in, and sat with the officers, to see the end.

Mark's Account.

Chap. 14.

53 And they led Jesus away to the high priest : and there come together with him all the chief priests and the elders and the scribes.

Luke's Account.

Chap. 22.

51 the high priest, and struck off his right ear. But Jesus answered and said, Suffer ye thus far, and he touched his
52 ear, and healed him. And Jesus said unto the chief priests, and captains of the temple, and elders, that were come against him, Are ye come out, as against a robber,
53 with swords and staves ? When I was daily with you in the temple, ye stretched not forth your hands against me : but this is your hour, and the power of darkness.

54 And they seized him, and led him *away*, and brought him into the high priest's house.

§ 150. Peter's Denial.

Matthew's Account.

Chap. 26.

Now Peter was sitting without in the court : and a 69 maid came unto him, saying, Thou also wast with Jesus the Galilæan.   But he denied before them all. 70

Mark's Account.

Chap. 14.

And Peter had followed him afar off, even within, into 54 the court of the high priest ; and he was sitting with the officers, and warming himself in the light *of the fire*.   Now 55 the chief priests and the whole council sought witness against Jesus to put him to death ; and found it not.

And as Peter was beneath in the court, there cometh 66 one of the maids of the high priest ; and seeing Peter 67 warming himself, she looked upon him, and saith, Thou also wast with the Nazarene, *even* Jesus.   But he denied, 68 saying, I neither know, nor understand what thou sayest : and he went out into the porch ; and the cock crew.

Luke's Account.

Chap. 22.

But Peter followed afar off.   And when they had 54 kindled a fire in the midst of the court, and had sat down together, Peter sat in the midst of them.   And a certain 56 maid seeing him as he sat in the light *of the fire*, and looking steadfastly upon him, said, This man also was with him.   But he denied, saying, Woman, I know him 57 not.   And after a little while another saw him, and said, 58 Thou also art *one* of them.   But Peter said, Man, I am not.   And after the space of about one hour another confidently affirmed, saying :

[*See duplicate page 215.*]

218

Matthew 26.

to seize me? I sat daily in the temple
56 teaching, and ye took me not. But all this
is come to pass, that the scriptures of the
prophets might be fulfilled: ᶜthis is your
hour and the power of darkness. ᵃThen all
the disciples left him, and fled. ᵇAnd a
certain young man followed with him,
having a linen cloth cast about him, over
his naked *body :* and they laid hold on him;
but he left the linen cloth, and fled naked.
12 ᵈSo the ¹band and the ²chief cap- **John 18.**
tain, and the officers of the Jews, seized
13 Jesus and bound him, and led him to Annas
first; for he was father in law to Caiaphas,
14 who was high priest that year. Now
Caiaphas was he who gave counsel to the
Jews, that it was expedient that one man
should die for the people.

§ 150. Peter's Denial.

John 18.

15 ᵈAnd Simon Peter followed Jesus, ᶜafar
off, ᵈand *so did* another disciple. Now that
disciple was known unto the high priest,
and entered in with Jesus into the court of
16 the high priest; but Peter was standing
at the door without. So the other disciple, who was known unto the high priest,
went out and spake unto her that kept
the door, and brought ın Peter, ᵃto see
17 the end. ᵈThe maid therefore that kept
the door saith unto Peter, Art thou also
one of this man's disciples? ᶜBut he denied
18 saying, Woman, ᵈI am not. Now the ³ser-
vants and the officers were standing *there,*
having made ⁴a fire of coals; for it was
cold; and they were warming themselves:
and Peter also was with them, standing
and warming himself: ᶜand the cock crew.

KᴇY.—ᵃ Matthew, ᵇ Mark, ᶜ Luke, ᵈ John.

¹ Or, *cohort.* ² Or, *military tribune.* Gr. *chiliarch*
³ Gr. *bondservants.* ⁴ Gr. *a fire of charcoal.*

§ 151. The First Trial of Jesus.*

John 18.

[d] The high priest therefore asked Jesus of 19 his disciples, and of his teaching. Jesus 20 answered him, I have spoken openly to the world; I ever taught in [1]synagogues, and in the temple, where all the Jews come together; and in secret spake I nothing. Why askest thou me? ask them that have 21 heard *me*, what I spake unto them: behold, these know the things which I said. And 22 when he had said this, one of the officers standing by struck Jesus [2] with his hand, saying, Answerest thou the high priest so? Jesus answered him, If I have spoken evil, 23 bear witness of the evil: but if well, why smitest thou me? Now Simon Peter was 25 standing and warming himself. They said therefore unto him, Art thou also one of his disciples? He denied [a] with an oath, [d] and said, I am not. [c] And after the space of about an hour, [d] one of the servants of the high priest, being a kinsman of him whose ear Peter cut off, saith, Did not I see thee in the garden with him? [a] Of a truth thou art also one of them: for thy speech betrayeth thee: [b] for thou art a Galilæan. But he began to curse and to swear, I know not this man of whom ye speak. And straightway the cock crew. [a] And Peter remembered the word which Jesus had said, Before the cock crow, thou shalt deny me thrice. And he went out and wept bitterly.

KEY.—[a] Matthew, [b] Mark, [c] Luke, [d] John.

[1] Gr. *synagogue*.   [2] Or, *with a rod*.

* Five separate trials or arraignments did Jesus suffer, as follows: First, before Annas; second, before Caiaphas, while it was yet dark, and no death sentence could be legal; third, the formal condemnation at dawn; fourth, the secular trial before Pilate, without whose sanction a capital sentence could not be executed; and fifth, before Herod, who returned him to Pilate, and the iniquity was completed.

§ 151. The First Trial of Jesus.

[And the Denial of Peter.]

Matthew's Account.

Chap. 26.

⁷⁰⁄⁷¹ Saying, I know not what thou sayest. And when he was gone out into the porch, another *maid* saw him, and saith unto them that were there, This man also was with

72 Jesus the Nazarene. And again he denied with an oath,

73 I know not the man. And after a little while they that stood by came and said to Peter, Of a truth thou also art

74 *one* of them ; for thy speech bewrayeth thee. Then began

75 he to curse and to swear, I know not the man. And straightway the cock crew. And Peter remembered the word which Jesus had said, Before the cock crow, thou shalt deny me thrice. And he went out, and wept bitterly.

57 And they that had taken Jesus, led him away to the house of Caiaphas the high priest, where the scribes and

59 the elders were gathered together. Now the chief priests and the whole council sought false witness against Jesus,

60 that they might put him to death; and they found it not, though many false witnesses came. But afterward came

61 two, and said, This man said, I am able to destroy the

62 temple of God, and to build it in three days. And the high priest stood up, and said unto him, Answerest thou

63 nothing ? what is it which these witness against thee ? But Jesus held his peace. And the high priest said unto him, I adjure thee by the living God, that thou tell us whether

64 thou be the Christ, the Son of God. Jesus said unto him,

Mark's Account.

Chap. 14.

69 And the maid saw him, and began again to say to them

70 that stood by This is *one* of them. But he again denied it. And after a little while again they that stood by said to Peter, Of a truth thou art *one* of them ; for thou art a

[Continued on duplicate page 215.]

§ 151. The First Trial of Jesus.—(*Continued.*)

Matthew's Account.

Chap. 26.

Thou hast said : nevertheless I say unto you, Henceforth
ye shall see the Son of man sitting at the right hand of
power, and coming on the clouds of heaven. Then the 65
high priest rent his garments, saying, He hath spoken
blasphemy : what further need have we of witnesses?
behold, now ye have heard the blasphemy: what think ye? 66
They answered and said, He is worthy of death. Then 67
did they spit in his face and buffet him: and some smote
him with the palms of their hands, saying, Prophesy unto 68
us, thou Christ: who is he that struck thee?

Chap. 27.

Now when morning was come, all the chief priests and 1
the elders of the people took counsel against Jesus to put
him to death.

Mark's Account.

Chap. 14.

Galilæan. But he began to curse, and to swear, I know 71
not this man of whom ye speak. And straightway the 72
second time the cock crew. And Peter called to mind
the word, how that Jesus said unto him, Before the cock
crow twice, thou shalt deny me thrice. And when he
thought thereon, he wept.

And some began to spit on him, and to cover his face, 65
and to buffet him, and to say unto him, Prophesy : and
the officers received him with blows of their hands.

Chap. 15.

And straightway in the morning the chief priests with 1
the elders and scribes, and the whole council, held a consultation.

Luke's Account.

Chap. 22.

Of a truth this man also was with him : for he is a 59
Galilæan. But Peter said, Man, I know not what thou 60
sayest. And immediately, while he yet spake, the cock
crew. And the Lord turned, and looked upon Peter. 61
And Peter remembered the word of the Lord, how that
he said unto him, Before the cock crow this day, thou
shalt deny me thrice. And he went out, and wept bit- 62
terly.

John's Account.

Chap. 18.

Annas therefore sent him bound unto Caiaphas the high 24
priest.

Mark 14.

53 ^dAnnas therefore ^bled Jesus away to the ^ahouse of Caiaphas the ^bhigh priest; and there came together with him all the chief priests, and the elders, and the
55 scribes. Now the chief priests and the whole council sought witness against Jesus to put him to death; and found it not, ^athough many false witnesses came.
56 ^bFor many bare false witness against him, and their witness agreed not together.
57 And there stood up certain, and bare false
58 witness against him, saying, We heard him say, I will destroy this [1]temple that is made with hands, and in three days I will
59 build another made without hands. And
60 not even so did their witness agree together. And the high priest stood up in the midst, and asked Jesus, saying, Answerest thou nothing? what is it which these
61 witness against thee? But he held his peace, and answered nothing. Again the high priest asked him, and saith unto him, ^aI adjure thee by the living God that thou tell us; ^dArt thou the Christ, the Son of
62 the Blessed ^aGod? ^bAnd Jesus said, I am: and ye shall see the Son of man sitting at the right hand of power, and coming with
63 the clouds of heaven. And the high priest rent his clothes, and saith, What further
64 need have we of witnesses? Ye have heard the blasphemy: what think ye? And they all condemned him to be [2]worthy of death.
63 **Luke 22.** ^cAnd the men that held [3]*Jesus* mocked him, and beat him, ^aand they did
64 spit in his face and buffet him. ^cAnd they blindfolded him, and asked him, saying, Prophesy ^aunto us, thou Christ: ^cwho is he

KEY.—^a Matthew, ^b Mark, ^c Luke, ^d John.

[1] Or, *sanctuary*.　　　[2] Gr. *liable to*.
[3] Gr. *him*.

that struck thee? And many other things 65
spake they against him, reviling him. ᵇ And
the officers received him with blows of
their hands.

And as soon as it was day,* the assembly 66
of the elders of the people was gathered
together, both chief priests and scribes;
and they led him away into their council,
saying, If thou art the Christ, tell us. But 67
he said unto them, If I tell you, ye will not 68
believe: and if I ask *you*, ye will not answer.
But from henceforth shall the Son of man 69
be seated at the right hand of the power of
God. And they all said, Art thou then the 70
Son of God? And he said unto them, ¹ Ye
say *it*, for I am. And they said, What 71
further need have we of witness? for we
ourselves have heard from his ρwn mouth.

§ 152. Remorse of Judas.

ᵃ Then Judas, who betrayed him, when 3
he saw that he was condemned, repented
himself, and brought back the thirty pieces
of silver to the chief priests and elders, say- 4
ing, I have sinned in that I betrayed ² innocent blood. But they said, What is that
to us? see thou *to it*. And he cast down 5
the pieces of silver into the sanctuary, and
departed; and he went away and hanged
himself. And the chief priests took the 6
pieces of silver, and said, It is not lawful
to put them into the ³ treasury, since it is
the price of blood. And they took coun- 7
sel, and bought with them the potter's
field, to bury strangers in. Wherefore 8

KEY.—ᵃ Matthew, ᵇ Mark, ᶜ Luke, ᵈ John.

¹ Or, *Ye say that I am.*
² Many ancient authorities read *righteous.*
³ Gr. *corbanas,* that is, *sacred treasury.*

* The formal sentence, according both to Jewish and
Roman law, could only be pronounced by day. The pro-
ceedings of the night were legalized by repetition in the
morning.

§ 153. Jesus before Pilate.

Matthew's Account.

And <u>they</u> bound him, and led him away, and <u>delivered</u> 2 him up to Pilate the governor.

Now Jesus stood before the governor: and the gov- 11 ernor asked him, saying, Art thou the King of the Jews? And Jesus said unto him, Thou sayest. And when he 12 was accused by the chief priests and elders, he answered nothing. Then saith Pilate unto him, Hearest thou not 13 how many things they witness against thee? And he 14 gave him no answer, not even to one word: insomuch that the governor marvelled <u>greatly</u>.

Mark's Account.

And bound Jesus, and carried him away, and delivered 1 him up to Pilate. And Pilate asked him, Art thou the 2 King of the Jews? And he answering saith unto him, Thou sayest.

Luke's Account.

And the whole company of them rose up, and brought 1 him before Pilate. And they began to accuse him; say- 2 ing, <u>We found this man perverting our nation, and forbid-</u> <u>ing to give tribute to Cæsar, and saying that he himself is</u> <u>Christ, a King.</u> And Pilate asked him, saying, Art thou 3 the King of the Jews? And he answered him <u>and said</u>, Thou sayest.

217

Matthew 27.

that field was called, The field of. blood,
9 unto this day. Then was fulfilled that
which was spoken through Jeremiah the
prophet, saying, And [1] they took the thirty
pieces of silver, the price of him that was
priced, [2] whom *certain* of the children of
10 Israel did price; and [3] they gave them for
the potter's field, as the Lord appointed
me.

§ 153. Jesus before Pilate.

John 18.

28 [d] They lead Jesus therefore [a] bound
[d] from Caiaphas into the [4] Prætorium [a] and
delivered him up to Pilate the governor:
[d] and it was early; and they themselves
entered not into the [4] Prætorium, that they
might not be defiled, but might eat the
29 passover. Pilate therefore went out unto
them, and saith, What accusation bring ye
30 against this man? They answered and
said unto him, If this man were not an
evil-doer, we should not have delivered
31 him up unto thee. Pilate therefore said
unto them, Take him yourselves, and
judge him according to your law. The
Jews said unto him, It is not lawful for us
32 to put any man to death: that the word of
Jesus might be fulfilled, which he spake,
signifying by what manner of death he
should die. [c] And they began to accuse
him, saying, We found this man perverting our nation, and forbidding to give tribute to Cæsar, and saying that he himself
is Christ a king.
33 [d] Pilate therefore entered again into the
[4] Prætorium, and called Jesus, and said unto him, Art thou the King of the Jews?

KEY.—[a] Matthew, [b] Mark, [c] Luke, [d] John.

[1] Or, *I took.*
[2] Or, *whom they priced on the part of the sons of Israel.*
[3] Some ancient authorities read *I gave.*
[4] Or, *palace.*

Jesus answered, Sayest thou this of thy- 34
self, or did others tell it thee concerning
me?   Pilate answered, Am I a Jew? 35
Thine own nation and the chief priests delivered thee unto me: what hast thou
done?   Jesus answered, My kingdom is 36
not of this world: if my kingdom were of
this world, then would my ¹servants fight,
that I should not be delivered to the Jews:
but now is my kingdom not from hence.
Pilate therefore said unto him, Art thou a 37
king then? Jesus answered, ²Thou sayest
it, for I am a king.   To this end have I
been born, and to this end am I come into
the world, that I should bear witness unto
the truth.   Every one that is of the truth
heareth my voice.   Pilate saith unto him, 38
What is truth?

And when he had said this, he went out
again unto the Jews, and saith unto them,
I find no crime in him.

ᵇAnd the chief priests accused **Mark 15.** 3
him of many things.   And Pilate again 4
asked him, saying, Answerest thou nothing? behold how many things they accuse
thee of.   But Jesus no more answered 5
anything; insomuch that Pilate marvelled
ᵃgreatly.   **Luke 23.**

ᶜAnd Pilate said unto the chief priests 4
and the multitudes, I find no fault in this
man.   But they were the more urgent, 5
saying, He stirreth up the people, teaching
throughout all Judæa, and beginning from
Galilee even unto this place.   But when 6
Pilate heard it, he asked whether the man
were a Galilæan.   And when he knew that 7
he was of Herod's jurisdiction, he sent him
unto Herod, who himself also was at Jerusalem in these days.

KEY.—ᵃ Matthew, ᵇ Mark, ᶜ Luke, ᵈ John.

¹ Or, *officers*: as in ver. 3, 12, 18, 22.
² Or, *Thou sayest that I am a king.*

§ 155. Barabbas Released.

Matthew's Account.

Chap. 27.

Now at the feast the governor was wont to release 15 unto the multitude one prisoner, whom they would. And 16 they had then a notable prisoner, called Barabbas. When 17 therefore they were gathered together, Pilate said unto them, Whom will ye that I release unto you? Barabbas, or Jesus who is called Christ? For he knew that for 18 envy they had delivered him up.

John's Account.

Chap. 18.

And when he had said this, he went out again unto 38 the Jews, and saith unto them, I find no crime in him. But ye have a custom, that I should release unto you one 39 at the passover: will ye therefore that I release unto you the King of the Jews? They cried out therefore again, 40 saying, Not this man, but Barabbas. Now Barabbas was a robber.

Mark's Account.

Chap. 15.

But the chief priests stirred up the multitude, that he 11 should rather release Barabbas unto them. And Pilate 12 again answered and said unto them, What then shall I do unto him whom ye call the King of the Jews? And they 13 cried out again, Crucify him. And Pilate said unto them, 14 Why, what evil hath he done? But they cried out exceedingly, Crucify him. And Pilate, wishing to content 15 the multitude, released unto them Barabbas, and delivered Jesus, when he had scourged him, to be crucified.

Luke's Account.

Chap. 23.

But they cried out all together, saying, Away with this 18 man, and release unto us Barabbas; one who for a cer- 19 tain insurrection made in the city, and for murder, was cast into prison. And Pilate spake unto them again, de- 20 siring to release Jesus; but they shouted, saying, Crucify, 21 crucify him. And he said unto them the third time, 22 Why, what evil hath this man done? I have found no cause of death in him: I will therefore chastise him and release him. But they were urgent with loud voices, ask- 23 ing that he might be crucified. And their voices prevailed. And Pilate gave sentence that what they asked 24 for should be done. And he released him that for insur- 25 rection and murder had been cast into prison, whom they asked for; but Jesus he delivered up to their will.

§ 154. Jesus sent unto Herod.

Luke 23.

8 ^cNow when Herod saw Jesus, he was exceeding glad: for he was of a long time desirous to see him, because he had heard concerning him; and he hoped to see
9 some ¹miracle done by him. And he questioned him in many words; but he an-
10 swered him nothing. And the chief priests and the scribes stood, vehemently
11 accusing him. And Herod with his soldiers set him at nought, and mocked him, and arraying him in gorgeous apparel sent
12 him back to Pilate. And Herod and Pilate became friends with each other that very day: for before they were at enmity between themselves.

§ 155. Barabbas Released.

Mark 15.

6 ^bNow at ²the feast he used to release unto them one prisoner, whom they asked of
7 him. And there was one called Barabbas, *lying* bound with them that had made insurrection, men who in the insurrection
8 had committed murder. And the multitude went up and began to ask him *to do* as
9 he was wont to do unto them. And Pilate answered them, saying, Will ye that I re-

KEY.—^a Matthew, ^b Mark, ^c Luke, ^d John.

¹ Gr. *sign.*
² Many ancient authorities read *I sent you to him.*
³ Or, *a feast.*

Mark 15.

lease unto you the King of the Jews? For 10
he perceived that for envy the chief priests
had delivered him up.

ᵃ And while he was sitting on **Matthew 27.** 19
the judgment-seat, his wife sent unto him,
saying, Have thou nothing to do with that
righteous man: for I have suffered many
things this day in a dream because of him.
ᶜAnd Pilate called together the **Luke 23.** 13
chief priests and the rulers and the people,
and said unto them, Ye brought unto me 14
this man, as one that perverteth the people;
and behold, I, having examined him before
you, find no fault in this man touching
those things whereof ye accuse him; no, 15
nor yet Herod: for he sent him back unto
us; and behold, nothing worthy of death
hath been done by him. I will therefore 16
chastise him, and release him. But they 18
cried out all together, saying, Away with
this man, and release unto us Barabbas.
ᵃ Now the chief priests and the **Matthew 27.** 20
elders persuaded the multitudes that they
should ask for Barabbas, and destroy Jesus. 21
But the governor answered and said unto
them, Whether of the twain will ye that I
release unto you? And they said, Barabbas. Pilate saith unto them, What then 22
shall I do unto Jesus who is called Christ,
ᵇwhom ye call the King of the Jews?
ᵃ They all say, Let him be crucified. And 23
he said, Why, what evil hath he done?
But they cried out exceedingly, saying,
Let him be crucified. So when Pilate saw 24
that he prevailed nothing, but rather that
a tumult was arising, he took water, and
washed his hands before the multitude,
saying, I am innocent ¹of the blood of this
righteous man: see ye *to it*. And all the 25
people answered and said, His blood *be* on
us, and on our children. Then released he 26

KEY.—ᵃ Matthew, ᵇ Mark, ᶜ Luke, ᵈ John.

Some ancient authorities read *of this blood: see ye &c.*

§ 156. Jesus Mocked.

Mark's Account.

And the soldiers led him away within the court, 16
which is the Prætorium; and they call together the whole
band. And they clothe him with purple, and plaiting a 17
crown of thorns, they put it on him; and they began to 18
salute him, Hail, King of the Jews! And they smote his 19
head with a reed, and did spit upon him, and bowing their
knees worshipped him.

John's Account.

Then Pilate therefore took Jesus, and scourged him. 1
And the soldiers plaited a crown of thorns, and put it on 2
his head, and arrayed him in a purple garment; and they
came unto him, and said, Hail, King of the Jews! and 3
they struck him with their hands.

Matthew 27.

unto them Barabbas ^c whom they asked for:
^a but Jesus he scourged and delivered ^c to
their will ^a to be crucified.

§ 156. Jesus Mocked.

Matthew 27.

27 ^a Then the soldiers of the governor took
Jesus into the [1] Prætorium, and gathered
28 unto him the whole [2] band. And they
[3] stripped him, and put on him a scarlet
29 robe. And they plaited a crown of thorns
and put it upon his head, and a reed in his
right hand ; and they kneeled down before
him, and mocked him, saying, Hail, King
30 of the Jews! And they spat upon him,
and took the reed and smote him on the
4 head. ^d And Pilate went out again, **John 19.**
and saith unto them, Behold, I bring him
out to you, that ye may know that I find
5 no crime in him. Jesus therefore came
out, wearing the crown of thorns and the
purple garment. And *Pilate* saith unto
6 them, Behold, the man ! When therefore
the chief priests and the officers saw him,
they cried out, saying, Crucify *him*, crucify *him*. Pilate saith unto them, Take him
yourselves, and crucify him : for I find no
7 crime in him. The Jews answered him,
We have a law, and by that law he ought
to die, because he made himself the Son of
8 God. When Pilate therefore heard this
9 saying, he was the more afraid ; and he
entered into the [1] Prætorium again, and
saith unto Jesus, Whence art thou ? But
10 Jesus gave him no answer. Pilate therefore saith unto him, Speakest thou not unto me ? knowest thou not that I have
[4] power to release thee, and have [4] power
11 to crucify thee ? Jesus answered him,
Thou wouldest have no [4] power against

KEY.—^a Matthew, ^b Mark, ^c Luke, ^d John.

[1] Or, *palace.*   [2] Or, *cohort.*
[3] Some ancient authorities read *clothed.*   [4] Or, *authority.*

me, except it were given thee from above :
therefore he that delivered me unto thee
hath greater sin. Upon this Pilate sought 12
to release him : but the Jews cried out,
saying, If thou release this man, thou art
not Cæsar's friend : every one that maketh
himself a king ¹ speaketh˅ against Cæsar.
When Pilate therefore heard these words, 13
he brought Jesus out, and sat down on the
judgement-seat at a place called The Pave-
ment, but in Hebrew, Gabbatha. Now it 14
was the Preparation of the passover : it
was about the sixth hour. And he saith
unto the Jews, Behold, your King ! They 15
therefore cried out, Away with *him*, away
with *him*, crucify him. Pilate saith unto
them, Shall I crucify your King? The
chief priests answered, We have no king
but Cæsar.

§ 157. The Journey to the Cross.

And when they had mocked him, they 20
took off from him the ᵃscarlet [and]*
ᵇpurple, and put on him his garments.
And they lead him out to crucify him.

And they ᵃcompel one passing by, Si- 21
mon of Cyrene, coming from the country,
the father of Alexander and Rufus, to go
with them, that he might bear his cross
ᶜafter Jesus.

ᶜAnd there followed him a great multi- 27
tude of the people, and of women who
bewailed and lamented him. But Jesus 28
turning unto them said, Daughters of
Jerusalem, weep not for me, but weep for
yourselves, and for your children. For 29
behold, the days are coming, in which they
shall say, Blessed are the barren, and the
wombs that never bare, and the breasts

KEY.—ᵃ Matthew, ᵇ Mark, ᶜ Luke, ᵈ John.

¹ Or, *opposeth Cæsar.*   ² Gr. *impress.*
* Word inserted by the compiler.

§ 157. The Journey to the Cross.

Matthew's Account.

Chap. 27.

31 And when they had mocked him, they took off from him the robe, and put on him his garments, and led him away to crucify him.

32 And as they came out, they found a man of Cyrene, Simon by name: him they compelled to go *with them*, that he might bear his cross.

Luke's Account.

Chap. 23.

26 And when they led him away, they laid hold upon one Simon of Cyrene, coming from the country, and laid on him the cross, to bear it after Jesus.

John's Account.

Chap. 19.

16 Then therefore he delivered him unto them to be crucified.

17 They took Jesus therefore: and he went out, bearing the cross for himself.

§ 158. The Crucifixion.

Mark's Account.

Chap. 15.

And they bring him unto the place Golgotha, which is, 22
being interpreted, The place of a skull. And they offered 23
him wine mingled with myrrh : but he received it not.
And they crucify him, and part his garments among them, 24
casting lots upon them, what each should take. And it 25
was the third hour, and they crucified him. And the su- 26
perscription of his accusation was written over, THE KING
OF THE JEWS. And with him they crucify two robbers; 27
one on his right hand, and one on his left. And they 29
that passed by railed on him, wagging their heads, and saying, Ha! thou that destroyest the temple, and buildest it
in three days, save thyself, and come down from the cross. 30
In like manner also the chief priests mocking *him* among 31
themselves with the scribes said, He saved others; himself he cannot save. Let the Christ, the King of Israel, 32
now come down from the cross, that we may see and believe. And they that were crucified with him reproached
him.

Luke's Account.

Chap. 23.

And when they came unto the place which is called The 33
skull, there they crucified him, and the malefactors, one
on the right hand and the other on the left. And Jesus 34
said, Father, forgive them; for they know not what they
do. And parting his garments among them, they cast
lots. And the people stood beholding. And the rulers 35
also scoffed at him, saying, He saved others; let him save
himself, if this is the Christ of God, his chosen. And the 36
soldiers also mocked him, coming to him, offering him
vinegar, and saying, If thou art the King of the Jews, 37
save thyself.

John's Account.

Chap. 19.

Unto the place called The place of a skull, which is 17
called in Hebrew Golgotha: where they crucified him, and 18
with him two others, on either side one, and Jesus in the
midst.

228

Luke 23.

30 that never gave suck. Then shall they begin to say to the mountains, Fall on us;

31 and to the hills, Cover us. For if they do these things in the green tree, what shall be done in the dry?

32 And there were also two others, malefactors, led with him to be put to death.

§ 158. The Crucifixion.

Matthew 27

33 ᵃAnd when they were come unto a place called Golgotha, that is to say, The place

34 of a skull, they gave him wine to drink mingled with gall: and when he had

35 tasted it, he would not drink. ᶜThere they crucified him, and the malefactors, one on the right hand, and the other on the left. And Jesus said, Father, forgive them; for they know not what they do.

19 ᵈAnd Pilate wrote a title also, **John 19.** and put it on the cross. And there was written, JESUS OF NAZARETH, THE KING OF

20 THE JEWS. This title therefore read many of the Jews: ¹for the place where Jesus was crucified was nigh to the city: and it was written in Hebrew, *and* in Latin, *ana*

21 in Greek. The chief priests of the Jews therefore said to Pilate, Write not, The King of the Jews; but, that he said, I am

22 King of the Jews. Pilate answered, What I have written I have written.

23 The soldiers therefore, when they had crucified Jesus, took his garments, and made four parts, to every soldier a part; and also the ²coat: now the ²coat was without seam, woven from the top throughout.

24 They said therefore, one to another, Let us not rend it, but cast lots for it, whose it shall be; that the scripture might be fulfilled, which saith,

KEY.—ᵃ Matthew, ᵇ Mark, ᶜ Luke, ᵈ John.

¹ Or, *for the place of the city where Jesus was crucified was nigh at hand.* ² Or, *tunic.*

They parted my garments among them,
  And upon my vesture did they cast lots.
These things therefore the soldiers did.   25
  ᵃ And they that passed by Matthew 27. 39
railed on him, wagging their heads, and 40
saying, Thou that destroyest the ¹temple,
and buildest it in three days, save thyself:
if thou art the Son of God, come down
from the cross. In like manner also the 41
chief priests mocking *him*, with the
scribes and elders, said, He saved others; 42
ᵃ himself he cannot save. He is ᵇ the
Christ, ᵃ the King of Israel; let him now
come down from the cross, and we will
believe on him. He trusteth on God; let 43
him deliver him now, if he desireth him:
for he said, I am the Son of God. ᵇ And
they that were crucified with him reproached him.* ᶜ And the soldiers also
mocked him, coming to him, offering him
vinegar, and saying, If thou art the King
of the Jews, save thyself.

§ 159. The Penitent Malefactor.

  ᶜ And one of the malefactors that were 39
hanged railed on him, saying, Art not thou
the Christ? save thyself and us. But the 40
other answered, and rebuking him said,
Dost thou not even fear God, seeing thou
art in the same condemnation? And we 41
indeed justly; for we receive the due reward of our deeds: but this man hath
done nothing amiss. And he said, Jesus, 42
remember me when thou comest ²in thy
kingdom. And he said unto him, Verily 43
I say unto thee, To-day shalt thou be with
me in Paradise.

KEY.—ᵃ Matthew, ᵇ Mark, ᶜ Luke, ᵈ John.

¹ Or, *sanctuary.*   ² Or, *can he not save himself?*
³ Some ancient authorities read *into thy kingdom.*
* Later the heart of one was changed. See § 159.

§ 160. The Death of Jesus.

Matthew's Account.

And Jesus cried again with a loud voice, and yielded up 50 his spirit.

Mark's Account.

And when the sixth hour was come, there was darkness 33 over the whole land until the ninth hour.   And at the 34 ninth hour Jesus cried with a loud voice, Eloi, Eloi, lama sabachthani? which is, being interpreted, My God, my, God, why hast thou forsaken me? And some of them 35 that stood by, when they heard it, said, Behold, he calleth Elijah.   And one ran, and filling a sponge full of vinegar, 36 put it on a reed, and gave him to drink, saying, Let be; let us see whether Elijah cometh to take him down.   And 37 Jesus uttered a loud voice, and gave up the ghost.   And 38 the veil of the temple was rent in twain, from the top to the bottom.   And when the centurion, who stood by over 39 against him, saw that he so gave up the ghost, he said, Truly this man was the Son of God.   And there were 40 also women beholding from afar: among whom *were* both Mary Magdalene, and Mary the mother of James the less and of Joses, and Salome; who, when he was in Galilee, 41 followed him, and ministered unto him; and many other women that came up with him unto Jerusalem.

Luke's Account.

And it was now about the sixth hour, and a darkness 44 came over the whole land until the ninth hour, the sun's 45 light failing.   And Jesus, crying with a loud voice, said, 46 Father, into thy hands I commend my spirit· and having said this, he gave up the ghost.   And the veil of the temple was rent in the midst.   And when the centurion saw 47 what was done, he glorified God, saying, Certainly this was a righteous man.   And all the multitudes that came 48 together to this sight, when they beheld the things that were done, returned smiting their breasts.   And all his 49 acquaintance, and the women that followed with him from Galilee, stood afar off, seeing these things.

John 19.

25 ^dBut there were standing by the cross of Jesus his mother, and his mother's sister, Mary the *wife* of Clopas, and Mary

26 Magdalene. When Jesus therefore saw his mother, and the disciple standing by, whom he loved, he saith unto his mother,

27 Woman, behold, thy son! Then saith he to the disciple, Behold, thy mother! And from that hour the disciple took her unto his own *home*.

§ 160. The Death of Jesus.

Matthew 27.

. 45 ^aNow from the sixth hour there was darkness over all the ¹ land, ^c the sun's light

46 failing ^a until the ninth hour. And about the ninth hour Jesus cried with a loud voice, saying, Eli, Eli, lama sabachthani? that is, My God, my God, ² why hast thou

47 forsaken me? And some of them that stood there, when they heard it, said, ^b Be-

48 hold, ^a this man calleth Elijah. And straightway one of them ran, and took a sponge, and filled it with vinegar, and put it on a reed, and gave him to drink.

49 And the rest said, Let be; let us see whether Elijah cometh to save him.

28 **John 19.** ^dAfter this Jesus, knowing that all things are now finished, that the scrip-ture might be accomplished, saith, I

29 thirst. There was set there a vessel full of vinegar: so they put a sponge full of the vinegar upon hyssop, and brought it to

30 his mouth. When Jesus therefore had re-ceived the vinegar, he said, It is finished! ^{c³}And Jesus, crying with a loud voice, said, Father, into thy hands I commend my spirit: and having said this, he ^d bowed his head and ^c gave up the ghost.

KEY.—^a Matthew, ^b Mark, ^c Luke, ^d John.

¹ Or, *earth.*   ² Or, *why didst thou forsake me?*
³ Or, *And when Jesus had cried with a loud voice, he said:*

Matthew 27.

^aAnd behold, the veil of the ¹ temple 51
was rent in twain from the top to the
bottom; and the earth did quake; and
the rocks were rent; and the tombs were 52
opened; and many bodies of the saints
that had fallen asleep were raised; and 53
coming forth out of the tombs after his
resurrection they entered into the holy
city and appeared unto many. Now the 54
centurion, and they that were with him
watching Jesus, when they saw ^b that he so
gave up the ghost, [and saw]* ^a the earthquake, and the things that were done,
feared exceedingly, saying, Truly this was
² the Son of God. And many women were 55
there beholding from afar, who had followed Jesus from Galilee, ministering unto
him: among whom was Mary Magdalene, 56
and Mary the mother of James and Joses,
and the mother of the sons of Zebedee,
^b and many other women that came up
with him unto Jerusalem.

^d The Jews therefore, because it John 19. 31
was the Preparation, that the bodies should
not remain on the cross upon the sabbath
(for the day of that sabbath was a high
day), asked of Pilate that their legs
might be broken, and *that* they might be
taken away. The soldiers therefore came, 32
and brake the legs of the first, and of the
other who was crucified with him: but 33
when they came to Jesus, and saw that he
was dead already, they brake not his legs:
howbeit one of the soldiers with a spear 34
pierced his side, and straightway there
came out blood and water. And he that 35
hath seen hath borne witness, and his witness is true: and he knoweth that he
saith true, that ye also may believe. For 36

KEY.—^a Matthew, ^b Mark, ^c Luke, ^d John.

¹ Or, *sanctuary*.   ² Or, *a son of God*.
* Words inserted by the compiler.

§ 161. The Burial of Jesus.

Matthew's Account.

Chap. 27.

And when even was come, there came a <u>rich man</u> from 57 Arimathæa, named Joseph, who also himself <u>was Jesus'</u> disciple: this man went to Pilate, and asked for <u>the body</u> 58 of Jesus. Then Pilate commanded it to be given up. And Joseph took the body, and wrapped it in a clean linen 59 cloth, and laid it in <u>his own</u> new tomb, which he had hewn 60 out in the rock: <u>and he rolled a great stone to the door of the tomb, and departed.</u> And Mary Magdalene was there, 61 and the other Mary, sitting over against the sepulchre.

Mark's Account.

Chap. 15.

And he brought a linen cloth, and taking him down, 46 wound him in the linen cloth, and laid him in a tomb <u>which had been hewn out of a rock</u> ; and he rolled a stone against the door of the tomb. And Mary Magdalene and 47 Mary the mother of Jesus beheld where he was laid.

Luke's Account.

Chap. 23.

And behold, a man named Joseph, who was a council- 50 lor, a good man and a righteous (<u>he had not consented to</u> 51 <u>their counsel and deed</u>), *a man* of Arimathæa, a city of the Jews, who was looking for the kingdom of God: this 52 man went to Pilate, and asked for the body of Jesus. And 53 he took it down, and wrapped it in a linen cloth, and laid him in a tomb that was hewn in stone, where never man had yet lain.

John's Account.

Chap. 19.

And after these things Joseph of Arimathæa, being a 38 disciple of Jesus, <u>but secretly for fear of the Jews,</u> asked of Pilate that he might take away the body of Jesus: and Pilate gave *him* leave. He came therefore, and took away his body.

John 19.

these things came to pass, that the scripture might be fulfilled, A bone of him
37 shall not be ¹ broken. And again another scripture saith, They shall look on him whom they pierced.

§ 161. The Burial of Jesus.

Mark 15.

42 ᵇAnd when even was now come, because it was the Preparation, that is, the day be-
43 fore the sabbath, there came ᵃa rich man, ᵇJoseph of Arimathæa, a councillor of honourable estate, who also himselfᵃwas Jesus' disciple, ᵈ but secretly, for fear of the Jews, [and]* ᵇwas looking for the kingdom of God; ᶜhe had not consented unto their counsel and deed; ᵇand he boldly went in unto Pilate,
44 and asked for the body of Jesus. And Pilate marvelled if he were already dead : and calling unto him the centurion, he asked him whether heᵃ had been any while dead.
45 And when he learned it of the centurion, he granted the corpse to Joseph.
39 ᵈAnd there came also Nicode- **John 19.** mus, he who at the first came to him by night, bringing a ᵃmixture of myrrh and
40 aloes, about a hundred pound *weight*. So they took the body of Jesus, and bound it in linen cloths with the spices, as the
41 custom of the Jews is to bury. Now in the place where he was crucified there was a garden; and in the gardenᵃ his †own ᵈnew tomb, ᵇ which had been hewn out of a rock, ᵈ wherein was never man yet laid.
42 There then because of the Jews' Preparation (for the tomb was nigh at hand) they laid Jesus, ᵃand rolled a great stone to the door of the tomb and departed.
55 **Luke 23.** ᶜAnd the women, that had come

KEY.—ᵃ Matthew, ᵇ Mark, ᶜ Luke, ᵈ John.

¹ Or, *crushed.*
² Many ancient authorities read *were already dead.*
³ Some ancient authorities read *roll.*
* Word inserted by the compiler.
† Joseph's.

with him out of Galilee, followed after, and beheld the tomb, and how his body was laid. And they returned, and prepared 56 spices and ointments.

And on the sabbath they rested according to the commandment.

ª Now on the morrow, which **Matthew 27.** 62 is *the day* after the Preparation, the chief priests and the Pharisees were gathered together unto Pilate, saying, Sir, we re- 63 member that that deceiver said, while he was yet alive, After three days I rise again. Command therefore that the sep- 64 ulchre be made sure until the third day, lest haply his disciples come and steal him away, and say unto the people, He is risen from the dead: and the last error will be worse than the first. Pilate said unto 65 them, ªYe have a guard: go, ªmake it *as* sure as ye can. So they went, and made 66 the sepulchre sure, sealing the stone, the guard being with them.

KEY.—ª Matthew, ᵇ Mark, ᶜ Luke, ᵈ John.

¹ Or, *Take a guard.*   ² Gr. *make it sure, as ye know.*

§ 162. The Women Visit the Sepulchre.

Matthew's Account.

Chap. 28.

Now late on the sabbath day, as it began to dawn toward 1
the first *day* of the week, came Mary Magdalene and the
other Mary to see the sepulchre. And behold, there was 2
a great earthquake; for an angel of the Lord descended
from heaven, and came and rolled away the stone, and
sat upon it. His appearance was as lightning, and his 3
raiment white as snow: and for fear of him the watchers 4
did quake, and became as dead men. And the angel an- 5
swered and said unto the women, Fear not ye: for I know
that ye seek Jesus, who hath been crucified. He is not 6
here; for he is risen, even as he said. Come, see the
place where the Lord lay. And go quickly, and tell his 7
disciples, He is risen from the dead; and lo, he goeth before you into Galilee; there shall ye see him: lo, I have

Mark's Account.

Chap. 16.

Now when he was risen early on the first day of the 9
week, he appeared first to Mary Magdalene, from whom
he had cast out seven demons. She went and told them 10
that had been with him, as they mourned and wept. And 11
they, when they heard that he was alive, and had been
seen of her, disbelieved.

Luke's Account.

Chap. 24.

But on the first day of the week, at early dawn, they 1
came unto the tomb, bringing the spices which they had
prepared. And they found the stone rolled away from 2
the tomb. And they entered in, and found not the body 3
of the Lord Jesus. And it came to pass, while they were 4
perplexed thereabout, behold, two men stood by them in
dazzling apparel: and as they were affrighted, and bowed 5
down their faces to the earth, they said unto them, Why
seek ye the living among the dead? He is not here, but is 6
risen: remember how he spake unto you when he was yet
in Galilee, saying that the Son of man must be delivered 7
up into the hands of sinful men, and be crucified, and the
third day rise again. And they remembered his words, 8

[*Continued on duplicate page* 230.]

PERIOD VI.

After the Resurrection.

[From the Resurrection to the Ascension; a period of forty days.]

§ 162. The Women Visit the Sepulchre.

Mark 16.

1 ^bAnd when the sabbath was past, ^dwhile it was yet dark, ^abehold, there was a great earthquake: for an angel of the Lord descended from heaven, and came and rolled away the stone, and sat upon it. His appearance was as lightning, and his raiment white as snow: and for fear of him the watchers did quake, and became as dead men.

^bMary Magdalene, and Mary the *mother* of James, and Salome, bought spices, that
2 they might come and anoint him. And very early on the first day of the week, they come to the tomb when the sun was
3 risen. And they were saying among themselves, Who shall roll us away the
4 stone from the door of the tomb? and looking up, they see that the stone is rolled back: for it was exceeding great. [Mary Magdalene] ^drunneth therefore, and cometh to Simon Peter, and to the other disciple whom Jesus loved, and saith unto them, They have taken away the Lord out of the tomb, and we know not where they have
5 laid him. ^bAnd entering into the tomb, they ^cfound not the body of the Lord Jesus. And it came to pass, while they were perplexed thereabout, [they]* ^b saw a young man sitting on the right side, ar-

KEY.—^a Matthew, ^b Mark, ^c Luke, ^d John.

* Word inserted by the compiler.

Mark 16.

rayed in a white robe; and they were
amazed. And he saith unto them, Be not 6
amazed: ^cwhy seek ye the living among
the dead: ^bye seek Jesus, the Nazarene,
who hath been crucified: he is risen; he
is not here: ^cremember how he spake unto you when he was yet in Galilee, saying
that the Son of man must be delivered up
into the hands of sinful men, and be crucified, and the third day rise again: ^bbehold,
the place where they laid him! But go, 7
tell his disciples and Peter, He goeth before you into Galilee: there shall ye see
him, as he said unto you. ^aAnd they departed quickly from the tomb with fear
and great joy; ^bfor trembling and astonish- 8
ment had come upon them: and they said
nothing to any one: for they were afraid,
^aand ran to bring his disciples word.

^dPeter therefore went forth, John 20. 3
and the other disciple, and they went
toward the tomb. And they ran both to- 4
gether: and the other disciple outran
Peter, and came first to the tomb; and 5
stooping and looking in, he seeth the linen
cloths lying; yet entered he not in. Simon 6
Peter therefore also cometh, following
him, and entered into the tomb; and he beholdeth the linen cloths lying, and the nap- 7
kin, that was upon his head, not lying with
the linen cloths, but rolled up in a place
by itself. Then entered in therefore the 8
other disciple also, who came first to the
tomb, and he saw, and believed. For as 9
yet they knew not the scripture, that he
must rise again from the dead. So the 10
disciples went away again unto their own
home.

But Mary was standing without at the 11
tomb weeping: so, as she wept, she stooped
and looked into the tomb; and she behold- 12

KEY.—^a Matthew, ^b Mark, ^c Luke, ^d John.

§ 162. The Women Visit the Sepulchre.—(*Continued.*)

Matthew's Account.

Chap. 28.

8 told you. And they departed quickly from the tomb with fear and great joy, and ran to bring his disciples word.

9 And behold, Jesus met them, saying, All hail. And they came and took hold of his feet, and worshipped him.

10 Then saith Jesus unto them, Fear not: go tell my brethren that they depart into Galilee, and there shall they see me.

Luke's Account.

Chap. 24.

9 and returned from the tomb, and told all these things to
10 the eleven, and to all the rest. Now they were Mary Magdalene, and Joanna, and Mary the *mother* of James: and the other women with them told these things unto
11 the apostles. And these words appeared in their sight as
12 idle talk; and they disbelieved them. But Peter arose, and ran unto the tomb; and stooping and looking in, he seeth the linen cloths by themselves; and he departed to his home, wondering at that which was come to pass.

John's Account.

Chap. 20.

1 Now on the first *day* of the week cometh Mary Magdalene early, while it was yet dark, unto the tomb, and seeth
2 the stone taken away from the tomb. She runneth therefore, and cometh to Simon Peter, and to the other disciple, whom Jesus loved, and saith unto them, They have taken away the Lord out of the tomb, and we know not where they have laid him.

John 20.

eth two angels in white sitting, one at the head, and one at the feet, where the body
13 of Jesus had lain. And they say unto her, Woman, why weepest thou? She saith unto them, Because they have taken away my Lord, and I know not where they have
14 laid him. When she had thus said, she turned herself back, and beholdeth Jesus standing, and knew not that it was Jesus.
15 Jesus saith unto her, Woman, why weepest thou? whom seekest thou? She, supposing him to be the gardener, saith unto him, Sir, if thou hast borne him hence, tell me where thou hast laid him, and I will
16 take him away. Jesus saith unto her, Mary. She turneth herself, and saith unto him in Hebrew, Rabboni; which is to
17 say, ¹ Master. Jesus saith to her, ² Touch me not; for I am not yet ascended unto the Father: but go unto my brethren, and say to them, I ascend unto my Father and your Father, and my God and your God. ᵃAnd behold Jesus met them * saying, All hail. And they came and took hold of his feet and worshipped him. Then saith Jesus unto them, Fear not; go tell my brethren that they depart into Galilee,
18 and there they shall see me. ᵈMary Magdalene cometh and telleth the disciples, I have seen the Lord; and *how that* he had said these things unto her.

ᵇAnd they, when they heard that he was alive, and had been seen of her, disbelieved.

[§ 163. The Story of the Guard.

Matthew 28.

11   ᵃNow, behold, some of the guard came into the city, and told unto the chief priests

Key.—ᵃ Matthew, ᵇ Mark, ᶜ Luke, ᵈ John.

¹ Or, *Teacher.*   ² Or, *Take not hold on me.*

* Doubtless the other women, who must have been separated from Mary Magdalene after the vision of angels.

all the things that were come to pass.
And when they were assembled with the 12
elders, and had taken counsel, they gave
large money unto the soldiers, saying, Say 13
ye, His disciples came by night, and stole
him away while we slept.   And if this 14
[1] come to the governor's ears, we will per-
suade him, and rid you of care.   So they 15
took the money, and did as they were
taught: and this saying was spread abroad
among the Jews, *and continueth* until this
day.

§ 164. The Journey to Emmaus.

[c]And behold, two of them were going 13
that very day to a village named Emmaus,
which was threescore furlongs from Jerusalem.   And they communed with each 14
other of all these things which had happened.   And it came to pass, while they 15
communed and questioned together, that
Jesus himself drew near, and went with
them.   But their eyes were holden that 16
they should not know him.   And he said 17
unto them, [2]What communications are
these that ye have one with another, as ye
walk?   And they stood still, looking sad.
And one of them, named Cleopas, answer- 18
ing said unto him, [3]Dost thou alone sojourn
in Jerusalem and not know the things
which are come to pass there in these days?
And he said unto them, What things? 19
And they said unto him, The things concerning Jesus of Nazareth, who was a
prophet mighty in deed and word before
God and all the people: and how the chief 20
priests and our rulers delivered him up to

KEY.—[a] Matthew, [b] Mark, [c] Luke, [d] John.

[1] Or, *come to a hearing before the governor.*
[2] Gr. *What words are these that ye exchange one with an-other.*
[3] Or, *Dost thou sojourn alone in Jerusalem, and knowest thou not the things.*

§ 164. The Journey to Emmaus.

Mark's Account.

Chap. 16.

12 And after these things he was manifested in another
form unto two of them, as they walked, on their way into
13 the country. And they went away and told it unto the
rest: neither believed they them.

be condemned to death, and crucified him.
21 But we hoped that it was he that should
redeem Israel. Yea and beside all this, it
is now the third day since these things
22 came to pass. Moreover certain women
of our company amazed us, having been
23 early at the tomb; and when they found
not his body, they came, saying, that they
had also seen a vision of angels, who said
24 that he was alive. And certain of them
that were with us went to the tomb, and
found it even so as the women had said:
25 but him they saw not. And he said unto
them, O foolish men, and slow of heart to
believe ¹ in all that the prophets have
26 spoken! Behoved it not the Christ to suffer these things, and to enter into his
27 glory? And beginning from Moses and
from all the prophets, he interpreted to
them in all the scriptures the things con-
28 cerning himself. And they drew nigh unto the village, whither they were going:
and he made as though he would go
29 further. And they constrained him, saying, Abide with us: for it is toward evening, and the day is now far spent. And
30 he went in to abide with them. And it
came to pass, when he had sat down with
them to meat, he took the ² bread and
blessed; and breaking *it* he gave to them.
31 And their eyes were opened, and they
knew him; and he vanished out of their
32 sight. And they said one to another, Was
not our heart burning within us, while he
spake to us in the way, while he opened to
33 us the scriptures? And they rose up that
very hour, and returned to Jerusalem, and
found the eleven gathered together, and
34 them that were with them, saying, The
Lord is risen indeed, and hath appeared to

KEY.—ᵃ Matthew, ᵇ Mark, ᶜ Luke, ᵈ John.

¹ Or, *after.* ² Or, *loaf.*

Luke 24,

Simon. And they rehearsed the things 35 *that happened* in the way, and how he was known of them in the breaking of the bread.

§ 165. Evening Revelation.

Luke 24.

ᶜAnd as they spake these things, he 36 himself stood in the midst of them, ᵈwhen the doors were shut where the disciples were, for fear of the Jews, ᶜ¹and saith unto them, Peace *be* unto you. But they 37 were terrified and affrighted, and supposed that they beheld a spirit. And he said 38 unto them, Why are ye troubled? and wherefore do questionings arise in your heart? See my hands and my feet, that 39 it is I myself: handle me, and see; for a spirit hath not flesh and bones, as ye behold me having. ²And when he had said 40 this, he shewed them his hands ᵈand his side, ᶜand his feet. And while they still 41 disbelieved for joy, and wondered, he said unto them, Have ye here anything to eat? And they gave him a piece of a broiled 42 fish³. And he took it, and did eat before 43 them.

And he said unto them, These are my 44 words which I spake unto you, while I was yet with you, how that all things must needs be fulfilled, which are written in the law of Moses, and the prophets, and the psalms, concerning me. Then opened he 45 their mind, that they might understand the scriptures; and he said unto them, Thus it 46 is written, that the Christ should suffer, and rise again from the dead the third day; and that repentance ⁴and remission of sins 47

KEY.—ᵃ Matthew, ᵇ Mark, ᶜ Luke, ᵈ John.

¹ Some ancient authorities omit *and saith unto them, Peace be unto you.*
² Some ancient authorities omit ver. 40.
³ Many ancient authorities add *and a honeycomb.*
⁴ Some ancient authorities read *unto.*

§ 165. Evening Revelation.

Mark's Account.

Chap. 16.

14 And afterward he was manifested unto the eleven themselves' as they sat at meat; and he upbraided them with
their unbelief and hardness of heart, because they believed
not them who had seen him after he was risen.

John's Account.

Chap. 20.

19 When therefore it was evening, on that day, the first
day of the week, and when the doors were shut where the
disciples were, for fear of the Jews, Jesus came and stood
in the midst, and said unto them, Peace *be* unto you.
20 And when he had said this, he showed unto them his
hands and his side.

284

Luke 24.

should be preached in his name unto all the
48 ¹nations, beginning from Jerusalem. Ye
49 are witnesses of these things. And behold, I send forth the promise of my
Father upon you : but tarry ye in the city,
until ye be clothed with power from on
high.
20 **John 20.** ᵈThe disciples therefore were
glad, when they saw the Lord. Jesus
21 therefore said to them again, Peace
be unto you : as the Father hath sent me,
22 even so send I you. And when he had said
this, he breathed on them, and saith unto
23 them, Receive ye the Holy Spirit : whose
soever sins ye forgive, they are forgiven
unto them ; whose soever *sins* ye retain,
they are retained.

§ 166. Revelation to Thomas.
John 20.
24   ᵈBut Thomas, one of the twelve, called
²Didymus, was not with them when Jesus
25 came. The other disciples therefore said
unto him, We have seen the Lord. But
he said unto them, Except I shall see in
his hands the print of the nails, and put my
finger into the print of the nails, and put
my hand into his side, I will not believe.
26   And after eight days again his disciples
were within, and Thomas with them.
Jesus cometh, the doors being shut, and
stood in the midst, and said, Peace *be*
unto you. Then saith he to Thomas,
Reach hither thy finger, and see my hands;
27 and reach *hither* thy hand, and put it into
my side : and be not faithless, but believing.
28 Thomas answered and said unto him,
29 My Lord and my God. Jesus saith unto
him, because thou hast seen me, ³thou hast

KEY.—ᵃ Matthew, ᵇ Mark, ᶜ Luke, ᵈ John.

¹ Or, *nations. Beginning from Jerusalem, ye are witnesses.*
² That is, *Twin.*   ³ Or, *hast thou believed ?*

believed : blessed *are* they that have not
seen, and *yet* have believed.

Many other signs therefore did Jesus 30
in the presence of the disciples, which are
not written in this book: but these are 31
written, that ye may believe that Jesus is
the Christ, the Son of God : and that believing ye may have life in his name.

§ 167. Revelation at the Sea-side.

^dAfter these things Jesus manifested 1
himself again to the disciples at the sea
of Tiberias ; and he manifested *himself* on
this wise. There were together Simon 2
Peter, and Thomas called ¹ Didymus, and
Nathaniel of Cana in Galilee, and the *sons*
of Zebedee, and two other of his disciples. Simon Peter saith unto them, I go 3
a fishing. They say unto him, We also
come with thee. They went forth, and
entered into the boat ; and that night they
took nothing. But when day was now break- 4
ing, Jesus stood on the beach : howbeit the
disciples knew not that it was Jesus. Jesus 5
therefore saith unto them, Children, have
ye aught to eat? They answered him,
No. And he said unto them, Cast the net 6
on the right side of the boat, and ye
shall find. They cast therefore, and now
they were not able to draw it for the multitude of fishes. That disciple therefore 7
whom Jesus loved saith unto Peter, It is
the Lord. So when Simon Peter heard
that it was the Lord, he girt his coat
about him (for he ²was naked), and cast
himself into the sea. But the other disci- 8
ples came in the little boat (for they were
not far from the land, but about two hundred cubits off), dragging the net *full* of

KEY.—^a Matthew, ^b Mark, ^c Luke, ^d John.

¹ That is, *Twin.*   ² Or, *had on his under garment only.*

9 fishes. So when they got out upon the land, they see ¹a fire of coals there, and
10 ²fish laid thereon, and ³bread. Jesus saith unto them, Bring of the fish which ye
11 have now taken. Simon Peter therefore went ⁴up, and drew the net to land, full of great fishes, a hundred and fifty and three: and for all there were so many,
12 the net was not rent. Jesus saith unto them, Come *and* break your fast. And none of the disciples durst inquire of him, Who art thou? knowing that it was the
13 Lord. Jesus cometh, and taketh the ⁵bread, and giveth them, and the fish like-
14 wise. This is now the third time that Jesus was manifested to the disciples, after that he was risen from the dead.

§ 168. Peter Confirmed.

15 ᵈSo when they had broken their fast, Jesus saith to Simon Peter, Simon, *son* of ⁶John, ⁷lovest thou me more than these? He saith unto him, Yea, Lord; thou knowest that I ⁷love thee. He saith unto him, Feed my lambs. He saith to him again a second time, Simon, *son* of ⁶John, ⁷lovest thou me? He saith unto him, Yea, Lord; thou
17 knowest that I ⁷love thee. He saith unto him, Tend my sheep. He saith unto him the third time, Simon, *son* of ⁶John, ⁷lovest thou me? Peter was grieved because he said unto him the third time, ⁷Lovest thou me? And he said unto him, Lord, thou knowest all things; thou ⁸knowest that I ⁷love thee. Jesus saith unto him, Feed
18 my sheep. Verily, verily, I say unto thee,

KEY.—ᵃ Matthew, ᵇ Mark, ᶜ Luke, ᵈ John.

¹ Gr. *a fire of charcoal.*   ² Or, *a fish.*
³ Or, *a loaf.*   ⁴ Or, *aboard.*
⁵ Or, *loaf.*   ⁶ Gr. *Joanes.*
⁷ *Love* in these places represents two different Greek words.   ⁸ Or, *perceivest.*

John 21.

When thou wast young, thou girdedst thyself, and walkedst whither thou wouldest:
but when thou shalt be old, thou shalt
stretch forth thy hands, and another shall
gird thee, and carry thee whither thou
wouldest not.   Now this he spake, signi- 19
fying by what manner of death he should
glorify God.   And when he had spoken
this, he saith unto him, Follow me. Peter, 20
turning about, seeth the disciple whom
Jesus loved following; who also leaned
back on his breast at the supper, and said,
Lord, who is he that betrayeth thee?
Peter therefore seeing him saith to Jesus, 21
Lord,¹ and what shall this man do?   Jesus 22
saith unto him, If I will that he tarry till I
come, what *is that* to thee? follow thou
me.   This saying therefore went forth 23
among the brethren, that that disciple
should not die: yet Jesus said not unto
him, that he should not die; but, If I will
that he tarry till I come, what *is that* to
thee?

This is the disciple who beareth witness 24
of these things, and wrote these things:
and we know that his witness is true.

And there are also many other things 25
which Jesus did, the which if they should
be written every one, I suppose that even
the world itself would not contain the
books that should be written.

§ 169.   Revelation on the Mountain.

Matthew 28.

ᵃ But the eleven disciples went into Gal- 16
ilee, unto the mountain where Jesus had
appointed them.   And when they saw 17
him, they worshipped *him*: but some
doubted.   And Jesus came to them and 18
spake unto them, saying, All authority

KEY.—ᵃ Matthew, ᵇ Mark, ᶜ Luke, ᵈ John.

¹ Gr. *and this man, what?*

Matthew 28.

 hath been given unto me in heaven and on earth.

§ 170. The Great Commission.

Mark 16.

15 [b]And he said unto them, Go ye into all the world, and preach the gospel to the
16 whole creation. He that believeth and is baptized shall be saved; but he that disbe-
17 lieveth shall be condemned. And these signs shall follow them that believe: in my name shall they cast out demons; they
18 shall speak with [1]new tongues; they shall take up serpents, and if they drink any deadly thing, it shall in no wise hurt them; they shall lay hands on the sick and they shall recover.

19 **Matthew 28.** [a]Go ye therefore, and make disciples of all the nations, baptizing them into the name of the Father and of the
20 Son and of the Holy Spirit: teaching them to observe all things whatsoever I commanded you: and lo, I am with you [2]alway, even unto [3]the end of the world.

6 **1 Cor. 15.** Then* he appeared to above five hundred brethren at once, of whom the greater part remain until now, but some
7 are fallen asleep; then he appeared to James; then to all the apostles.

4 **Acts 1.** And [4]being assembled together with them, he charged them not to de-part from Jerusalem, but to wait for the promise of the Father, which, *said he*, ye
5 heard from me: for John indeed baptized with water; but ye shall be baptized [5]in the Holy Spirit not many days hence.

6 They therefore, when they were come together, asked him, saying, Lord, dost thou at this time restore the kingdom to

KEY.—[a] Matthew, [b] Mark, [c] Luke, [d] John.

[1] Some ancient authorities omit *new*.
[2] Gr. *all the days*.   [3] Or, *the consummation of the age*.
[4] Or, *eating with them*.   [5] Or, *with*.
* This is probably the revelation on the mountain or as he descended from it.

Israel? And he said unto them, It is not 7
for you to know times or seasons, which
the Father hath [1] set within his own
authority. But ye shall receive power, 8
when the Holy Spirit is come upon you:
and ye shall be my witnesses both in Jerusalem, and in all Judæa and Samaria, and
unto the uttermost part of the earth.

§ 171. The Ascension.

Luke 24.

[c]And he led them out until *they were* 50
over against Bethany: and he lifted up his
hands, and blessed them. And it came 51
to pass, while he blessed them, he parted
from them, [2] and was carried up into
heaven, and a cloud received him Acts 1. 10
out of their sight. And while they were
looking steadfastly into heaven as he went,
behold, two men stood by them in white
apparel; who also said, Ye men of Galilee, 11
why stand ye looking into heaven? this
Jesus, who was received up from you into
heaven, shall so come in like manner as ye
beheld him going into heaven.

[b] So then the Lord Jesus after he Mark 16. 19
had spoken unto them, was received up into
heaven, and sat down at the right hand of
God. [c]And they [3] worshipped him, and
returned to Jerusalem with great joy: and
were continually in the temple, blessing
God. [b]And they went forth, and preached 20
everywhere, the Lord working with them,
and confirming the word by the signs
that followed. Amen.

KEY.—[a] Matthew, [b] Mark, [c] Luke, [d] John.

[1] Or, *appointed by.*
[2] Some ancient authorities omit *and was carried up into heaven.*
[3] Some ancient authorities omit *worshipped him, and.*

ALPHABETICAL INDEX.

Lightning Source UK Ltd.
Milton Keynes UK
UKHW022251291018
331422UK00008B/297/P